Reinventing Revolution

Reinventing Revolution
The Renovation of Left Discourse
in Cuba and Mexico

Edward J. McCaughan

WestviewPress

A Division of HarperCollins*Publishers*

Copyright © 1997 by Westview Press, A Division of HarperCollins Publishers, Inc.

Published in 1997 in the United States of America by Westview Press, 5500 Central Avenue, Boulder, Colorado 80301-2877, and in the United Kingdom by Westview Press, 12 Hid's Copse Road, Cumnor Hill, Oxford OX2 9JJ

A CIP catalog record for this book is available from the Library of Congress.
ISBN 0-8133-6907-X

The paper used in this publication meets the requirements of the American National Standard for Permanence of Paper for Printed Library Materials Z39.48-1984.

10   9   8   7   6   5   4   3   2   1

The Revolution has not triumphed.
In your hands is the will and the power to save it;
but if, unfortunately, you do not,
the shades of Cuauhtémoc, Hidalgo, and Juárez
and the heroes of all times will stir in their tombs to ask:
What have you done with the blood of your brothers?

Emiliano Zapata

Fidel . . . Fidel . . .
your coffin passes by
thru lanes and streets you never knew
thru day and night, Fidel
While lilacs last in the dooryard bloom, Fidel
your futile trip is done
yet is not done
and is not futile
I give you my sprig of laurel

Lawrence Ferlinghetti

This wind,
born below the trees,
will come down from the mountains;
it whispers of a new world,
so new that it is but an intuition in the collective heart.

Subcomandante Marcos

Contents

Preface

Loss, Renewal, and Frida's Blue House

I awoke early on my first morning of vacation in Oaxaca, Mexico to radio news of a military coup in the Soviet Union. Abandoning plans to sleep late, I rushed into the already crowded streets to buy a newspaper. There are only a couple of good dailies in Mexico, and in this nation of Kafkaesque centralization, the likes of which Soviet planners only dreamed, such newspapers are flown in from Mexico City. The plane hadn't yet arrived, so I had to settle for one of the local rags, which offered five-inch high, screaming headlines about the coup but no story to speak of. The paper did provide the official line on the "overwhelming victory" of the long-ruling Institutional Revolutionary Party (PRI) in the mid-term elections that August of 1991. This was the first major electoral contest since fraud robbed Cuauhtémoc Cárdenas of the presidency in 1988 and encouraged the formation of the Party of the Democratic Revolution (PRD), contemporary Mexico's first viable left opposition party. I was soon on my way to Oaxaca's Pacific coast for a couple of days in a remote beach town with my new lover, so I would have to wait for my return to Mexico City for any more substantive analysis of the Soviet coup and the Mexican elections.

Once back in the capital, I obsessively read the papers and magazines and talked to many old friends trying to sort out what was happening. Press coverage and commentary, as well as our conversations, inevitably focussed on these two seemingly unrelated events, the attempted overthrow of Gorbachev and the PRD's electoral defeat. The mood was decidedly glum. Gorbachev's reforms had kindled hopes among the world left that it might still be possible to democratize the Soviet Union while avoiding the headlong rush toward radical "free market" capitalism that seemed to be occurring in the other nations of the old socialist bloc. The coup threatened a return to authoritarianism and orthodoxy.

Left intellectuals in Mexico that August did their best to find a silver lining behind the dark events in the East. Sociologist Jaime Osorio brought me an opinion piece on the former Soviet bloc that he had just written for the Mexican daily *La Jornada*. Jaime is a Chilean who, like so many other Latin American leftists, has made Mexico City his home. He fled Chile, together with his young wife and infant daughter, after Pinochet's bloody takeover in 1973. His article focussed on the impressive civilian resistance to the Soviet coup, expressing great optimism for the democratization and mobilization of civil society taking place in Eastern Europe. Pablo González Casanova, one of Mexico's most prominent scholars, similarly held out hope; the Soviet military had not received the mass support it had counted on, making any return to the old rule far less likely. Yet, in their heart of hearts, they knew that the new leader, Boris Yeltsin, was no democrat, and their eyes spoke the fears that their words wouldn't or couldn't yet express.

The PRI's declaration of victory in the mid-term elections also proved disconcerting to my friends in Mexico City. The massive popular movement organized around the 1988 Cárdenas presidential campaign and the subsequent unification of most left currents into the PRD created great expectations for democratizing what Peruvian-born novelist Mario Vargas Llosa once called "the perfect dictatorship." After the August 1991 elections, however, democratization of Mexico seemed much further away than many had hoped and expected. My old friend, Raúl Alvarez Garín, a prominent figure in the Mexican left since his days as a leader of the 1968 student movement, picked me up at my gloomy budget hotel near el Monumento de la Revolución; for the first time, I noticed signs of age and fatigue in the face of this invariably ebullient organizer. As he honked and cursed our way through Mexico City traffic, he described how the PRI had pulled out all the stops to "win" the elections through "a tremendous, sophisticated fraud," and how the regime had been aided, once again, by splits within the left and by the incompetence of some of the PRD's own "opportunist" candidates.

A couple of days later, over coffee in the Bellas Artes cafeteria, Carlos Monsiváis, Mexico's famous chronicler of popular culture and one never known to mince words, offered his succinct explanation of the PRI's victory: "80 percent fraud; 90 percent errors of the left." The election results, he feared, would contribute to "cynicism and fatalism." And while Monsiváis made no explicit connection between the Mexican elections and the Soviet coup, two separate comments offered in the course of our conversation brought those events together. At one point he declared that Mexico's then president, Carlos Salinas, "is absolutely power-hungry and has placed all his eggs in George Bush's basket." Later, sinking into an even darker mood, he observed, "The collapse of Gorbachev's power and the rise of Yeltsin leave Bush absolutely unchallenged."

While conversations and news coverage that week revolved mainly around these two developments, a third source of disquiet inevitably made its presence felt: Cuba. For the Latin American left, as well as for me, the Cuban Revolution had long been a more important, and more immediate, point of reference than the Soviet Union. Several of the people I spoke with in Mexico City that August had also been with me in Havana earlier in the year attending a Latin American sociology conference. There were some positive signs coming from the island, mainly a sense of "fresh air," as González Casanova put it, an abandoning of the stale old discourse of "scientific socialism" and an openness to new ideas and language. In that regard, the collapse of Communism in the East seemed to have a healthy effect on Cuba.

But there were also the undeniable signs of crisis, particularly the grave economic situation provoked by the rapid disintegration of Cuba's main trading partners and source of economic aid. Questions about the future of the Cuban Revolution wove themselves in and out of our conversations about the Soviet coup and the Mexican left. Monsivaís, for one, was furious with Cuba's cautious declaration that the coup was a Soviet problem to be resolved by the Soviets; he thought Castro should have minimally signaled to Gorbachev that Cuba was critical of the coup, rather than leaving the impression that a return of the military hardliners might actually be considered to Cuba's advantage. Other long-time supporters of Cuba had begun to make severe public criticisms: Mexican Communist Pablo Gómez, for example, had written about the revolution's "senility" in a column in *La Jornada*. González Casanova, on the other hand, still expressed optimism about the island's future, pointing to the legacy of moral ethics running throughout the history of popular struggle in Cuba.

After several days of such conversations, I was frankly at a loss. Thinking I would clear my head, I decided to be tourist for a day, and set off for Frida Kahlo's house-museum in Coyoacán, the southern Mexico City neighborhood where I had lived in the early 1970s. Back then, relatively few people outside of Mexico had heard of Kahlo, the now internationally recognized painter and icon. I visited her house frequently in 1973, since it was free and only a few minutes walk from my apartment. I was fascinated by the haunting paintings of this pain-ridden Communist who seemed inclined to break all taboos. I have always associated Frida's bright blue home with that defining period of my youth when I first became friends with some of the brightest of Mexico's new left, first visited Cuba, began to seriously study Marxism, wrote my first published research with Peter Baird for the North American Congress on Latin America (NACLA), and helped organize a campaign to free my college classmate and dear friend, Olga Talamante, from an Argentine prison. Olga and her companion Patricia Ann were with me when I returned to Frida's blue house for the first time in nearly twenty years, hoping, I suppose, that memories of those youthful days when wrong and right seemed crystal clear would lift the clouds of doubt hanging in the air that August of 1991.

But Frida's house was closed. After pounding on the huge doors, we managed to get in with a hefty bribe to the guard. The house was in disarray, under renovation before reopening to Kahlo's vastly enlarged public, who would soon pay a steep admission fee beyond the reach of most Mexicans. Many of Frida's paintings had been removed for an exhibit abroad and the remaining ones were on the dusty floor, leaning against peeling walls. Suddenly, I was flooded with unexpected memories of an old college friend, Eddie Escobedo, who had helped organize one of the first exhibits of Frida Kahlo's work in Los Angeles in the early 1980s. Eddie waged a battle to have Frida's paintings displayed in the working class, Mexican barrio of Santa Ana, rather than exclusively in the elite haunts of postmodern LA. Eddie's life was cut far too short by AIDS, but at least he didn't have to witness the subsequent crass commercialization of Frida Kahlo, whose paintings now fetch the highest prices of any Latin American artist, whose home can no longer be visited by Mexicans who can't afford the price of admission, and whom the Material Girl herself, Madonna, now wants to portray on the silver screen. From Communist militant to Hollywood vamp was not, I thought, what Eddie had in mind. The clouds had not lifted.

From Frida's blue house we walked the few blocks to the house-museum of her old friend, Leon Trotsky. After being exiled from the Russian Revolution he helped create, Trotsky spent the last years of his life in this house. The curators have preserved his study, his bedroom, even a closet with a few drab clothes. Loneliness and betrayal are the pervasive feelings generated by such surroundings. I walked outside into the extensive gardens, trying to picture the happier Trotsky portrayed in a scene from Paul Leduc's film about Frida, in which the aging revolutionary and the beautiful young artist stroll peacefully, even coquettishly through the woods. The image was quickly shattered as I found myself before Trotsky's tomb: It had been exactly 51 years to the day since Trotsky was assassinated, apparently with the collaboration of Mexican Communists. Now the Soviet Union was self-destructing, in large part due to errors denounced by Trotsky, who paid the price of dissent with exile and death. My own history in the sectarian U.S. left did not leave me predisposed to sympathy for Trotsky, but I sat and wept.

Early the next morning, nursing a hangover from my unsuccessful attempts to clear away a nagging sense of loss, I learned that Gregorio Selser, the great Argentine journalist, had thrown himself out a window in Mexico City the same day I visited Frida's blue house and Trotsky's tomb. Another exiled, brilliant, left intellectual who had found a second home in Mexico. Another creative, productive life cut short. Newspapers quoted friends as saying that Selser had found himself in too much pain from a long-term, debilitating disease, that he could no longer write and therefore could no longer live. When Jaime Osorio arrived at my hotel later that morning, I assumed he had heard the news, and I wondered aloud why Selser had made the decision to end his life on that particular day, that month of August in 1991. Frida had never chosen suicide, despite debilitating pain. Didn't Selser's decision surely have something to do with the state of the world, the state of the left, as much as with the state of his health? Jaime, in fact, had not heard about his friend's suicide, and as he absorbed what I was saying, he was left absolutely without words to explain the death or express his own sense of loss.

It had been an unsettling week. An historical era in eclipse, a super power self-destructing, the left's renewed electoral hopes dashed, friends disconcerted, unexpected memories reencountered, a life surrendered. Like Jaime Osorio, I found myself without words to explain or express the sense of loss. When I said goodbye to González Casanova that summer, he said, and with an uncommon sadness in his voice, I thought, "The next time you come, we'll have you and some others over to the house for taquitos. We need new friends." The ambiguous statement, "we need new friends," seemed an apt, even poignant, expression of what I was feeling and of what I sensed my other friends on the left also felt. We were not yet able to clearly articulate the extent to which the left had lost an entire paradigm, a way of thinking about the world, of how it would change, of how we would intervene to change it. But we sensed that there was a void that needed to be filled.

It was not an altogether unfamiliar ache: we had all known loss before, when our homelands expelled us, when sectarian disputes divided us, when our best-laid plans failed us, when our enemies overwhelmed us, when diseases devastated us. Time and again, we had answered painful loss with painful renewal. We knew what to do, almost instinctively. We needed to revisit some old friends and reaffirm the too often unacknowledged value of certain long-time companions. We needed to give up finally on a few false, or simply fickle friends. And, indeed, we needed some new friends, new ideas, new understandings, new plans, new actions. We understood, I thought, what the process of renewal demands, but I wondered if we were still, again, up to the task.

Edward J. McCaughan
Cuernavaca, Mexico

Acknowledgments

This research would not have been possible without the cooperation of the seventy-four Cubans and Mexicans who generously gave their time and ideas for the interviews that form the heart of the data presented herein. In Cuba, I am especially indebted to: Julio Carranza, Rafael Hernández, Santiago Pérez, and Juan Valdés Paz of the Centro de Estudios Sobre América (CEA), who greatly facilitated my research; Elena Díaz and Beatriz Díaz of the Centro de Estudios Sobre el Desarrollo (DES), who arranged a crucial six-week stay in Havana in 1993; and Juan Antonio Blanco, director of the Centro Felix Varela, who offered many invaluable insights. In Mexico, special thanks must go to: Alejandro Alvarez, Raúl Alvarez Garín, and Cristina Laurell, *compañeros de siempre*; Pablo González Casanova, director of the Centro de Investigaciones Interdisciplinarias en Humanidades at the Universidad Nacional Autónoma de México, who always made available his time and the facilities of his institute; and Jaime, Patricia, Daniela, and Alejandra Osorio for giving me a family and home away from home.

Thanks also to professors Walter Goldfrank, Sonia Alvarez, and Paul Lubeck at the University of California, Santa Cruz, for their critical help in formulating this project and for reading the book's many drafts. Tony Platt, under no obligation other than loyal friendship, also read every word, providing indispensable criticism and warm support. Long-time *compañeras* Susanne Jonas and Elizabeth Martínez also gave their valuable feedback on various chapter drafts. Harriet Swift copyedited the manuscript and provided astute criticism in the process. And John Kaine, whose brilliant artwork graces the cover, kept me dancing through it all, insisting that we hit the clubs at least once a month.

Finally, I am grateful to the following institutions for their financial support: the Fulbright-García Robles Program; the Cuban Studies Program of the Johns Hopkins University, in conjunction with the Ford Foundation; the Chicano/Latino Research Center at the University of California, Santa Cruz; the University of California Consortium on Mexico and the United States (UC MEXUS); the James D. Kline Fund for International Studies; and the Sociology Board and Division of Social Sciences of the University of California, Santa Cruz.

E.J.M.

CHAPTER 1. INTRODUCTION

Global Change, Paradigm Crisis, and the Renovation of Left Discourse

Thomas Kuhn observed that research scientists formulate their questions, experiments, and theories within a socially constructed paradigm, that is, within a broadly accepted framework of thought, language, and methodology. A given paradigm, proven fruitful through practice and reinforced by institutional resources, endures until a sufficient accumulation of problems, which are seemingly unresolvable within the prevailing paradigm, begins to sow doubts and provoke criticisms within the discipline. A paradigm crisis thus ensues, leading to an overthrow of the long-accepted framework, a period of confusion, contestation, debate, struggle, and, eventually, the construction of a new paradigm.[1]

What follows is an exploration, based on two national case studies (Cuba and Mexico), of the paradigm crisis facing left forces throughout the world today.[2] I am using "left" to refer broadly to those (including Marxists, socialists and communists, social democrats, revolutionary nationalists, populists, labor and social movements activists) who traditionally were guided by ideological and ethical principles that stressed social equality and social justice. This book presents an empiri-

---

1. Thomas Kuhn, *The Structure of Scientific Revolutions* (Chicago: University of Chicago Press, 1962).

2. Cuban social scientist Juan Valdés Paz has offered a definition of what he calls "the substantive left," which is "constituted on the basis of a scale of values, among which stand out full human dignity, altruism, and equality. [The left's] interpretation of reality places it in opposition to a society based on relations of exploitation and/or domination among men [sic] and states. Its historical objectives are aimed at overcoming such relations, at the radical transformation of societies based on them. Its praxis is expressed in programs of struggle for the constitution of new social relations and to represent the interests of the exploited, marginalized, and dominated sectors of historical societies." Juan Valdés Paz, "La Izquierda Hoy en América Latina," manuscript (1993). *Please note* that quotes from Spanish-language texts and interviews have been translated by the author unless indicated otherwise.

cal account, in a form rather like a multi-voiced conversation based on interviews with seventy-four intellectuals in Cuba and Mexico, of how left discourse, ideology, and strategy in these countries have been affected by major changes in the structures and practices of the world-system since the 1980s. More specifically, this book asks how the globalization of the world-economy, the rise of neoliberal ideology and policy, and the collapse of state socialism have challenged the left's long-prevailing world view. Because the relationship between socioeconomic *structures* and discursive *representation* is a two-way street, this book also examines how the left's traditional ideology and political culture mediate the ways it understands, assesses, and responds to these global changes.

Additionally, this book is about the current process of formulating a new left paradigm, a task described by Mexican scholar Raquel Sosa Elízaga as "a collective affair of long duration."[3] It is an effort that reflects the current state of the collectivity, its mode of living and understanding its contradictions, and the degree to which it has come to resolve those contradictions.[4] These case studies of Cuba and Mexico allow us to examine in depth one part of a larger worldwide process of articulating critical, oppositional ideologies and strategies that have the potential to challenge the status quo of the capitalist world-system more effectively than did left movements of the last 150 years. We are observing two national components of a global process understood by Immanuel Wallerstein as a quest for the "formulation of a clear antisystemic strategy for an era of disintegration."[5] That quest has been underway for some thirty years; it was given new impetus by the "world revolution of 1968" and will likely require at least another twenty years to complete.[6] As interpreted by Wallerstein:

> [A]bove all, 1968 had one crucial outcome. It launched a strategic debate among the movements in the same sense and to the same degree as had [the revolutions of] 1848. We know the outcome of the post-1848 debate. By the 1880s the movements had agreed on their basic *middle-run* strategy: they would seek to attain state power by political means. The revolution of 1968 challenged this nineteenth-century consensus on middle-run strategy. As a result, today we are in the midst of a re-

---

3. Raquel Sosa Elízaga, "La llamada crisis de los paradigmas," *Memoria* (Mexico), No. 55, June 1993, p. 24.

4. Ibid.

5. Immanuel Wallerstein, "The Collapse of Liberalism," in R. Miliband and L. Pantich, eds., *Socialist Register 1992* (London: Merline, 1992), p. 108.

6. Ibid.

newed debate about middle-run strategy. It is not yet clear how and where this new debate will come out.[7]

The Search for Alternatives Did Not End with the Cold War

Indeed the debate about how to create a more equitable, just, and democratic society is taking place throughout the world, although the reader might be excused for assuming these issues were settled with the end of the Cold War. Many academics, political leaders, and journalists, particularly in the United States and Western Europe, seem to have turned Francis Fukuyama's claim that history ended with the final trumph of capitalism and electoral democracy into a mantra, as though repeating it often enough would make it true.[8] Yet events around the globe belie such assertions of consensus. In virtually all of the societies once associated with the former Soviet bloc, for example, intense political and social struggles are being waged over whether and how to regulate the new market-oriented economies so as to protect fundamental social rights. Having overthrown apartheid, South African society is now grappling with how to create political and economic institutions that will best allow the poor, black majority finally to take full control of its future. Indian society, a major political, cultural, and economic force within Asia, is far from reconciled about abandoning its nationalist and quasi-socialist approach to social and economic issues in favor of en vogue tenents of radical free market capitalism.

Throughout Latin America, hard-won and still fragile transitions to democratic rule remain highly contested processes in which very different conceptions of democracy vie for influence. To be sure, Latin America in recent years has witnessed a flurry of neoliberal policies to end programs and institutions that characterized the region's post-Great Depression nationalist development schemes, such as protective trade policies designed to promote national industry, state control over strategic resources and economic sectors, and social welfare aimed at moderating the extreme inequality and conflict associated with capitalism in the Third World. Neoliberalism is still liberalism in its emphasis on the centrality of the market and the entrepreneurial drive of the free individual, but it is "neo" or new in its abandonment of old liberal reforms which

---

7. Immanuel Wallerstein, "Antisystemic Movements: History and Dilemmas," in Samir Amin, et al., *Transforming the Revolution. Social Movements and the World-System* (New York: Monthly Review Press, 1990), p. 40.

8. Francis Fukuyama, "The End of History," reprinted in S. Hall, et al., *Modernity and Its Futures, Modernity and Its Futures* (Cambridge: Polity Press, 1992), p. 48.

once sought to ameliorate the social and political upheaval produced by the expansion of capitalism. The implementation of neoliberal policies by technocratic Latin American governments faithful to the new doctrine of transnational capital should not be mistaken as a sign of consensus; to the contrary, the neoliberal restructuring of Latin America remains unpopular and fiercely challenged by a great variety of social and political forces.[9]

In all of the examples cited above, left political forces continue to play a significant role in shaping the debates over the future direction of society's economic and political systems. In the United States, where the left has very little impact on public discourse, it may be easier to accept the notion that history has indeed ended, that radical free-market capitalism has triumphed, that mean-spirited individualism has captured society's soul. However, if we take seriously what is occuring in the world beyond the United States, particularly within the semiperiphery (or middle strata nations) of the world-system, it is evident that the debate over the future of human society is far from settled and that the left's contribution remains relevant. Viewed within this global panorama of ongoing struggle, the following case studies of Mexico and Cuba take on significance beyond their national horizons. They help us shed light on what is a world-historic process of reassessing the shortcomings of old left paradigms and of articulating new visions of society still informed by the desire for greater social equality, justice, and democracy.

This book focuses on the *left's* efforts to formulate those new visions, but, as political scientist Sonia Alvarez wisely observed, the issues explored herein "are crucial for theorizing viable alternatives to the deep crises that afflict not only the left but also, importantly, contemporary Latin American societies (and exploited and oppressed folks everywhere in general)."[10] A few statistics buttress her point:

> According to a recent study published at the University of Miami's North-South Center, gross national income per capita fell by more than 14 percent from 1981 to 1991 in every Latin American country (21 percent in the Caribbean). The ranks of the poor (defined in terms of the money income sufficient to cover the cost of basic foods, goods, and services) increased in every Latin American country during the 1980s. Today, over half of the Latin American population lives below the pov-

---

9. A dramatic example of opposition to neoliberal policies in the region was an international meeting held in Chiapas, Mexico, in August, 1996. The Intercontinental Encounter for Humanity and Against Neoliberalism was called by the Zapatista Army of National Liberation (EZLN) and attended by hundreds of participants from throughout the Americas.

10. Sonia E. Alvarez, personal correspondence with author, March 8, 1995.

erty line (80 to 90 percent in several countries). The share of the population living in "abject poverty," i.e., unable to afford a basic minimum diet, has also risen substantially, in some countries including over two-thirds of the population.[11]

Indeed, it is not only the left's old paradigms and strategies that are in crisis. Ruling elites everywhere are without alternatives to the deep social crises afflicting Latin America and most of the world's peoples.

Wallerstein has made the case, quite persuasively, that liberalism and national developmentalism have collapsed along with communism.[12] Mexico's long-ruling Partido Revolucionario Institucional (PRI), having abandoned its decades-old developmentalist strategy in favor of radical free-market policies, is deeply divided. The party stubbornly clings to power, while self-destructing in spiraling scandals of corruption, drug trafficking, and assassinations. Meanwhile, the economy staggers and an ever greater portion of the population slips into desolate poverty. The thirty-five-year-old communist regime in Cuba is desperately attempting to apply old liberal prescriptions to a collapsed socialist economy, risking the revolution's impressive social achievements, yet resisting fuller democratization, and watching national consensus erode. Having rejected New Deal liberalism, neither Democrats nor Republicans in the United States offer any alternative to the nation's social disintegration. Internationally, the "last great superpower" appears semi-paralyzed in the face of numerous military conflicts abroad and holds firm only on the issues of an irrational, inhumane, and ineffective trade embargo against Cuba and more-of-the-same neoliberalism for Mexico. Global earth summits and social summits are organized with great fanfare and hope, only to end with pitiful, half-hearted proposals.[13] Such efforts seem inevitably hobbled by the unwillingness of the wealthy and powerful to cede even a smidgen of their wealth and power. Ruling elites offer no solutions, but they try to convince us all that there is no alternative to the status quo.

---

11. Susanne Jonas and Edward J. McCaughan, "Introduction: The Quest for Social Transformation in Latin America," in S. Jonas and E. McCaughan, eds., *Latin America Faces the Twenty-First Century. Reconstructing a Social Justice Agenda* (Boulder: Westview Press, 1994), p. 1.

12. See Immanuel Wallerstein, "The Collapse of Liberalism," op. cit.; I. Wallerstein, "The Concept of National Development, 1917-1989. Elegy and Requiem," *American Behavioral Scientist*, Vol. 35, No. 4/5, March/June 1992; and I. Wallerstein, "Marxism After the Collapse of Communism," *Economic Review*, February/March 1992.

13. See, for example, William Felice, "The Copenhagen Summit: A Victory for the World Bank?" *Social Justice*, Vol. 24, No. 1 (Spring 1997).

Sonia Alvarez is quite right when she observes that the findings of this study are "also a response to the doom-sayers of both the right and the left who argue that the left is dead, that there are no pathways out of the current crises, that there are, in short, no alternatives to neoliberalism and restricted democracy."[14]   In fact, as we will see, out of the left's paradigm crisis, there are emerging some renovative ideas that contribute to alternative strategies for transcending "an era of disintegration" and contributing to a more humane world order. The potential impact of these ideas is heightened by the crisis facing ruling elites, by which I mean their failure, as yet, to replace the old cooptive strategies of liberalism (in the core) and developmentalism (elsewhere) with equally effective modes of domination. The conjunctural preference among Western political leaders for neoliberalism will undoubtedly wane as the full impact of neoliberalism's social and environmental devastation is more broadly acknowledged.   As the neoliberal consensus breaks down, the many serious conflicts already evident among the world's ruling classes (on everything from trade policy to armed conflict settlement to boundary disputes to the role of the United Nations) will most likely deepen. Throughout history, as sociologist Robert Wuthnow has observed, the emergence of new, critical discourses has been facilitated by division among ruling elites.[15]   The left, as this study suggests, has already begun to seriously reassess the failures of its old paradigms and to suggest the outlines of alternative modes of subsistence and governance. These new ideas, I argue, form the kernel of the new critical discourses that will likely gain influence as the ideology and strategy of the old ruling strata lose coherence.   Thus these two case studies contribute to a clearer conceptual understanding of the process by which new discourses emerge to challenge old orthodoxies, as well as to a better practical understanding of potential, progressive alternatives to the crisis-prone capitalist world-system.

Paradigm Crisis and the Latin American Left

The paradigm informing the international left's old middle-run strategy was shared by broad sectors of Latin America's progressive forces, from those of clear Marxist-Leninist orientation, to social

---

14. Sonia E. Alvarez, personal correspondence, op. cit.

15. Robert Wuthnow, *Communities of Discourse. Ideology and Social Structure in the Reformation, the Enlightenment, and European Socialism* (Cambridge: Harvard University Press, 1989).

democrats, to those of more nationalist and/or populist persuasion. Despite important distinctions and conflicts among Latin America's various nationalist, populist, and/or socialist regimes and movements throughout the twentieth century, they embraced a developmental paradigm that placed the state at the heart of progressive change.

The state was at the center of most projects for development and social or political change in Latin America from the 1930s through the 1980s, whether it be the nationalist populism of Mexico's Lázaro Cárdenas, Brazil's Getulio Vargas, or Argentina's Juan Perón, the economic reforms advanced by the Economic Council for Latin America (CEPAL), the more radical nationalism of the *dependencia* school, the Cuban revolution's tropical version of state socialism, or the eclectic experiments of the Chilean Popular Unity government or the Nicaraguan Sandinistas.

In economic terms, an active, interventionist state was seen by the left as the key to autonomous development in a world-economy dominated by the United States and transnational capital. The importance placed on the state's economic role was reinforced by the experience of the Soviet Union's impressively rapid industrialization and rise to superpower status, as well as by the generalization of Keynesian economic policies after the Great Depression.

In political terms, the radical left's attention was on proletarian revolution, understood as seizure of the state by the working class. Even the more social democratic left was preoccupied primarily with increasing the working class's representation in government and influence over the state. For most of the left, the state was the almost exclusive focus of national politics, to be supported, influenced, seized, or smashed, depending on the conjuncture and particular strategic vision of a given left current.

More recently embraced considerations about the autonomy of civil society, the many forms of political struggle outside of the state, and the importance of democratic procedures and rule of law generally took back seat to the left's concern with overthrowing, constructing, or preserving a strong state. This dimension of the left's paradigm has loomed especially large in Latin America, and particularly so in Cuba and Mexico, given the reality of joint hemispheric tenancy with an often belligerent, powerful Northern neighbor, whose presence seemed to demand a strong, unified nation.

Within the lefts of Western Europe and the United States, the old paradigm's statism was substantially challenged from the late 1960s on by new poltical and ideological currents such as feminism, new social movements theories, post-Marxism, poststructuralism, and postmodernism.[16] These cultural challenges to the left's historical statism also influenced progressive forces in Latin America to one degree or another. In particular, important aspects of the "new social movements" paradigm and feminism were adapted by sectors of the Latin American left to the conditions of their world, helping to broaden and enrich the left's traditional emphasis on the struggle of class forces over state power.[17] However, the structural realities of the South limit the extent to which the more radically antistatist versions of Northern-born postmodernism and poststructuralism are directly applicable in nations such as Cuba and Mexico. The continued relevance of class analysis and state power are readily apparent in the highly stratified and still relatively authoritarian societies of Latin America. Consequently, the Latin American left often gave more attention to renovating Marxism than to employing the various "post" paradigms.[18] This had the great advantage of helping to preserve Marxism as a useful tool of analysis that has been discarded by much of the United States and European left. At the same time, it meant that many aspects of the left's old statist paradigm went unchallenged in Latin America until quite recently.

A brief historical summary of how left discourse evolved in Cuba and Mexico from the 1960s through the world-shaking events of the late 1980s is presented in Chapter Two. For now, suffice it to say that the old left paradigm, already shaky since 1968, was then quite substantially undermined by three global developments that culminated at the end of the 1980s: the restructuring of a globalized world-economy, the rise of neoliberal ideology, and the collapse of the state socialist regimes in the Soviet Union and Eastern Europe. The accelerated globalization of economic processes undermined the state's capacity to regulate or direct the national economy. Neoliberalism's assault on socialist and even Keynesian notions about the interventionist state posed a considerable

---

16. For a review of such developments, see, e.g., the essays in Stuart Hall, et al., *Modernity and Its Futures* (Cambridge: Polity Press, 1992).

17. Regarding the influence of new social movements theories on the Latin American left, see Arturo Escobar and Sonia E. Alvarez, eds., *The Making of Social Movements in Latin America. Identity, Strategy, and Democracy* (Boulder: Westview Press, 1992). Regarding the influence of feminism, see Norma Stoltz Chinchilla, "Marxism, Feminism, and the Struggle for Democracy in Latin America," in ibid.; Isabel Larguía, "Why Political Feminism?" in S. Jonas and E. McCaughan, *Latin America Faces the Twenty-First Century*, op. cit.; and Margaret Randall, *Gathering Rage. The Failure of 20th Century Revolutions to Develop a Feminist Agenda* (New York: Monthly Review Press, 1992).

18. See, e.g., Agustín Cueva, "El marxismo latinoamericano: historia y problemas actuales," *Contrarios* (Madrid), No. 3, November 1989, pp. 21-34.

challenge to progressive ideas about the state's social responsibilities. The sudden demise of the Soviet bloc seemed to tarnish the legitimacy even of those left forces that had consistently disavowed Stalinism. Combined with events more particular to national developments in Cuba and Mexico, these global changes contributed to a critical accumulation of doubts among the broadly-defined left in those nations.

As I began to interview and study the current writings of left intellectuals in Cuba and Mexico in the early 1990s, an acute awareness of paradigm crisis was frequently expressed, as reflected in the following comments.

- From a high-level official in the International Relations Department of the Cuban Communist Party Central Committee, who specializes in the Central American left:

The Latin American left is facing a very difficult moment. Seldom has the left had such a clear picture of the inability of capitalism to solve our problems and such prospects for power. But the left is facing many moral, political, social, ideological, and psychological problems. Until a few years ago, Latin America found in the socialist camp, in Marxism, in Marxism-Leninism, at least an ideological point of reference. Now that's been shattered, leading to a left crisis of identity.[19]

- From a Cuban intellectual once associated with the University of Havana's Philosophy Department, closed in 1971 for its heterodoxy :

There is a paradigm crisis, requiring a reencounter with Marxism. Marxism as a theory is not finished, and its liberal framework is not clear. Cuba doesn't have the answers, but at least Cuba is now asking the questions. But the process is slow; orthodoxy doesn't allow for such criticisms.[20]

- From a Cuban political scientist and researcher:

Today the paradigms of "real socialism" do not exist, and for the common citizen there remain few doubts that the supposed superiority and irreversibility of the socialism [of the Eastern bloc] were no more than a mythological construction.[21]

---

19. Ramiro Abreú, interview with author, Havana, March 8, 1993.
20. Aurelio Alonso, interview with author, Havana, February 23, 1993.
21. Haroldo Dilla Alfonso, "Cuba: La Crisis y la Rearticulación del Consenso Político (Notas Para Un Debate Socialista)," manuscript (1993).

- From a leading intellectual of Mexico's revolutionary nationalist tendency, who became a supporter of the neoliberal Carlos Salinas administration:

Politically, the Mexican left had already abandoned political paradigms associated with the USSR. But economically, the left has real problems. We haven't taken up the lessons of, one, the collapse of the Soviet economy and central planning, and, two, the crisis of the Mexican model of development. The left is very weak in the face of neoliberal discourse. For the left, the collapse of the Soviet bloc has led to a sense of futility in trying to imagine a future with a radical alternative to further integration with the United States.[22]

- From a Maoist-influenced sociologist active in the Mexican labor movement:

There is no Marxist discourse in the left now. The fall of the Berlin Wall had a huge impact here, because much of the left believed that these socialisms were reformable. Many have become exceedingly pragmatic. Marxist reflection is at its worst moment.[23]

- From a Marxist professor at the University of Guadalajara, who has written extensively on the Cuban revolution and the Latin American left:

There is confusion and paralysis in the Latin American left as a result of the events in Eastern Europe. However, there is also a tendency to reject the thesis that magnifies the extent to which the problems of the Latin American left developed in close relationship to the crisis of the socialist paradigm in Europe.[24]

---

22. Rolando Cordera, interview with author, Mexico City, September 2, 1992.

23. Enrique de la Garza Toledo, interview with author, Mexico City, August 10, 1993.

24. Jorge Alonso, "Alternativas para un socialismo posible," manuscript (n.d.). An example of what Alonso means when he refers to a tendency to play down the significance for the Latin American left of the collapse of the Eastern European regimes is the following statement from a leading figure in the PRD: "My first experience with a socialist country was in Eastern Europe, and it was the first place I'd ever had a machine gun pointed at me. The experience left a lasting, negative impression. So I never saw the Soviet bloc states as a model, and in that sense their demise has no consequence for me." (Cristina Laurell, interview with author, Mexico City, August 6, 1992.)

Utopia Unarmed or Renovated?

The crisis facing the Latin American left has been documented and analyzed by several writers, most notably Jorge Castañeda in his acclaimed book, *Utopia Unarmed*.[25] Castañeda's synoptic, interpretative study of current trends and shifts in the political thinking of the Latin American left is an indispensable point of reference. This book, however, differs from *Utopia Unarmed* in terms of both methodology and findings. Castañeda offers a sweeping, panoramic view of Latin America's left forces and tends to focus on the politics of parties in the formally political sphere. My study is situated within regional developments but focuses on the left in just two countries, Cuba and Mexico, and it examines a broader slice of the left, including social movements activists. Castañeda provides crucial insights into the thinking of a number of prominent political players, based on his lifelong association with many of the Latin American lefts' most celebrated intellectual and political figures. My interpretations are drawn from interviews with nearly seventy-five leftists. Some of them are renowned national figures and others are lesser known movement activists, party cadre, or university researchers.

More importantly than the methodological differences (elaborated below) between this study and Castañeda's, the findings of my research differ considerably from those of *Utopia Unarmed*. Castañeda emphasizes the extent to which a significant current of the Latin American left has rejected the possibility of revolutionary change. Instead, he says, they have settled for what he considers a more viable, pragmatic strategy of reforming the region's political and economic systems into a Latin American version of social democracy: a decidedly more humane, more just, and more inclusive brand of capitalism, but capitalism nonetheless. My research also identifies this liberal-minded reformism as an important and growing tendency among left intellectuals in Cuba

---

25. Jorge Castañeda, *Utopia Unarmed. The Latin American Left After the Cold War* (New York: Alfred A. Knopf, 1993). Other interpretations of the Latin American left's crisis can be found in: Barry Carr and Steve Ellner, *The Latin American Left. From the Fall of Allende to Perestroika* (Boulder: Westview Press, 1993); Richard L. Harris, *Marxism, Socialism and Democracy in Latin America* (Boulder: Westview Press, 1992); Marta Harnecker, *América Latina, Izquierda y Crisis Actual* (Mexico: Siglo XXI, 1990); Joan Alcázar Garrido, "La crisis histórica de las izquierdas latinoamericanas," *Memoria* (Mexico), No. 57, August 1993; Guillermo Zamora, *La caída de la hoz y el martillo* (Mexico: Edamex, 1994); and Susanne Jonas and Edward J. McCaughan, *Latin America Faces the Twenty-first Century*, op. cit.

and Mexico, which coexists with more orthodox socialist tendencies. However, in addition, my study identifies a third current of thought not clearly present in Castañeda's book, which is neither orthodox socialist nor liberal but rather renovative, and potentially far more significant. I use the term renovative to refer to those leftists who still emphasize social goals and social, even collectivist, political and economic visions, and who are critical of both statist-socialist and liberal approaches. These three typologies (or ideal types), orthodox socialist, liberal, and renovative, do not correspond neatly to past political militancy or ideological orientation, but rather reflect the genuine shake-up of long-held positions and the process of renovation indicative of a true paradigm crisis and shift.

The orthodox current of the left retains much of the traditional socialist discourse about the dangers of private property, market relations, and "bourgeois" democracy. The renovators have much in common with the reform-minded, liberal left represented by Castañeda. They embrace the democratic aspects of liberal political traditions and reject the extreme statism of the centrally planned economies of the former Soviet bloc. In the short-run, liberals and renovators within the left can agree on many of the reforms needed to make their societies more democratic, more just, and more egalitarian. However, as should become clear in the following chapters, the long-term vision of the renovators is still inspired by a belief in the possibility and the necessity of something more than reformed capitalism. The emerging renovative left is sustained by the ideal, utopian perhaps, of an egalitarian, socially just, and democratic, *noncapitalist* world-system. In this regard, the discourse and strategy of the renovative left remain what Wallerstein would call "antisystemic" rather than reformist. They are, as Carl Boggs has observed of similar critical intellectual currents elsewhere in the world today, both post-(not *anti*-)Marxist and postliberal.[26]

I am inclined to agree with Wallerstein's analysis that liberalism, "the politics of constant rational reform," the dominant ideology of this century, is as dead as Leninism. Liberalism gained very broad acceptance, according to Wallerstein, when growth and expansion of the capitalist world-economy made belief in inevitable progress and integration seem reasonable. However, he argues, it is no longer possible to continue to reallocate political power and economic benefits without disrupting accumulation within the capitalist world-system. Therefore, liberal reform is no longer a viable, long-term option.

---

26. Carl Boggs, *Intellectuals and the Crisis of Modernity* (Albany: State University of New York Press, 1993), pp. 5-6.

> The period from 1968-1989 has seen the steady crumbling of what remained of the liberal consensus. . . . The world's dominant strata have lost any possibility to control the world's working classes other than by force. Consent is gone, and consent has gone because bribery has gone. But force alone . . . is insufficient to permit political structures to survive very long.[27]

It is in this sense that I argue that the presence and growth of an antisystemic, renovative left tendency in Latin America is potentially more significant in the long run than the new reform-oriented pragmatism highlighted by Castañeda, which, in essence, is little more than an attempt to revive liberalism. (Indeed, the revival of liberalism seems a rather utopian scheme under the conditions of late twentieth-century Latin America.) Moreover, I expect that the same typology identified in this study, orthodox, liberal, and renovative, can be accurately applied to left forces in other regions of the world-system, such as Eastern Europe or India, where similar structural conditions and conjunctural contradictions prevail and limit the applicability of liberalism, even as left orthodoxy is rejected.[28] Furthermore, the renovative ideas and evolving strategic vision explored herein are important beyond the left, particularly given the dearth of alternatives to neoliberalism being offered by any other political forces. Mexican novelist Carlos Fuentes wrote not long ago:

> Today, the programs and activities of the left in Latin America are more important than ever. . . . Only the left can make sure that capitalism without safeguards, perpetuating our ancient social evils, is not imposed in Latin America. And only the left can prevent a bureaucratic and unproductive populist state from suffocating society.[29]

Despite repeated proclamations that "The Left Is Dead," not only is the left increasingly important in Latin America, the Latin American left is increasingly important as an inspiration for noncapitalist alternatives to crises that are global in scope. Note the comments of Latin Americanist scholar Goran Therborn :

---

27. Immanuel Wallerstein, "The Collapse of Liberalism," op cit., pp. 103-104.

28. The applicability of this typology to the Eastern European lefts struck me as reasonable following personal conversations with European participants in an international conference on "Democracy in Post-Communist and Market Socialist Regimes," organized by the Cultural Studies Center, University of California, Santa Cruz, February 1996.

29. Carlos Fuentes, "The Left Is Not Dead," *World Press Review*, March 1991, p. 64.

The core values of socialist culture—universal equality and solidarity—remain intact. The increasingly global nature of social problems—of poverty/migration and of the environment, for example—and the existence of global communication networks, make it likely that these values will gain adherents and therefore strength rather than the opposite. The classical left is likely to be reconstituted on that basis in the next century. What it will look like we cannot say. But it seems probable that the future of the European socialist left will be more in the image of *the left of the New Worlds of the Americas* than in that of the classical left of European industrial capitalism. It will be more heterogeneous, both in its concerns and core identities, as well as in its long-term perspectives; more influenced by exogenous cultural tendencies; looser and more democratically organized; more pragmatic in practice.[30]

In the following chapters, we will explore in detail the ideas of the lefts that are being reconstituted in two nations of the Americas. Chapter Two will first present a brief historical account of the evolution of the left's paradigm crisis in Cuba and Mexico from the 1960s through the end of the 1980s, highlighting the impact of global changes during the past decade. Then, in Chapter Three, we will examine those currents of today's left which still formulate their conceptions of democracy largely in terms of old socialist and liberal orthodoxies. Chapter Four then presents the renovative left's efforts to define a democracy that is fuller and broader than the restricted models offered by liberal and socialist doctrines and practices. Chapters Five and Six explore these same tendencies with regards to their views on socialism, market economies, and alternative economic models. Chapters Seven and Eight address the issues of national sovereignty and the importance of asserting the autonomy of the nation-state within the world-system. Around these questions there remains considerable consensus and thus fewer clear-cut ideological differences. The concluding chapter offers a multidimensional explanation of the existence and influence of the orthodox, liberal, and renovative currents and the trend of each toward ascendency or decline in their respective national contexts.

Methodology

Cuba and Mexico were chosen as case studies for several reasons. First, these nations produced the two most thorough (in terms of socio-

---

30. Goran Therborn, "The Life and Times of Socialism," *New Left Review*, No. 194, July-August 1992, p. 32, (my emphasis).

economic and political transformation) and enduring revolutions in Latin America. They were revolutions guided by the old statist paradigm shared by much of the nationalist and socialist left. In many regards, the Mexican and Cuban revolutions are two of the most successful examples of the old middle-run strategy: the popular classes were incorporated into the political system; left-associated ethical values of social justice and equality were substantially incorporated into the postrevolutionary national culture; state-led, economic development strategies lifted both nations out of the periphery; and national sovereignty was defended with relative success in the shadow of an aggressively expansive superpower. The cohesiveness and stability of their postrevolutionary societies allowed Mexico and Cuba to avoid brutal and traumatic ruptures like those caused by the military dictatorships that ruled many Latin American nations throughout much of the 1970s and 1980s.

Clearly, there were important countervailing constraints on their respective national-revolutionary projects. The United States reasserted its influence over Mexico in the 1920s and again in the 1940s and '50s, and Cuba slipped into quasi-dependence on the Soviet bloc after the early 1960s. At the same time, the historical trajectory of both revolutions attest to the most serious deficits of the old statist paradigm: the postrevolutionary political systems evolved into increasingly authoritarian state-party regimes, and the state-centered economies were ill-equipped to adapt to the sweeping global changes of recent decades. Today, the postrevolutionary regimes of both nations, Cuba with a left still in power and Mexico with a strong left in opposition, confront profound socioeconomic and political crises reflecting the deficiencies of the old strategy and the difficulty of creating a progressive alternative to neoliberal restructuring.

As case studies Cuba and Mexico will allow us to examine two historically important lefts that exhibit compositional integrity over time (undisturbed by the violent national traumas experienced elsewhere) and which are today facing serious conjunctural crises and readjustment. Furthermore, by focussing on the paradigm crisis and shift underway within the lefts of just these two countries, it is possible to present a more nuanced analysis than that offered in *Utopia Unarmed's* sweeping, panoramic view of the Latin American left.

Another methodological difference between this study and Castañeda's book is that my research is based on a larger and broader sample of the left: I interviewed seventy-four Cubans and Mexicans for this book, a purposive sample selected to reflect the range of relevant political and ideological currents and generations. With few exceptions, the individuals interviewed are not government officials, but neither are they isolated, "ivory-tower" academics. Their ideas and activities are highly relevant in the politics of their nations. Those interviewed include members of the highest policy-making bodies of the ruling Cuban Communist Party (PCC) and of Mexico's main left opposition Partido de la Revolución Democrática (PRD). They include important Mexican opinion-makers who write regular columns in the Mexican press, lend moral authority as well as strategic vision to the opposition, serve as national mediators in the conflict in Chiapas and as opposition legislators in the national Congress, help set the agenda of national universities, and advise labor unions, women's organizations, and urban popular movements. The Cubans interviewed include policy advisers who have the ear of the nation's highest officials on a broad range of issues from reforms of the economy, the Constitution, and the criminal justice system to policies on culture and the arts. Specifically, I interviewed forty-three Cubans, including: three members of the PCC Central Committee (two of whom were part of the revolution's historic leadership); four high-level PCC functionaries; five ministerial functionaries (including one minister of state); two Communist Youth cadre; six intellectuals from the arts/cultural sphere; twenty-five academics from various university departments and research centers; and two members of the small, social democratic opposition. I interviewed thirty-one Mexicans, representing Communist, Trotskyist, Maoist, revolutionary nationalist, and independent socialist currents, former members of the ruling PRI and current PRI sympathizers, left party militants as well as unaffiliated academics and other sectors of the intelligentsia. Fifteen of the Mexicans interviewed are currently active in the main left opposition party, Partido de la Revolución Democrática, ten of them in national leadership positions. Many of these seventy-four people were interviewed more than once.

The interviews were based on a questionnaire divided into five sets of issues: (1) the international situation, particularly the implications of a post-Cold War order for traditional nationalist aspirations; (2) political economy and development, including the role of the state, planning, and markets, as well as questions regarding the viability of socialism and the meaning of "development" and "progress"; (3) democratization, conceptions of democracy, and state-party-civil society relations; (4) the emergence of new social actors and changing concepts of who constitutes the "*sujeto histórico*" of social change; and (5) ideology per se, including Marxism, Leninism, revolutionary nationalism, liberalism, and neoliberalism. Interview data is supplemented with an extensive bibliography of recent written materials from the Cuban and Mexican lefts. This empirical data, essentially ideas and discourse, provide the heart of the study, which is a description and analysis of the current process of ideological redefinition and reassessment among left intellectuals in Cuba and Mexico.[31]

Theoretical Perspectives

Although this is a study of ideas, it is primarily an empirical rather than a theoretical work. Nevertheless, my analysis is clearly informed by theoretical perspectives, particularly those associated with two distinct traditions within sociology: (1) the sociology of knowledge, ideology, and intellectuals, and (2) the historical political economy of world-systems theory. The combining of these two traditions is somewhat rare, and this study represents one of the few empirical studies of ideology and discourse written from a world-systems perspective.

The sociology of knowledge and ideology, dating back to Karl Mannheim, attempts to explain how historical, social settings help determine "the subject's whole mode of conceiving things."[32] In Mannheim's words "the conditions of existence affect not merely the historical genesis of ideas, but constitute an essential part of the products of thought and make themselves felt in their content and form."[33] From Marx's observations about "false consciousness," through Mannheim's preference for the more neutral formulation of "perspective," via the work of Georg Lukács, Louis Althusser, Clifford Geertz, and into the present, a great debate has persisted about the definition of ideology, which ultimately "revolves around one single question: should ideology be defined according to the criterion of truth or falsehood?"[34] In other words, does ideology merely reflect the current realities of society or is it distortion (conscious or otherwise)?

---

31. One reader of an earlier draft of this book was critical of what he considered my immersion in "very parochial literature" and my inattention to the work of "leading scholarly experts on Cuba and Mexico." Most of the literature cited herein is only parochial by the most U.S.-centric standards, and indeed much of the work cited is written by leading experts on Cuba and Mexico, most of them *from* Cuba, Mexico, or other Latin American countries. It is hoped that this study will help expose more U.S. scholars to the important ideas of their Latin American colleagues.

32. Karl Mannheim, *Ideology and Utopia. An Introduction to the Sociology of Knowledge* (New York: Harcourt, Brace & World, Inc., 1936), p. 266.

33. Ibid., p. 279.

34. Raymond Boudon, *The Analysis of Ideology* (Chicago: University of Chicago Press, 1989), p. 24.

So many theorists have added their opinions to this debate, that the proverbial angels dancing on the pinhead have come to resemble a heavy-metal mosh pit, one into which I have neither the courage nor the inclination to hurl myself. Besides which, I am reasonably satisfied with the resolution to this debate suggested in a recent work by John Thompson, who claims to offer a "critical conception of ideology," which, "can be used to refer to the ways in which meaning serves, in particular circumstances, to establish and sustain relations of power . . . . Ideology, broadly speaking, is *meaning in the service of power.*"[35] I would add but one qualification, ideology may also be meaning in the service of *undermining* power; that is, there are antisystemic (in Wallerstein's terms), or counterhegemonic (in Gramscian parlance), as well as dominant ideologies. This study is about both the decline of old ideologies that served to sustain relations of power (i.e., liberalism and Marxism-Leninism), as well as about efforts to construct new antisystemic ideologies.

In recent years, discourse analysis has reminded us again about the importance of meaning and representation in sustaining power; occasionally, however, in its tendency to read all social phenomenon as text, discourse analysis loses sight of the other historical, structural conditions in which discursive representation is formed. Fortunately, Robert Wuthnow has provided a marvelous, structurally-grounded, historical account of how three major world ideologies emerged as critical discourses and then became institutionalized: the Reformation, the Enlightenment, and European Socialism.[36]

Wuthnow had the great advantage over this author of examining historically consolidated ideologies, whereas the present study is about a process of ideological change still very much underway. Nevertheless, many of Wuthnow's general findings are applicable to the developments described herein. Particularly helpful is Wuthnow's insistence on examining the "concrete living and breathing communities [in which] discourse becomes meaningful":

> Discourse subsumes the written as well as the verbal, the formal as well as the informal, the gestural or ritual as well as the conceptual. It occurs, however, within communities in the broadest sense of the word: communities of competing producers, of interpreters and critics, of

---

35. John B. Thompson, *Ideology and Modern Culture* (Stanford: Stanford University Press, 1990), pp. 6-7.

36. Robert Wuthnow, *Communities of Discourse. Ideology and Social Structure in the Reformation, the Enlightenment, and European Socialism,* op cit.

audiences and consumers, and of patrons and other significant actors who become the subjects of discourse itself.[37]

Therefore, "to understand how an ideology is shaped by its social environments, one must . . . examine the specific circumstances under which these expressions come into being."[38] Among those circumstances, Wuthnow highlights two factors that are especially pertinent to the cases examined here: (1) divisions within the ruling elite, which were identified as a prominent feature of the political conditions giving rise to each of the cultural innovations analyzed in *Communities of Discourse*, and (2) the availability of resources to support the diffusion of new ideologies.

We will return to these issues in the concluding chapter, when we explore (1) the ways in which divisions within, and the absence of viable alternatives from, ruling elites in Cuba and Mexico, as well as in core nations like the United States, have contributed to a conjuncture in which a renovative left discourse appears and asserts itself, and (2) how the different resources available in each national situation condition the relative strength of renovative, liberal, and orthodox perspectives.

The sociology of intellectuals provides another important thread of the theoretical cloth in which this study is wrapped. Carl Boggs' recent book, *Intellectuals and the Crisis of Modernity*, presents intellectuals as important "agents of legitimation and delegitimation."[39] After summarizing the negative dimensions of "modernity" and "progress," understood in Enlightenment terms as technological control over nature and material abundance, Boggs argues that:

> The implications of all this for the role of intellectuals are dual and contradictory: the rise of a hegemonic technocratic intelligentsia accompanied by its negation in the social forces that grow out of the conditions [of the late twentieth century]. The crisis of modernity generates an epochal conflict between technocratic and critical modes of thought, between structures of domination and embryonic forms of opposition visible in the emergence of new social movements.[40]

The Gramscian-influenced Boggs is particularly concerned with the hegemony exercised by increasingly technocratic intellectuals and the declining role of traditionally critical intellectuals, because without

---

37. Ibid., p. 16.
38. Ibid., p. 540.
39. Carl Boggs, op cit., p. 2.
40. Ibid., p. xiii.

"critical modes of thought . . . no effective social transformation can occur."[41]

The critical role of intellectuals has been especially important in the history of Latin America. Latin Americanist scholar Jean Franco recently observed that Latin America's intelligentsia helped sustain utopian visions and "shaped the identity of nations."

> It was they who acted as the critical consciousness of society, as the voice of the oppressed, as the teachers of future generations. They were held—and held themselves—in high regard. Indeed, Cuban independence hero José Martí is still referred to as "the apostle," the Mexican José Vasconcelos compared himself to Moses . . . . This prestige has to be understood in the context of societies with high levels of illiteracy. The intelligentsia were not only major actors in the public sphere, but also—at least in public perception—mediators for the popular classes and advocates of social change.[42]

That historical role is in question today, according to Franco, not only because of factors such as the disillusionment with socialism, the electoral defeat of the Sandinistas in Nicaragua, and the collapse of communism, but also because of the eclipse of the print media and the globalization of the electronic media. "The extinction that threatens the intelligentsia," notes Mexico's Roger Bartra, "has caused great alarm in Latin America, possibly because this is one of the regions of the world that has best preserved these relics of the past that are the public or organic intellectuals."[43]

Bartra is right, but why has the critical role of the intelligentsia been better preserved in Latin America? Most sociological works on intellectuals, including the excellent books by Wuthnow and Boggs, focus largely, if not exclusively, on intellectuals of Western Europe and the United States, the core of the modern world-system. To understand the particular role that left intellectuals continue to play in Mexico and Cuba, and to appreciate the likelihood that a new antisystemic or counterhegemonic discourse may emerge in such areas of the world, it is necessary to situate this study within the framework of world-systems analysis.

---

41. Ibid., p. xii.

42. Jean Franco, "What's Left of the Intelligentsia? The Uncertain Future of the Printed Word," *NACLA Report on the Americas*, Vol. XXVIII, No. 2 (Sept./Oct. 1994). An excellent Spanish translation of Franco's piece also appeared in *La Jornada Semanal* (Mexico), No. 291 (January 8, 1995).

43. Roger Bartra, "Cuatro Formas de Experimentar la Muerte Intelectual," *La Jornada Semanal* (Mexico), No. 291 (January 8, 1995).

World-systems scholars argue that, since the sixteenth century, there has existed a single world-system, consisting of a political network of nation-states and "one capitalist economic system with different *sectors* performing different functions."[44] Those sectors have been labeled core, periphery, and semiperiphery. The core, including the United States, Western Europe, and Japan, is characterized by the most advanced technologies of the world-economy, global military power, strong states and stable political systems, and a large middle class. The periphery, including most African states and many Latin American and Asian nations, reflect the opposite characteristics: poor, often single-crop agricultural economies, weak and unstable states, a small, extravagantly wealthy elite alongside an extremely impoverished, largely marginalized majority. Semiperipheral sectors of the world-economy are generally characterized by older industrial technologies formerly limited to the core. Semiperipheral states are relatively strong and stable (often authoritarian), and the population of the semiperiphery includes a substantial middle class, generally associated with the public sectors, and a significant industrial working class. Much of the current discussion about "globalization," a process anticipated by and contained within the world-system analysis of capitalism, gives little attention to the ways in which interstate competition and the unequal division of labor (represented by the core, periphery, and semiperiphery) render the nature and effects of globalization quite different from one region to another. That is why this analysis is situated within the world-system framework rather than within the less precisely elaborated notion of "globalization."

The semiperiphery is a category of particular importance in world-systems theory because of its dual role as political buffer in the interstate system and as site of new, profitable investment opportunities no longer available in the core. The semiperiphery includes large parts of Latin America, Southeast Asia, South Africa, India, and Eastern Europe. Mexico is one of the classic semiperipheral nations. Cuba, as I will argue, also exhibits many of the qualities associated with the semiperiphery, even though it has not commonly been described in this way and currently risks being reperipheralized. I will contend that the semiperipheral status of Cuba and Mexico, which places them above the most extreme conditions of abject poverty that contribute to the social disintegration so pervasive in the periphery but not within reach of the material abundance that tends to placate citizens of the core, helps explain the reluctance of the lefts in those nations to embrace liberalism and their efforts to renovate an antisystemic strategy.

---

44. Immanuel Wallerstein, *The Capitalist World Economy* (Cambridge: Cambridge University Press, 1980), p. 68.

The structural position of Cuba and Mexico within the world-system also affects the very nature and role of intellectuals, distinguishing them from their counterparts in the core. Samir Amin notes that the intelligentsia outside the core is defined by:

> (i) its anticapitalism; (ii) its openness to the universal dimension of the culture of our time and, by this means, its capacity to situate itself in this world, analyze its contradictions, understand its weak links, and so on; and (iii) its simultaneous capacity to remain in living and close communion with the popular classes, to share their history and cultural expression.[45]

In contrasting the twentieth-century history of traditional European intellectuals with that of Third World intellectuals, Boggs observes that the latter "were more integral to political struggles of the post-War period, more keenly focussed on the unity of knowledge and power—owing in part to their sense of national subordination within the global order."[46] Thus when this book focuses on left intellectuals in Cuba and Mexico, it is not examining the ideas of isolated academics or technocrats. It is exploring the thinking of a politically influential and engaged intelligentsia closely associated with parties and social movements that intervene in national politics.

The question of political struggle and its relationship to the role of intellectuals and the construction of discourse brings us to a final theoretical concern running throughout this study: the relationship between structure and agency. Elsewhere I have reviewed the contribution of some of sociology's greatest thinkers to our understanding of how human agency is exerted within and, at pivotal moments, against historical structures.[47] The question is relevant here regarding: (1) the power of discourse itself as subject, not merely as a reflection of existing structures, and (2) the critical role of political struggle in altering both ideology and material structures. Although dogmatic interpretations of Marxism have often zigzagged between extreme economic determinism and idealistic voluntarism, the founders of Marxism attempted to strike a balance. Marx believed that human beings make history, but he warned that they do not always do so under their conditions-of-choice. And Engels

---

45. Samir Amin, "The Social Movements in the Periphery: An End to National Liberation," in S. Amin, et al., *Transforming the Revolution*, op. cit., p. 136.

46. Carl Boggs, *Intellectuals and the Crisis of Modernity*, op. cit., p. 13.

47. Edward J. McCaughan, "Race, Ethnicity, Nation, and Class within Theories of Structure and Agency," *Social Justice*, Vol. 20, Nos. 1-2 (Spring 1993).

acknowledged that "ideological conception . . . reacts in its turn upon the economic basis and may, within certain limits, modify it."[48]

Wuthnow writes about the "reciprocal influence (a kind of feedback mechanism) of ideas on the social environment."[49] Based on his historical studies, Wuthnow argues that, once institutionalized, an ideology "may play a decisive role in acting back on its environment."[50] Regarding the role of intellectuals and associated political actors and movements, the important agents of ideology and social change, Wuthnow concludes from his study:

> [H]istory is not determined by the invisible dynamics of capitalist development; it is made by actors who exercise choice on the basis of partial information; but it is also shaped within the constraints defined by tradition, special interests, economic conditions, and political circumstances. . . . In each historical episode the leading contributors to the new cultural motifs recognized the extent to which the institutional conditions of their day were flawed, constraining, oppressing, arbitrary. . . . The strength of their discourse lay in going beyond negative criticism and beyond idealism to identify working models of individual and social action for the future.[51]

What are the implications of these observations for this study? If the renovative left currents identified in Mexico and Cuba successfully institutionalize their discourse into viable political organizations, economic programs, social modes of existence, and cultural expressions, the future of those nations and of their relationship to the world-system could be significantly altered. Whatever the ultimate outcome of their efforts, as the dust settles from the simultaneous collapse of socialism and liberal reformism, and as neoliberalism's sudden ascendancy continues to wreak social and economic havoc, the political intellectuals examined herein are most certainly responding to Wallerstein's call to help formulate "a clear antisystemic strategy for an era of disintegration."

---

48. Frederick Engels, "Letters on Historical Materialism," in Robert C. Tucker, *The Marx-Engels Reader* (New York and London: W.W. Norton and Co., 1978), p. 763.

49. Robert Wuthnow, *Communities of Discourse*, op. cit., p. 548.

50. Ibid.

51. Ibid., pp. 582-83.

CHAPTER 2. THE BACKDROP

From the Revolutionary 1960s to the Neoliberal 1980s—What's Left?

In Cuba and Mexico, the left's historical, statist paradigm took on added weight as a result of the nationalist revolutions that constitute the key defining moments of their twentieth-century life (Mexico from 1910 through the 1930s, Cuba from 1959 through the 1970s[1]). A quick review of major trends in left thought in these countries will allow a better appreciation of the extent to which global events of the 1980s shattered the old paradigm.

The Sovietization of the Cuban Revolution

In the first years following the 1959 seizure of state power, the Cuban revolution was not dominated by any one ideological current. Fidel Castro's Twenty-Sixth of July Movement was politically dominant as a result of Castro's charismatic leadership, the movement's successful guerrilla campaign against the Batista dictatorship, and the relative weakness of Cuba's dominant social classes.[2] However, Castro's was an ideologically diverse movement, including socialists, nationalists, and various vaguely-defined democrats. Cuba's historic communist party,

---

1. The ending dates of both revolutions are debatable. For the Mexican revolution, the Lázaro Cárdenas government of the 1930s marked a period of significant institutionalization and consolidation of the new regime and the last of the major social reforms sparked by the revolution. Cuba's revolution carried out the bulk of its most radical economic and social changes during the 1960s and underwent a substantial process of institutionalization in the 1970s. In that regard, I offer these decades as markers of the end of the actual revolutionary periods of profound socioeconomic and political change.

2. See Marifeli Pérez Stable, *The Cuban Revolution. Origins, Course, and Legacy* (Oxford: Oxford University Press, 1993) for an insightful analysis of the failure of Cuba's upper classes to articulate and carry out their own program for nonrevolutionary change, of the sort undertaken elsewhere in Latin America (e.g., under Getulio Vargas in Brazil and Juan Perón in Argentina).

the Popular Socialist Party (PSP), was far more cohesive but had played a less decisive role in the military campaign and was unable to dominate politically. The rocky process of unifying these diverse forces into a single party of the revolution would take more than five years, including the short-lived Organizaciones Revolucionarias Integradas (ORI) and eventually the founding of the new Cuban Communist Party (PCC) in 1965.

Partly as a result of the early diversity of the revolution, the 1960s were a period of great effervescence, creativity, and debate. It would be a mistake to romanticize the 1960s, since they were also marked by bitter disputes, purges, defections, chaos, economic difficulties, and the threat of U.S. intervention. Nevertheless, the period also generated great enthusiasm among the popular classes and radical intelligentsia, as the Cuban revolution actively experimented with various economic and political notions, in search of an independent, uniquely Cuban socialism. The agrarian reforms combined small private, collective, and state forms of property. Efforts at import-substitution industrialization accompanied an expansion and modernization of the traditional sugar economy. The relative merits of moral and material incentives were endlessly argued, as were theories of value and systems of accounting and pricing.

In the political realm, utopian notions of direct democracy gradually gave way to an emphasis on popular participation through mass organizations of workers, peasants, women, artists, and intellectuals. Literature and the arts flowered. New currents of progressive thought from around the world influenced the academy, perhaps most notably at the University of Havana's Philosophy Department, and were reflected in heterodox journals such as *Pensamiento Crítico*. The countercultural values of the "world revolution of 1968" echoed strongly within sectors of the Cuban revolution as well, according to philosopher Juan Antonio Blanco. But, he laments, the invasion of Czechoslovakia by Cuba's new Soviet patrons "destroyed the hopes of 1968."[3] For Cuban historian Jorge Ibarra, "The Cuban revolution was made during the first ten years. Since 1970, it has mainly lost time."[4]

---

3. Juan Antonio Blanco, presentation on Cuba and the 1960s, Casa de las Américas, Havana, February 9, 1993.

4. Jorge Ibarra, interview with author, Havana, February 12, 1993. For early assessments of the first decade of the Cuban Revolution, see Sheldon B. Liss, *Roots of Revolution: Radical Thought in Cuba* (Lincoln: University of Nebraska Press, 1987); Lionel Martin, *The Early Fidel. Roots of Castro's Communism* (Secaucus, N.J.: Lyle Stuart Inc., 1978); Elizabeth Sutherland, *The Youngest Revolution* (New York: The Dial Press, Inc., 1969); Leo Huberman and Paul M. Sweezy, *Cuba: Anatomy of a Revolution* (New York: Monthly Review Press, 1968); James O'Connor, *The Origins of Socialism in Cuba* (New York: Monthly Review

Again, I do not want to suggest that the Cuba of the 1960s perfectly embodied the idealistic aspirations of that revolutionary decade. Cubanist scholar Carollee Bengelsdorf offers a sober assessment, particularly of the leadership's failure to establish a solid framework for democratic input into the direction of the revolution:

> The Cuba of the 1960s had taken the emancipatory message of the classical Marxist heritage concerning the postcapitalist state and simply followed its spirit. The solution to the problem of its silences and contradictions and, above all, to its incarnation in the political and economic structures of Eastern Europe and the Soviet Union was, in effect, not to create any permanent state institutions. . . . The absence of forms to insure any kind of popular input into decision making had led, by the end of the 1960s, to a situation in which the leadership—ever more concentrated around the figure of Fidel—had separated itself entirely from the population, a population that had been left virtually without a voice and without a path by which to read this leadership.[5]

The period of institutionalization that followed, together with the relative stability and economic well-being of the 1970s, were no doubt experienced by many Cubans as a much-needed order and respite from the upheaval of the previous decade. But the price of calm and institutionalization may well have been a lost opportunity to break with the more orthodox features of state socialism. The discourse and strategy of the Cuban revolution thereafter were increasingly confined within a relatively more humane, more participatory, and therefore more popular version of the Soviet model. Several developments combined to cut short the revolution's early phase of diverse experimentation and move it increasingly in the direction of a more rigid, more authoritarian system patterned after the Soviet Union. In addition to the unambiguous signal to fall in step sent by the Soviets with the invasion of Czechoslovakia, at least five other factors contributed to the jelling of a more statist society:

1. The unrelenting hostility of the United States, even after the defeat of the internal counterrevolution, seemed to justify an emphasis on defense, unity, discipline, and certain authoritarian

---

Press, 1970). For more recent and more sobering looks back on that decade, see Marifeli Pérez Stable, *The Cuban Revolution*, op. cit., especially chapters 3, 4, and 5; Susan Eva Eckstein, *Back from the Future: Castro Under Cuba* (Princeton, N.J.: Princeton University Press, 1994); and Carollee Bengelsdorf, *The Problem of Democracy in Cuba. Between Vision and Reality* (New York and Oxford: Oxford University Press, 1994).

5. Carollee Bengelsdorf, ibid., p. 100.

measures. More-over, the economic disruptions caused by the U.S. trade embargo made central planning and an alliance with the Soviet Union an option increasingly difficult to avoid.

2. The death of Ernesto (Che) Guevara in 1967, and his increasing absence from Cuba in the preceding years, deprived the revolution's leadership of a creative, unorthodox voice who was highly critical of the Soviet system and represented a counterbalance to the orthodoxy of Cuba's historic Communists and to the realpolitik pragmatism of Castro.[6]

3. In 1970, Fidel Castro and his supporters threw all of the island's resources into attempting a record 10-million ton sugar harvest. This was understood as Cuba's last, best effort to pursue an independent path by maximizing its natural advantage and generating the capital needed for autonomous development. When the effort failed, and in the absence of Guevara, Castro was left without any clear alternative to a strategic alliance with the Soviets. Moreover, his own authority was undermined by the failure of the sugar harvest, opening room for greater influence by more orthodox, pro-Soviet leaders from the former PSP.

4. Following the failure of the 1970 harvest, and in the face of the U.S. trade embargo, Cuba decided to join the Soviet bloc's economic system, the Council for Mutual Economic Assistance (CMEA). Joining CMEA implied making the island's systems of economic planning, management, financing, pricing, and so on, compatible with that of the Soviet and Eastern European economies. A Soviet-style, five-year plan was adopted in Cuba, and criticism of the revolution's new patrons was increasingly discouraged.

5. As the revolution began a process of political institutionalization in its second decade, those with the acknowledged organizational skills and experiences were largely cadre from the former PSP. The organization of the new Communist Party, its structure, procedures, educational program, ideological manuals, and the like, was left to a considerable extent in the

---

6. On the thought of Ernesto (Che) Guevara and his influence on the Cuban Revolution, see Carlos Tablada, *Che Guevara: Economics and Politics in the Transition to Socialism* (Sydney: Pathfinder Press, 1989); and Various, *Pensar Al Che* (Havana: Centro de Estudios Sobre América/Editorial José Martí, 1989). On the thought of Fidel Castro, see Sheldon B. Liss, *Fidel! Castro's Political and Social Thought* (Boulder: Westview Press, 1994); Fidel Castro, *Ideología, conciencia y trabajo político/1959-1986* (Havana: Editorial Pueblo y Educación, 1991); and Lionel Martin, op. cit.

hands of pro-Soviet, orthodox militants of the PSP. The discourse of the Cuban revolution became increasingly stamped with the stale language of "scientific socialism."[7]

This combination of factors led to a more rigid, more authoritarian system and to the elimination of institutional centers representing alternative perspectives (e.g., the University of Havana's Philosophy Department and *Pensamiento Crítico* were both closed down in 1971).[8] That is not to say that all efforts at autochthonous innovation were eliminated. The formation of Cuba's national political system of Poder Popular in 1975 reflected a commitment to genuine popular participation, particularly at the local levels, that distinguished it from the Soviet model. Nevertheless, prevailing political discourse continued to spurn "bourgeois" or "liberal" democracy as meaningless formalities, and a multiparty system was condemned as counterrevolutionary or at best dismissed as unnecessary.

Periodic campaigns against bureaucratization, abuses of technocratic power, and corruption (the most recent of which was the "Rectification" begun in 1986) kept Cuba's economic enterprises more honest and participatory than their Eastern counterparts.[9] However, the dominant so-

---

7. According to Jorge Castañeda, "Castro was forced to use PSP cadres as professionals fled the island en masse. And even after the purges of 1962 and 1968, PSP Communists filled positions of responsibility well beyond what their actual participation in the revolution entitled them to. Similarly, the policies Cuba followed domestically, particularly after 1968, came uncannily to resemble what the PSP would have called for if it had survived as a separate entity." Jorge Castañeda, *Utopia Unarmed* (New York: Alfred A. Knopf, 1993), p. 32.

8. In Juan Antonio Blanco's account, through the Philosophy Department and *Pensamiento Crítico*, "we were trying to create a Cuban Marxist school of thinking, using a nondogmatic approach to Marxism. . . . Throughout the 1960s, we tried to update the Cuban population on the major trends of thinking of our time . . . . All this was something totally 'abnormal' for a proper, prudent Soviet socialist publication. . . . All of a sudden the direction of the department changed, a new curriculum was imposed, and *Pensamiento Crítico* was shut down." Juan Antonio Blanco, "Cuba: Crisis, Ethics, and Viability," in S. Jonas and E. McCaughan, *Latin America Faces the Twenty-First Century* (Boulder: Westview Press, 1994), p. 192.

9. On "Rectification," see Fidel Castro, *Rectificación: Sobre el proceso de rectificación en Cuba 1986-1990* (Havana: Editorial Política, 1990); Jorge Alonso, *Cuba: La Rectificación* (Guadalajara: Universidad de Guadalajara, 1990); Marifeli Pérez Stable, *The Cuban Revolution*, op cit.; Susan Eva Eckstein, *Back From the Future*, op cit.;and various articles in Sandor Halebsky and John M. Kirk, *Transformation and Struggle: Cuba Faces the 1990s* (New York: Praeger, 1990);

cialist discourse did not allow any consideration of private property or market relations. Even private snow-cone vendors were regarded as a potential threat to the revolution's goal of a classless society. On the cultural front, despite censorship and with considerable effort and courage, Cuba's film makers, literary community, and artists generally managed to produce in refreshing, often brilliant modes far removed from the stilted socialist realism of the East.[10]

The revolution and its leadership continued to enjoy broad popular support, despite the lack of democracy and space for individual initiative, in large part because of the regime's real achievements in the areas of universal health care and education. Perhaps to an even greater extent, the revolution and Fidel Castro retained legitimacy because they were seen as having finally secured Cuba's long frustrated national independence and sovereignty, particularly *vis a vis* the United States.[11] When all was said and done, however, from the mid-1970s until the world-shaking events of the late-1980s, the Cuban revolution and the vast majority of its intellectuals never seriously challenged the authoritarian, paternalistic, and highly centralized statist paradigm that had emerged from both Marxist-Leninist and nationalist traditions. What began as a peoples' revolution evolved into a relatively monolithic state-party regime.[12]

The term "state-party regime" perhaps has been most clearly defined by Adolfo Gilly in relation to the system that eventually emerged from the Mexican revolution and against which a majority of today's Mexican left is mobilized:

> [A state-party regime] is a political regime in which the ruling party forms a single body with the administrative and coercive apparatus of

---

Sandor Halebsky and John M. Kirk, *Cuba in Transition: Crisis and Transformation* (Boulder: Westview, 1992).

10. See, for example, Luis Camnitzer, *New Art of Cuba* (Austin: University of Texas Press, 1994) and the series of articles on Cuban culture in S. Halebsky and J. Kirk (eds.), *Cuba: 25 Years of Revolution, 1959-1984* (New York: Praeger Publishers, 1985) and in J. Griffiths and P. Griffiths (eds.), *Cuba: The Second Decade* (Britain-Cuba Scientific Liason Commitee, 1982).

11. See Marifeli Pérez Stable, *The Cuban Revolution*, op. cit., for an insightful analysis of what she describes as Cuba's "mediated sovereignty," identified along with Cuba's sugar-centered development, uneven modernization, a crisis of political authority, the weakness of the economic classes, and the relative strength of the popular classes as six factors in the twentieth century which "interacted to render Cuba susceptible to radical revolution," p. 7.

12. On developments in the Cuban revolution in the 1980s and early 1990s, see the Halebsky and Kirk collections, ibid.; Marifeli Pérez Stable, *The Cuban Revolution*, op cit.; and Susan Eva Eckstein, *Back From the Future*, op cit.

the state, acts as its political organ, obtains its resources from state fi-
nances and excludes the possibility of alternation of other parties in the
executive branch or in the formation of a majority in the legislature.
Such a regime can take the form of a single party that is constitutionally
established [e.g., Cuba] or that of a state party with symbolic opposition
parties that cannot, de facto or de jure, aspire to occupy the executive or
to share the status and privileges of the ruling party [e.g., Mexico].[13]

A large majority of Cuba's left has remained loyal to the state-party
regime created by the revolution, and Cuba's dissident left is a small but
growing minority. In contrast, while the Mexican left's relationship to its
nation's postrevolutionary regime has always been fraught with contradictions, the great bulk of left forces today are in the opposition, and only
a small, albeit influential, minority of leftists remain sympathetic to the
ruling Partido Revolucionario Institucional (PRI). As a left-in-opposition,
Mexicans, unlike their Cuban counterparts, broke with certain political
aspects of the old paradigm and embraced more liberal notions about
democracy. Like the Cubans, however, Mexican leftists have been slow
to question the statism of the old economic strategy.

The Mexican Left: Democracy Revalued, Statism Unchallenged

Of the various historic currents making up the Mexican left today,
three are particularly important: (1) the Communists, whose party was
founded in 1919, (2) the revolutionary nationalists and *cardenistas*, who
achieved their greatest influence and clearest articulation during the
Lázaro Cárdenas government of the 1930s, and (3) the various strands of
the new left that emerged from the 1968 student movement. These currents remained sharply divided through the 1970s, but during the 1980s,
a series of difficult, on-again-off-again mergers helped create a more
unified left. The massively-supported 1988 presidential campaign of
Cuauhtémoc Cárdenas, a prominent center-left political figure (and son
of Lázaro) who broke with the ruling PRI, was decisive in further uniting
these left currents together with broad sectors of Mexico's popular and
social movements into the Partido de la Revolución Democrática (PRD)
in 1989.

During the Lázaro Cárdenas government in the 1930s, much of the
communist and revolutionary nationalist left in Mexico actively supported the progressive nationalism of the regime. Left support of the

---

13. Adolfo Gilly, "The Mexican Regime and Its Dilemma," *Journal of
International Affairs*, Vol. 43, No. 2 (Winter 1990), p. 274.

PRI dwindled from the 1940s through the 1960s, as the state-party regime (the bases of which, ironically, were established by Lázaro Cárdenas) became more authoritarian, more representative of national and international business interests, and less responsive to popular sectors. As a result, the question of democracy and democratization, including the formal and procedural issues of multiparty, electoral systems, took on a greater significance for the Mexican left than it has, until very recently, for Cuban revolutionaries. Particularly after the Mexican government's bloody repression of the 1968 student movement, a watershed event for the nation as a whole, demands for democratization became an increasingly important component of the left's discourse.

As a left-in-opposition, the differences among Mexican leftists have been more transparent than the divisions within the highly disciplined Cuban Communist Party. As a result, there has never been one, official left discourse on democracy in Mexico. Different interpretations of the nature of Mexico's postrevolutionary state produced quite different strategies for political and social change in contemporary Mexican society. Those differences were initially sharpened by the government's limited political reforms of the mid-1970s (prompted by the fall-out of 1968) and by the worsening economic situation in the early 1980s, following the 1982 debt crisis.

Differences within the Mexican left over political strategy can be seen in the important debates over the question of electoral politics. One position stressed the importance of the electoral arena from the beginning of the political reforms in the 1970s. The Mexican Communist Party (PCM), for example, argued that by participating in the state-engineered political reforms, the PCM was able to broaden the scope of the reforms. The fight for the Communists' legal and electoral status became a primary focus of the PCM in the mid-1970s. Similarly, revolutionary nationalists grouped at the time within the Movimiento de Acción Popular (MAP) also emphasized the importance of the electoral arena, maintaining that, despite the government's control over the electoral process, the 1977 reforms did substantially advance the conditions in which to consolidate political and ideological pluralism and help regularize political confrontation.

Another position, held by various independent socialist formations of the post-'68 left, such as Punto Crítico, maintained that the political reforms, in the context of economic crisis and vast impoverishment, offered little to the popular masses. Rather, these forces argued that the limited reforms threatened the independence of the left and encouraged it to abandon popular struggles and the struggle for socialism. Save specific exceptional cases, according to this position, conditions in Mexico were not appropriate for electoral contests in the late 1970s and early

1980s; these forces consequently were very selective in their electoral participation.

However, Mexico's changing political and economic context demanded new political practices, which in turn contributed to ever more fully elaborated and nuanced strategies and tactics. By the mid-1980s, differences over whether or not to participate in elections had become less important than differences over the relative importance given electoral work over mass organizing. Revolutionary nationalists of MAP saw the importance of the electoral arena *expanding* after the 1982 debt crisis, given divisions within the PRI and a resurgent right-wing PAN (Partido de Acción Nacional). They viewed elections as an increasingly effective means of confirming the illegitimacy of the PRI. Organizations such as Punto Crítico also came to view the potential of the electoral arena more favorably, but for quite different reasons. In their view, the emergence of new social movements and popular organizations, many of which had important ties with groups such as their own, changed the prospects for popular intervention in electoral struggle, at least on the local and regional level.

For each political tendency within the Mexican left, the increasing importance of the electoral arena was greatly underscored by Cuauhtémoc Cárdenas's 1988 presidential campaign, and seemed to be the logical outcome of its initial strategy. Those, like the PCM members, who participated in the political reforms from the beginning could argue that they had indeed substantially opened up the electoral arena to progressive forces. Those of the MAP, who privileged the state as the key site of social struggle, felt vindicated by the fissures that were deepening within the state party, making electoral politics more effective. Those active in Punto Crítico, who had criticized the reforms and emphasized mass organizing, could claim to have helped alter the social correlation of forces in Mexico, thereby changing the context in which electoral work could be pursued. Thus, by the time Cuauhtémoc Cárdenas and other PRIistas of the center-left Corriente Democrática decided to break with the ruling party, most significant sectors of the Mexican left had already embraced electoral politics in one form or another.

Consequently, by the late 1980s, the reality of being a left-in-opposition against a postrevolutionary, state-party regime led large sectors of the Mexican left to question important political aspects of the old left paradigm. Specifically, the Mexican left demonstrated an appreciation for the formal, procedural aspects of representative, electoral political systems that had long been discarded by much of the left, including the Cubans in particular, as the meaningless trappings of "bourgeois" democracy. The Mexican left's revaluation of democracy had also been reinforced by the experience of South American leftists who suffered terribly under the military dictatorships that ruled most of the region in the 1970s and 1980s, many of whom made their lives-in-exile in Mexico.

In reassessing the old, statist political paradigm, the Mexican left enjoyed at least one significant advantage over their Cuban counterparts. Many social movements flourished in Mexico in the mid-1980s, including a women's movement that made feminism an influential component of revitalized left discourse. This is not to say that consciousness about women's equality has not been present in the Cuban Revolution; the status of Cuban women was considerably advanced over the past 35 years in terms of integration into the work force and mobility, access to child care, birth control and excellent health services, and legislative reinforcement of men's responsibility in the home. But these developments, not without their contradictions, were not achieved as the result of an autonomous women's movement guided by a feminist critique of authoritarianism at all levels of society. Women's gains in Cuba came about within the paternalistic and authoritarian system of the postrevolutionary state-party regime.[14]

Something quite different began to occur elsewhere in the region, including Mexico, in the 1980s. As a result of the influence of new social movements, and feminism in particular, Norma Stoltz Chinchilla argues that:

> There is a growing convergence of thinking on issues that once divided or were the source of serious tension: the importance of pluralism and democracy and its relationship to the idea of plural (potentially revolutionary) social subjects or actors (such as women) and the relationship of democracy to the principle of autonomy for popular organizations (such as those composed of women) in relationship to the state and to political parties.[15]

Consequently, by the late 1980s, the process of reassessing the left's old paradigms was more advanced in Mexico than in Cuba, in large part because of the strong presence of autonomous popular movements and

---

14. For a critique of the failure of the Cuban revolution, and other socialist regimes, to fully incorporate women and a feminist perspective, see Margaret Randall, *Gathering Rage: The Failure of Twentieth Century Revolutions to Develop a Feminist Agenda* (New York: Monthly Review Press, 1992). Randall, as well as Marfeli Pérez Stable (*The Cuban Revolution*, op. cit.), emphasize the critical lack of autonomy for mass organizations in Cuba, which has prevented the emergence of broader social movements there.

15. Norma Stoltz Chinchilla, "Marxism, Feminism, and the Struggle for Democracy," in A. Escobar and S. Alvarez, eds., *The Making of Social Movements in Latin America* (Boulder: Westview Press, 1992), p. 39.

critical discourses such as feminism. Nevertheless, in many regards, the Mexican left's "middle-run strategy" continued to be, as Wallerstein argues it has been the world over since the last century, "to attain state power by political means."[16] In that sense, the Mexican left had only partially reassessed the basic political assumptions of the old paradigm by the end of the 1980s.

Moreover, before 1990, there had been an even less thorough reassessment by the Mexican left of the *economic* aspects of the old paradigm (associated both with the state socialist regimes and the nationalist developmentalism of *cardenismo*). The discourse of much of the Mexican left still reflected considerable confidence in long-held ideas about the central role of the state and planning in the economy, the inevitably negative consequences of unregulated markets, competition and private property, and the teleology of inexorable progress through the harnessing of science and technology.

To be sure, criticism of the Soviet system had been raised by reform tendencies within the Mexican Communist Party, by Trotskyist intellectuals, and by sectors of the post-'68 left (although the Cuban Revolution remained a sacred cow among the Mexican left until very recently). The most notable critique of the dogmatization of Communist thought in Mexico was probably that made by the well-known writer and political activist José Revueltas in the early 1960s.[17] Likewise, the nationalist Lázaro Cárdenas government subsequently had been criticized for establishing corporatist control over the working class and laying the bases for an unequal, industrial capitalism in Mexico. But the Mexican left had remained so far from power for so long that it had never been faced with the need to elaborate a truly viable, alternative economic program for the nation. As a result, much of the economic aspects of the left's statist paradigm remained nearly as unexamined in Mexico as in Cuba until the current decade. Indeed, as neoliberal policies were implemented during the Miguel de la Madrid and Carlos Salinas administrations (1982-1994), the Mexican left, more often than not, found itself the most vocal defenders of state-owned enterprises and state intervention in the economy more generally.[18]

---

16. Immanuel Wallerstein, "Antisystemic Movements: History and Dilemmas," in Samir Amin, et al., *Transforming the Revolution. Social Movements and the World-System* (New York: Monthly Review Press, 1990), p. 40.

17. See José Revueltas, "A Headless Proletariat in Mexico," translated and reprinted in Luis A. Aguilar (ed.), *Marxism in Latin America* (New York: Alfred A. Knopf, 1968), pp. 240-244.

18. The above summary of the Mexican left prior to the 1990s is based largely on Edward J. McCaughan, *The Mexican Left Between the Fall of State Socialism and the Rise of Neoliberalism* (Santa Cruz, Calif.: Chicano/Latino

Global Challenges to the Statist Paradigm

Until quite recently, then, much of the left's traditionally statist paradigm remained substantially unchallenged in Cuba and Mexico. The most significant exception was the extent to which a number of national developments in Mexico had broadened the left's strategy to include aspects of electoral, representative democracy, historically more associated with liberalism, and a greater appreciation of pluralism generated by the new social movements. However, significant changes in the economic, political, and cultural structures and practices of the world-system were accelerating throughout the 1980s, influencing the more strictly national developments highlighted in this brief sketch of the lefts in Cuba and Mexico. The accumulation of global changes eventually contributed to a genuine paradigm crisis, as expressed by the left intellectuals quoted in Chapter One.

This was not the first time, of course, that major changes in the world-system combined with signficant regional developments to provoke serious debate and rethinking within the Latin American left. The 1920s and '30s were rich with efforts by political intellectuals to develop a more organic Latin American leftism, such as Haya de la Torre's populist nationalism and José Carlos Mariátegui's attempts at a more indigenous socialism.[19] In some regards, the political-intellectual work of these

---

Research Center, University of California, Santa Cruz, 1993). For more detailed information and analysis about the evolution of left thought in Mexico since the 1960s, also see: Cuauhtémoc Cárdenas, et al., *Corriente Democrática: Alternativa Frente a la Crisis* (Mexico: Costa-Amic Editores, 1987); Barry Carr, *Marxism and Communism in Twentieth-Century Mexico* (Lincoln: University of Nebraska Press, 1992); Jorge Castañeda, *Utopia Unarmed,* op. cit.; Rolando Cordera Campos, et al., *México: El reclamo democrático* (Mexico: Siglo XXI, 1988); Rolando Cordera Campos and Carlos Tello, *México: La Disputa por la Nación* (Mexico: Siglo XXI, 1981); Joe Foweraker and Ann L. Craig, *Popular Movements and Political Change in Mexico* (Boulder: Lynne Rienner Publishers, 1990); Enrique Semo, *Viaje alrededor de la izquierda* (Mexico: Editorial Nueva Imagen, 1988); Jorge Tamayo Rodríguez, "Los movimientos sociales y el proceso electoral de 1988 en México," in *Memoria* (Mexico), Vol. IV, No. 29 (Jan-Feb. 1990).

19 William Rowe and Vivian Schelling revisit in a useful way the contributions and contradictions of Haya de la Torre and Mariáteugi in the context of Antonio Gramsci's ideas about the "national-popular collective will" in Chapter 3 of their *Memory and Modernity. Popular Culture in Latin America* (London: Verso, 1991). Other useful sources on historical debates within Latin American left thought are Luis E. Aguilar, *Marxism in Latin America,* op. cit.; Sheldon B. Liss, *Marxist Thought in Latin America* (Berkeley: University of California Press, 1984); and Michael Löwy, *El marxismo en América Latina* (Mexico: Ediciones ERA, 1982).

men, which represents efforts to articulate a more distinctly Latin American left discourse, can be seen as precursors to current developments in the Latin American left. However, these and other historical debates within Latin American leftism (such as over Peronism or Revueltas's critique of the Communist Party) do not appear to be significant points of reference in the reassessment taking place today. In part, I suspect that is because those earlier debates themselves remained confined within the statist world-view now being questioned. Moreover, there is a sense that the world has changed fundamentally in the intervening decades, necessitating a bolder departure from past ideological schemes.

As noted earlier, long before the dramatic events associated with the fall of the Berlin Wall in 1989, challenges from within the left itself had begun to fray some threads of the old statist paradigm: particularly the antiauthoritarian and countercultural movements of 1968 and more recent social movements. However, Stoltz Chinchilla reminds us that "Democracy and feminism were not topics of serious discussion" among the Latin American left until the 1980s. These are quite new developments. Moreover, the various strands of more radically antistatist postmodern and poststructuralist theories about the "decentering of the subject" and the failure of modernity's Enlightenment project, as well as claims that we have entered a postcapitalist era, were relatively less influential in Latin America than in Western Europe and the United States.[20] The structural realities of the semiperiphery (extreme class inequalities, increasing poverty, and national subordination to core states and international capital) continued to correspond more closely to the traditional Marxist and nationalist paradigm than to any postmodern, postindustrial vision. Consequently, up through the 1980s, the process of renovation within the Latin American lefts was only partial.

Then, three concomitant, global developments in particular culminated at the end of the 1980s to bring about a full-blown paradigm crisis among the left in Latin America: the accelerated globalization and restructuring of the world-economy, the near-hegemonic rise of neoliberal ideology, and the sudden collapse of the former Soviet bloc.

All of Latin America has been deeply affected by the restructuring of the world-economy, which began at the initiative of core nations and

---

20. A particularly lucid and insightful analysis of these developments and their challenge to the paradigms associated with modernity, and therefore with the left, can be found in Stuart Hall, "The Question of Cultural Identity," in S. Hall, et al., *Modernity and Its Futures* (Cambridge: Polity Press, 1992).

core-based capital in response to the profit crisis of the 1970s. As the restructuring coincided with the exhaustion of national developmentalist projects in Latin America, severe financial crises emerged in the newly developing nations of the region. Even for the most successful national-ist development models, such as Mexico's post-1930s, import-substitu-tion industrialization, such restructuring and financial crisis have gener-ally involved a relative subordination of national policies to international financial institutions. This often contributed to (1) devastating declines in wages and living standards, (2) abandonment of the internal market in favor of export activities, (3) dismantling of national welfare states, (4) destruction of small and medium national industries, and (5) absorption of the most dynamic economic sectors by transnational capital. Since the collapse of the Soviet Union, even Cuba's once protected economy has been gradually subjected to restructuring along lines more acceptable to international banks and investors. The ability of individual nation-states to regulate or ameliorate these developments has been further undermined by the accelerated internationalization of capital.[21]

Globalization and restructuring of the world-economy also posed challenges to the strong national cultures of Latin America, particularly in Cuba and Mexico where revolutions had been waged in assertion of national identities. As Stuart Hall has observed:

[A] nation is not only a political entity but something which produces meanings—a system of cultural representation. People are not only le-gal citizens of a nation; they participate in the *idea* of the nation as rep-resented in its national culture.[22]

The global process of integrating regional economies brought with it "the consequent interpenetration of cultures and customs,"[23] threatening the traditional nationalism of countries like Cuba and Mexico. Thus the challenges posed to the Latin American left by global economic restruc-turing were cultural and ideological as well, unraveling the very "idea" of the nation-state.

---

21. On world economic restructuring and its impact on developing nations, see, e.g., R. Jenkins, *Transnational Corporations and Uneven Development: The Internationalization of Capital and the Third World* (London: Methuen, 1987); A. Lipietz, *Mirages and Miracles: The Global Crisis of Fordism* (London: Verso, 1987); A. Alvarez, *La crisis global del capitalismo en México, 1968-1985* (Mexico City: Ediciones Era, 1987); and Edward J. McCaughan, "Mexico's Long Crisis: Toward New Regimes of Accumulation and Domination," *Latin American Perspectives*, Vol. 20, No. 3, Summer 1993.

22. Stuart Hall, "The Question of Cultural Identity," op. cit., p. 292.

23. Adolfo Gilly, "The Mexican Regime in Its Dilemma," op cit., p. 276.

One of the most unsettling ideological developments accompanying economic restructuring has been the aggressive neoliberal ideological offensive, which gained considerable strength during the Ronald Reagan and Margaret Thatcher administrations and was supported by the intellectual and policy-making cadre of international financial institutions. Neoliberalism remains within the tradition of liberalism in its emphasis on free enterprise, the market, and individual initiative and responsibility. It is "neo" in its abandonment of twentieth-century liberalism's "politics of constant rational reform," which aimed at avoiding extreme social conflict through the integration of larger sectors of the population into the system, both nationally (through the welfare state and universal suffrage) and internationally (through national self-determination and developmentalism).[24]

The neoliberal offensive proved to be astonishingly successful and further undermined left confidence in the Latin American state's capacity to shepherd economic development and social transformation.[25] In little more than a decade, broad sectors of intellectuals and policy makers around the world, including many leftists in Latin America, were apparently convinced that the eighteenth century ideologies of Adam Smith and David Ricardo would lead the way into the third millennium (even as nineteenth century Marxism was pronounced dead). This was particularly true in the Southern Cone nations of Chile and Argentina, where brutal military dictatorships devastated the historical lefts and ruptured strong national political cultures, leaving them particularly open to the influence of neoliberalism.[26] Looking at the recent trajectory of the left in those nations, one might be tempted to accept Francis Fukuyama's now famous assertions about the end of history and the final universalization of free-market economies and restricted electoral democracy.[27] However, I will argue that, while radical "free-market" tenets

---

24. See Immanuel Wallerstein, "The Collapse of Liberalism," op. cit.

25. On the influence of neoliberalism worldwide, see, e.g., S. Hall, *The Hard Road to Renewal* (London: Verso, 1988); J. Valenzuela Feijóo, *Crítica del modelo neoliberal* (Mexico: Fac. de Economía, UNAM, 1991); F. Hinkelammert, "Our Project for the New Society in Latin America: The Regulating Role of the State and Problems of Self-Regulation in the Market," in S. Jonas and E. McCaughan, eds., *Latin America Faces the Twenty-First Century*, op. cit.

26. Rhoda Rabkin has written a persuasive analysis of the importance of "ideas" in influencing center-left forces in Chile to embrace neoliberal economic policies; see R. Rabkin, "How Ideas Become Influential. Ideological Foundations of Export-Led Growth in Chile (1973-1990)," in *World Affairs*, Vol. 156, No. 1 (Summer 1993).

27. Francis Fukuyama, "The End of History," reprinted in S. Hall, et al., *Modernity and Its Futures*, op. cit., p. 48.

have been taken up more recently by some leftists in Cuba and Mexico, the nationalist and social justice values of these nations' deeply rooted political and popular cultures, as well as the structural realities of the semiperiphery, continue to mediate the degree to which neoliberalism is accepted there.

The Fall of State Socialism

Associated with both global economic restructuring and the rise of neoliberalism is the collapse of the Soviet bloc. For Cuba, the demise of the Soviet and Eastern European regimes brought immediate, very material consequences, including the loss of more than three-fourths of its markets and once uniquely favorable terms of trade. But the sudden fall of state socialism reverberated beyond socialist Cuba, throughout much of the world's left, including in countries like Mexico which were never part of the Soviet bloc. The East's debacle swept away any remaining illusions harbored by some of the left that an alternative socialist world-system was in the making. It eliminated the hope that state socialism might be reformed into a more democratic and humane alternative to capitalism. For others, the collapse of the Soviet bloc was the nail in the coffin of the state-centered models of economic development and progressive social change long embraced by the left.[28]

As Immanuel Wallerstein has argued, because socialist revolutions took place not in the core nations of the world-system but in the periphery and semiperiphery, the "construction of socialism" in practice "became the process by which (semi) peripheral states would catch up with the core zones of the capitalist world economy."[29] The Soviet "program for national development" was greatly admired throughout the Third World, even by nationalist governments (like that of Lázaro

---

28. Useful accounts of how the disintegration of the socialist bloc affected the world's left can be found in: David Held, "Liberalism, Marxism and Democracy," in S. Hall, et al., *Modernity and Its Futures* (Cambridge: Polity Press, 1992); Carl Boggs, *Intellectuals and the Crisis of Modernity* (Albany: State University of New York Press, 1993); Immanuel Wallerstein, "Marxism After the Collapse of Communism," *Economic Review* (February/March 1992); Immanuel Wallerstein, "The Concept of National Development, 1917-1989. Elegy and Requiem," *American Behavioral Scientist*, Vol. 35, No. 4/5 (March/June 1992); Samir Amin, et al., *Transforming the Revolution. Social Movements and the World-System* (New York: Monthly Review Press, 1990); and Carlos Antonio Aguirre Rojas, "1989 En Perspectiva Histórica," *La Jornada Semanal* (April 4, 1993).

29. Immanuel Wallerstein, "Marxism After the Collapse of Communism," op. cit., p. 34.

Cárdenas) and left forces that remained highly critical of the Soviet bloc. The Soviet Union's sudden collapse symbolized for some of the left a great defeat for the very idea of national development.

Moreover, though sectors of the Latin American left were heartened by the "democratic revolutions" that swept through the East in 1989-1990, the uncertain post-Cold War order appeared ominous to many. This was particularly true given how the collapse of the Soviet bloc coincided with disturbing events such as the Persian Gulf War and, regionally, the U.S. invasion of Panama and the electoral defeat of the Sandinistas in Nicaragua (following a punishing war financed and directed by the United States). The demise of the Soviet Union therefore also suggested to many on the left the unpleasant prospect of a unipolar world, of an unrestrained United States with its long history of aggression in Latin America.

All of these changes clearly pose enormous challenges to the traditional paradigms of the Latin American left, particularly its emphasis on the state. Within Cuba and Mexico, the challenges of world-systemic changes appeared especially unsettling given the serious domestic problems faced by their respective state-party regimes. As Gilly has noted, pressures from worldwide economic restructuring contributed to a crisis of postrevolutionary political regimes, because, "beyond state coercion and force, these regimes are also based on 'social pacts.'"[30] Their historic social pacts cannot be sustained with neoliberal policies. In Cuba, where the loss of Soviet support and a tightening of the U.S. trade embargo have forced the state to adopt austerity measures, the social pact of the revolution has been weakened, and divisions over policy and long-term strategy have become more apparent within the regime, opening space for greater questioning of the old dogmas. In Mexico, extensive neoliberal restructuring throughout the 1980s far more seriously eroded the long-stable social pact dating from the 1930s, leading important center-left forces to break with the regime and greatly strengthen the opposition, but within a context in which the left opposition's traditional program was in doubt.

As the century began its final decade, the old paradigm that had oriented and given identity to left intellectuals in Cuba and Mexico was shattered. While attending a play about Christopher Columbus in Mexico City in August, 1992, on the 500th anniversary of his fateful encounter with the indigenous peoples of the Americas, I unexpectedly found this paradigm crisis expressed in the program notes. Playwright Héctor Ortega explained:

---

30. Adolfo Gilly, "The Mexican Regime in Its Dilemma," op cit. p. 277.

My melancholy reflections about utopias and their collapse were influenced by the sudden fall of "real socialism," the loss of power from one day to the next of Gorbachev, the creator of "perestroika and glasnost," that is, the proposal for a democratic socialism that never came to be.

The effects of these changes on our country, as well as the Persian Gulf War with its fireworks that liquidated 250,000 human beings, whom we never saw and whose death we never learned about on television, the globalization of the planet, the birth or definition of its commercial nuclei as a threat to the concept of the nation, etc., have forced us to rapidly redefine ourselves.[31]

The following chapters examine in depth how the left's paradigm crisis has provoked serious redefinition and ideological realignments on the key issues of democracy, socialism, and national sovereignty.

---

31. Héctor Ortega, program notes to "El Huevo de Colon," Teatro Juan Ruiz de Alarcón, Centro Cultural Universitario, Mexico City, August 1992.

CHAPTER 3. DEMOCRACY I

The Persistence of
Socialist and Liberal Orthodoxies

The left's conceptions of democracy have long suffered from a Manichean liberalism-socialism opposition. The world-systemic discourses of liberalism, democracy, socialism, and nationalism tended to become reified and polarized in the power struggles of the Cold War. Political and intellectual prolocutors of the Western core powers successfully fused the liberal ideology of the capitalist world-economy with the notion of democracy, when, in fact, as Chilean sociologist Jaime Osorio reminds us:

> At least until the mid-19th century, the terms liberalism and democracy were in conflict. The first called attention to liberties and gave special emphasis to economic freedom. Liberalism's defenders rejected democracy because they believed that the search for equality under governments of the majorities would call liberal principles into question.[1]

Nevertheless, as Immanuel Wallerstein explains, following the emergence in Europe of a conscious workers movement and the revolutionary upheavals of 1848, a broad consensus emerged among the dominant classes in the core around liberalism as a politics of "constant rational reform." If the capitalist economy was to be stabilized, the "dangerous classes" had to be incorporated into the political system. Democracy, conceived in terms of "one citizen-one vote" electoral participation, seemed the best way of integrating the rebellious working classes without jeopardizing the capitalist nature of the economy. Liberalism, thus associated with gradual and limited democratic reforms, became "the overwhelmingly dominant ideology" for the next hundred years.[2]

---

1. Jaime Osorio, "Liberalism, Democracy, and Socialism," in S. Jonas and E. McCaughan, eds., *Latin America Faces the Twenty-First Century: Reconstructing a Social Justice Agenda* (Boulder: Westview Press, 1994), p. 28.
2. Immanuel Wallerstein, "The Collapse of Liberalism," in R. Miliband and L. Pantich, eds., *Socialist Register 1992* (London: Merlin, 1992), pp. 98-100.

In the course of the twentieth century, liberal discourse, inadvertently aided by Lenin, Stalin, and the experiences of the Soviet bloc, also effectively presented socialism and Marxism as the antithesis of democracy. Socialism, in practice and in ideological mutation, became identified with authoritarian statism, and the nationalist, anti-imperialist struggles of the South gradually suffered from guilt-by-association in the global ideological wars. In Latin America, for instance, reform-minded nationalists, like Guatemalan President Jacobo Arbenz in the 1950s, were vilified as communists and removed by armies dispatched by liberal democracies like the United States.

If nationalist struggles for independence and autonomous development generated strong interventionist states that restricted the reign of transnational capital and core nation-states, then Third World nationalism, like socialism, was viewed as the enemy of liberalism and democracy. Liberalism = capitalism = freedom = democracy. Socialism = nationalism = statism = authoritarianism. There was just sufficient reality to the democratic freedoms of Western capitalist societies and more than ample evidence of authoritarianism in state socialist and nationalist regimes to make the forced, dichotomous pairings stick. One of the defining characteristics of world hegemony, of course, is that the hegemon's ideology appears not as ideology but as common sense.

In Latin America, the glaring economic and political inequalities of "really existing world capitalism" were enough to make the left wary of such simplistic formulations. Indeed, liberalism has never enjoyed quite the same popular acceptance in the South as it has in the North. Benito Juárez, for example, the great liberal reformer who broke up Mexico's vast semifeudal estates and church-owned landholdings in the mid-1800s, is highly revered as a national hero. At the same time, Mexicans generally acknowledge that Juárez's liberal reforms also helped to destroy the collective landholdings of ancient, indigenous communities, thereby aiding in the creation of a landless, rural work force to be exploited by the new Mexican and foreign *hacendados* who quickly reconcentrated the nation's best agricultural lands. This and many other historical experiences have made the Janus-faced nature of liberalism a prominent feature of Latin America's collective memory.

This did not mean, however, that Latin American thought escaped the ideological dualisms of the Cold War. More often than not, and especially during the 1960s and 1970s, the Latin American left was trapped by the same discursive sleight of hand that allowed liberalism to claim democracy as its own legitimate child. The current process of rethinking democracy in Cuba and Mexico revolves around the tension of the liberalism-socialism, or more accurately, in practice, a liberalism-statism dichotomy.

Historically, the Latin American left, with a few notable exceptions, gave relatively less emphasis to the liberal ideals of political democracy than it did to the national and social goals of justice, equality, and development. Jorge Castañeda's assessment of this history is shared by broad currents of today's Latin American left:

> Much of the left wrongly dismissed representative democracy for many years as a sham: a bureaucratic, corrupt device invented by local elites and foreign agents to trick the Latin masses into tolerating forms of government and domination contrary to their interests.[3]

Not that the left's dismissal of political democracy wasn't partly justified by the twisted forms it has taken in the region. Castañeda is quick to clarify that "the left has a point . . . representative democracy in Latin America has functioned poorly at best, and mostly when reduced to a meaningless exercise."[4]

However, during the difficult struggles against brutal, authoritarian military regimes that ruled much of the region from the mid-1960s through the mid-1980s, large sectors of the Latin American left developed a new appreciation for liberal political democracy.[5] As tens of thousands of democratic activists were jailed, tortured, disappeared, or murdered during the dark decades of military rule, it became starkly clear that individual rights and guarantees, independent judiciaries, and legislative checks on executive power do make a difference.

More broadly, the left began to question a commonly held assumption, reinforced by the harsh realities of Latin American politics, that "the only power worth winning was the one that sprang from the barrel of a gun."[6] Writing in 1983 about the lessons drawn by the Brazilian left in its struggle against the generals, Francisco Weffort explains:

> The discovery of the value of democracy is inseparable, within the opposition, from the discovery of civil society as a political space. More

---

3. Jorge Castañeda, *Utopia Unarmed: The Latin American Left After the Cold War* (New York: Alfred A. Knopf, 1993), p. 327.

4. Ibid., p. 357.

5. Robert Barros ("The Left and Democracy: Recent Debates in Latin America," *Telos*, No. 68, 1986, p. 49) began his widely discussed 1986 assessment of the Latin American left's changing view of democracy by observing, "In Brazil, Chile, Uruguay, and Argentina the experience of authoritarian rule during the past decade has produced a fundamental re-valuation of the importance of civil and political rights for protecting individual lives and the possibility of politics."

6. Jorge Castañeda, *Utopia Unarmed*, op. cit., p. 335.

than the "economic miracle," the terror years produced a real "political miracle," by undermining traditional ideas on the relations between State and society. And the concept of politics was placed on its true foundations.[7]

In Mexico, the increasingly authoritarian nature of the postrevolutionary regime was made painfully clear to broad segments of society during the brutal repression of the 1968 student movement. The Mexican left subsequently became ever-more focussed on the struggle for democratization of state and civil society throughout the 1970s and 1980s.[8]

Cuban revolutionaries remained generally skeptical about the long-term prospects for political liberalization in Latin America and frequently expressed concern about the left's growing preoccupation with electoral politics. Nonetheless, within the very different context of their own socialist regime, the Cuban left also gave considerable attention in the 1970s and 1980s to elaborating what it considered the more substantive, participatory democracy of Cuba's Poder Popular.[9]

Despite the impressive early efforts of far-sighted thinkers such as Francisco Weffort, Pablo González Casanova, and Carlos Pereyra,[10] until recently much of the discussion and debate about democracy was often limited to lining up behind one or the other side of rigidly dichotomous labels: bourgeois v. socialist democracy, formal v. substantive democ-

---

7. Francisco Weffort, "Why Democracy?" in Alfred Stepan, ed., *Democratizing Brazil: Problems of Transition and Consolidation* (New York and Oxford: Oxford University Press, 1989), p. 345.

8. See Edward J. McCaughan, "The Mexican Left Between the Fall of State Socialism and the Rise of Neoliberalism: Some Observations," *Working Paper No. 2* (Santa Cruz: Chicano/Latino Research Center, University of California, Santa Cruz, 1993).

9. See, for example, Olga Fernández Ríos and Gaspar J. García Gallo, "The State and Democracy in Cuba," *Contemporary Marxism*, No. 1, Spring 1980, pp. 81-88. A critical and thorough treatment of the Cuban regime's largely unsuccessful efforts to address the democracy question, see Carollee Bengelsdorf, *The Problem of Democracy in Cuba: Between Vision and Reality* (New York and Oxford: Oxford University Press, 1994).

10. See, e.g., Francisco Weffort, "Why Democracy?," op. cit.; Pablo González Casanova, *Democracy in Mexico* (New York: Oxford University Press, 1972); P. González Casanova, "The Crisis of the State and the Struggle for Democracy in Latin America," *Contemporary Marxism*, No. 1, Spring 1980, and "Foreign Debt, the Threat of Foreign Intervention, and Democracy in Latin America," *Contemporary Marxism*, No. 14, Fall 1986; and Carlos Peyera, *Sobre la democracia* (Mexico: Cal y Arena, 1990), a posthumously published collection of his writings on democracy from the 1980s.

racy, liberal v. participatory democracy, ad infinitum.[11] The quality of the search for a meaningful Latin American democracy was not improved by the rapid ascendency of neoliberal notions of restricted, free-market democracy that accompanied the economic crisis and restructuring of the 1980s. The influence of that perspective, backed by the economic and political muscle of the United States and the international financial system, skewed the discussion toward one extreme pole.[12] Advocates of a narrowly-defined electoral democracy, preoccupied almost exclusively with issues of order, continuity, and governability (rather than popular participation and representation), then gained further, at least momentary, advantage over left proponents of a fuller, social democracy when the communist regimes of Eastern Europe and the Soviet Union disintegrated.

The debate was also often limited by poorly understood or articulated distinctions among state, political regime, and government, despite the fact that such differentiation is common in political science. Sonia Alvarez, a political scientist from that rare breed called the Cuban-American left, uses the strikingly visual metaphor of an edifice to illustrate these distinctions. The *state*, she suggests, is like the building's foundation and weight-bearing frame, the structure that remains intact, defining the core shape and size of the structure, however much interior remodeling may be done. Including institutions like the military, courts, and the bureaucracy, the state represents the fundamental pact of class, race, and gender domination, which is maintained through a variety of coercive, regulatory, and distributive/redistributive methods. It is the basic structure of politics and the most difficult to transform. The *political regime*, according to Alvarez's metaphor, functions like the doorways, corridors, and stairways of the building, determining who participates

---

11. For three interesting collections in English of writings on democracy from some of Latin America's most notable left intellectuals in the 1980s, see *Contemporary Marxism*, No. 1 Spring 1980, *Contemporary Marxism*, No. 14 Fall 1986, and *Latin American Perspectives*, Issue 65, Vol. 17, No. 2, Spring 1990. These collections include some of the most sophisticated thinking about democracy by the left from the late 1970s through the mid-1980s, demonstrating both the serious limitations imposed by some of the left's traditional discourse as well as the evolution of new concepts.

12. Writing reflecting a more restricted vision of democracy, concerned more with institutionality and governability than with popular representation and participation, can be found in Larry Diamond, Juan J. Linz, and Seymour Martin Lipset, eds., *Democracy in Developing Countries* (Vol. 4): *Latin America* (Boulder: Lynne Rienner and London: Adamantine Press, 1989); and Robert A. Pastor, ed., *Democracy in the Americas: Stopping the Pendulum* (New York and London: Holmes & Meier, 1989).

and who gains access to how much political, economic and cultural power. The regime—including institutional arrangements such as the political party system, types of labor unions, balance of legislative and executive power—mediates and shapes relations between the state and society. Institutional and constitutional changes of the regime occur more frequently than changes in the state, adjusting to and accommodating social and political struggles. Finally, the *government* is the "super," the building superintendent, the incumbents of political power who try to make the edifice function.[13]

At two extremes of the left, the most orthodox, statist perspectives, associated with some Communists and revolutionary nationalists, and the most liberal-influenced social democratic views, there is often little appreciation of such distinctions and relationships. The orthodox perspective tends to overemphasize the state and underestimate the importance of the political regime. This has sometimes contributed to skepticism about the value of democratic reforms of the political system. For example, a case has been made by some Latin American leftists and left Latin Americanists in the United States that the transitions to civilian rule in countries like Brazil, Chile, and Argentina have been of limited significance because the class nature of the state remained fundamentally unchanged. Such a critique tends to ignore the real difference such liberalization of the political system has meant for the democratic opposition.[14]

At the same time, this underestimation of the political regime's importance relative to the state has led some orthodox leftists to an uncritical defense of "revolutionary" states, such as those of socialist Cuba or *cardenista* Mexico in the 1930s. Stressing that those states successfully restructured power relations in favor of a social pact encompassing the popular majority, such a perspective often fails to question why those revolutionary states also helped produce political regimes that have proven to be authoritarian and resistant to democratization.[15] To be fair

---

13. This summary of Alvarez's formulation is based on a lecture given by her at the University of California, Santa Cruz, September 27, 1990.

14. See, for example, Germán Sánchez, "Problemas de la democracia en Nuestra América," *Revista Casa de las Américas* (Havana), Año XXXII, Nú. 186, January-March 1992; Tomás A. Vasconi, "Democracy and Socialism in South America," *Latin American Perspectives*, Issue 65, Vol. 17, No. 2, Spring 1990; James Petras, "The Redemocratization Process," *Contemporary Marxism*, No. 14, Fall 1986; Ronald H. Chilcote, "Post-Marxism: The Retreat from Class in Latin America," *Latin American Perspectives*, Issue 65, Vol. 17, No. 2, Spring 1990.

15. Regarding Cuba, see, e.g., Olga Fernández Ríos and Gaspar J. García Gallo, op. cit., or the editorial, "Ironías de la OEA," in the Mexican journal, *Estrategia*, No. 100, July-August 1991, that defends Cuba as the most democratic of

to the Mexican and Cuban lefts, distinguishing between state, regime, and government has not been an easy task, given that the three have been attached at the hip like Siamese triplets in the state-party regimes that have ruled for more than 60 years in Mexico and for nearly 40 years in Cuba.[16]

Based on interviews and recent writings in Mexico and Cuba, I will now present a fuller picture of two currents within the left of the 1990s whose conceptions of democracy still adhere closely to the historical orthodoxies of socialism and liberalism. The following chapter examines the renovative current, which seeks to transcend the old dualisms. The liberal, orthodox, and renovative tendencies do not correspond precisely with past political or ideological affiliations, or with generations, but rather reflect the left's paradigm crisis and its shake-up and realignment in response to recent changes inside Mexico and Cuba and worldwide.

Orthodox Socialist Perspectives

Orthodox left perspectives from the traditions of statist socialism tend to define democracy in the broadest of terms, extending beyond the formal political arena to include the substantive goals of economic equality and social justice (not as prerequisites for democracy but as part of its very definition).[17] Moreover, in the experience of state socialism and the ideological legacies of Lenin and Stalin, the left's historical concern with social and collectivist ideals has tended to become associated primarily

---

all Latin American countries. Similarly uncritical views of the state and political regime forged by Lázaro Cárdenas in the 1930s are expressed by Cuauhtémoc Cárdenas, Porfirio Muñoz Ledo, and Ifigenia Martínez in their interviews with Andrew Reding in *World Policy Journal*, Vol. V, No. 2, Spring 1988; they are hard-pressed to account, theoretically or conceptually, for how the revolutionary state became "increasingly divorced from the interests of the people," as Cuauhtémoc Cárdenas puts it.

16. See Chapter 2 for a definition of the concept "state-party regime."

17. Three Cuban scholars, for example, have written that Marxist-Leninist conceptions of democracy "surpass the limitations of democracy [understood] in terms of government or participation in political activities and in the superstructural sphere, to include, besides government, popular participation and citizen rights in economic activity. That is, they consider economic democracy as consubstantial to democracy and give it its most complete, real, and legitimate meaning when also extending the analysis to the liberation struggles of the oppressed peoples." Olga Fernández Rios, Romelia Pino Freyre, and Hernán Llanes, "Cuba: Socialismo, democracia y soberanía," manuscript (Havana), April 1991.

with the state, often to the exclusion of the political system or even civil society. Thus, the orthodox left's perspective on democracy is inclined to underplay the significance of reforming the political system or enhancing the individual rights and obligations of citizens, focusing more on the class nature of the state. Democratization is understood more in terms of greater social equality and the state's defense or advocacy of working class interests. This view, as sociologist Walter Goldfrank points out, tends to conceal the party's domination and its privileges in acting as the working class's fiduciary.[18] The participatory aspect of democracy is frequently emphasized but without reference to the need for civil society's autonomy from state and ruling party. These more orthodox views encompass ideological positions that hold Leninist ideas about the state and vanguard party and that justify rather than criticize the past.

In Cuba, the orthodox, statist view on issues of the political system and democracy remain very influential but no longer hegemonic among the revolution's intellectuals. In essence, this perspective says the Cuban political system is the most democratic, most participatory in the world, requiring only fine-tuning: "The Eastern European regimes were perfectly democratic and it would be difficult to come up with a more participatory system than Cuba's Poder Popular."[19] "I don't know of a better system. Besides, the youth are not concerned with 'democracy,' which is a foreign discourse used against Cuba."[20] As ultimate proof of the extent of Cuban democracy, individuals from this perspective offer that the Cuban people are armed and therefore quite able to turn against the state if they think it is acting against their interests. For example, the distinguished Cuban intellectual and political leader Carlos Rafael Rodríguez in his opening address to a huge gathering of Latin American intellectuals, challenged the "so-called" multiparty democracies to arm their workers and peasants and then see what would happen to their regimes.[21]

For this tendency, the experience of liberal democracy has relatively little to offer Cuba: "Our experience with the U.S.-style political system has been mainly negative and not a point of reference."[22] "In Cuba, the

---

18. Wally Goldfrank, personal communication with author.

19. Herminio Camacho, Communist Youth official for Havana Province, interview with author, March 11, 1993.

20. Cristina Pedroza, president of a local Communist Youth branch, interview with author, Havana, March 9, 1993.

21. Carlos Rafael Rodríguez, "Intervención en la apertura del XVIII Congreso de ALAS," manuscript (Havana), May 28-31, 1991.

22. Ramiro Abreú, Central America specialist in the Central Committee's international relations department, interview with author, Havana, March 8, 1993.

multiparty project is inevitably counterrevolutionary."[23] As Carollee Bengelsdorf has pointed out, such disregard for liberal conceptions of democracy stems not only from their reading of Marxist precepts but also from their experience with the ways in which José Martí's political ideals "had been corrupted in the bankrupt political structures of the Cuban republic."[24]

There is a tendency to view liberalism, but not Marxism, as a foreign ideology. Armando Hart, a member of the revolution's historic leadership who did not come out of the Communist tradition and is reportedly a liberal influence on the reform process, still shares the orthodox tendency's dismissal of liberal democracy:

> Today there is an attempt to impose a model on us, one that is not our own. We have no liberal bourgeois tradition here. The great deficit of Western political culture is that it does not take 'the social' adequately into account. The great social drama is not at the center of analysis in Western political culture; even economic analyses lose the social context.[25]

The orthodox perspective in Cuba is also informed by an overriding concern with order, governability, and the avoidance of radical ruptures in the political system. In this regard, some Cubans are impressed with the ability of restricted liberal democracies to marginalize radical dissent by establishing the hegemony of liberal discourse. Juan Antonio Blanco, a philosopher and historian who is far from orthodox on most issues, leans in that direction on the questions of power and dissent:

> Bourgeois democracy is both things: democratic (a certain level of pluralism) and bourgeois. The limits of accepted pluralism, determined either by force or by cultural hegemony, exclude nonbourgeois alternatives. A socialist democracy should also be both things: democratic (tolerance of a pluralism of ideas), but within a socialist option and with the same possibilities of excluding bourgeois options. If socialist hegemony were sufficiently solid, as bourgeois hegemony is in the U.S., you could probably tolerate a bourgeois party (as in the U.S., where little left parties participate in elections).[26]

It is interesting to note that containing dissent within institutional frameworks, governability, the stability of the state, and avoidance of rupture, are of particular concern to *orthodox* left forces in Cuba and, as

---

23. Olga Fernández, interview with author, Havana, February 16, 1993.
24. Carollee Bengelsdorf, *The Problem of Democracy in Cuba*, op cit., p. 9.
25. Armando Hart, interview with author, Havana, March 11, 1993.
26. Juan Antonio Blanco, interview with author, Havana, March 4, 1993.

we shall see below, *liberal* left forces in Mexico. The orthodox left has long enjoyed state power in Cuba, and Mexico's liberal left arguably sees its best hope for a bigger share of power in a negotiated pact for co-governing with the PRI. It is not that renovative leftists in these countries are unconcerned with avoiding violent upheaval in the transitions to democracy, but they stand to gain little if the current state-party regimes are not thoroughly transformed or dismantled. Thus one's relationship or potential relationship to political power clearly helps determine one's take on issues such as containing dissent and assuring institutional continuity and governability.

The following comments by Darío Machado, a member of the Cuban Communist Party's Central Committee, illustrate various elements of the most orthodox, statist perspectives on democracy in Cuba:

> There has never been any sign of discontent with the structure of Poder Popular [Cuba's system of legislative bodies]. Sovereignty in Cuba rests where popular representation is located (in the Poder Popular), unlike in a country like the United States where a Supreme Court that can impose its will over the President and the legislature. There is no supra-popular power in Cuba. We have a more democratic system. The U.S. President has enormous power on the basis of being elected by the majority; he can declare war, name and remove ambassadors, etc. This is not true of the Cuban President [Fidel Castro], who is not elected directly by the people. The President here has to rule collegially; he doesn't concentrate an enormous amount of power, because he has to share it with the rest of the Council of State. This is more democratic than a President who is able to declare war on his own. Here there is a distribution of power, not a concentration in one figure.[27]

In addition to their uncritical devotion to Cuba's political model, orthodox intellectuals are reluctant to give up key Leninist doctrines. For example, Gladys Hernández, a young economist, told me, "I don't agree with the criticisms of Marxism-Leninism. The principles are objective. The dictatorship of the proletariat has worked in Cuba."[28] In another example, Darío Machado concludes his study of the problems of bureaucracy by reasserting the importance of democratic centralism.[29]

---

27. Darío Machado, interview with author, Havana, February 26, 1993. Of course, it should be noted that the U.S. president in fact does not have authority to declare war; only Congress can do so, which is not to say that U.S. presidents have not effectively done end-runs around Congress to prosecute local wars.

28. Gladys Hernández Pedraza, interview with author, Havana, March 2, 1993.

29. Darío L. Machado, *Burocracia y Burocratismo* (Havana: Editorial Política, 1990).

However, some reassessment of such ideas is under way even among more orthodox intellectuals. The process of change is producing a range of attitudes that move from the absolute defenses of Leninist orthodoxy cited above, to cautious reassessment of the left's "tactical" errors, to criticisms that are more thorough but still within the framework of Marxism-Leninism. Isabel Rauber, for example, an Argentinian who has lived in Cuba for two decades and is married to a high-ranking Communist Party official, agrees that the Latin American left undervalued democratic and electoral forms of struggle. *But,* she says, it did so for historically justified reasons, and the problem now is that the Right is able to use democratic discourse against the left.[30] Rauber says she has not yet rejected the dictatorship of the proletariat: "The problem is how to transform the theory into a political project. That's been the problem of all twentieth-century Marxism, how to apply the theoretical model to reality." [31]

Recent writings by Marta Harnecker, something of a living icon for Latin America's Marxist-Leninist left, are indicative of a process of reflection and change that is still incomplete. Harnecker argues that the left's project must include political democracy, social or substantive democracy, and participatory democracy, which she understands as government of, for, and by the people, respectively.[32] Yet Harnecker still wants to uphold the dictatorship of the proletariat as a valid theoretical discourse, even if it is no longer viable as political discourse:

> From the theoretical point of view, in order for a democratic political system to reflect the interests of the majority of its people, it is necessary to limit the realization of the interests of those who oppose measures beneficial to the people. . . . If the minority were to voluntarily submit to the interests of the popular majority in power, the majority could implement a democracy without limits. . . . The dictatorship of the proletariat is simply the other side of the coin of broader popular democracy, i.e., the strength of the majority.[33]

---

30. Isabel Rauber, *Proyecto, Sujeto y Poder: Desafíos Actuales del Movimiento Popular Latinoamericano* (Santo Domingo: Colección Debate Popular, 1992), pp. 35-36.

31. Isabel Rauber, interview with author, Havana, February 16, 1993.

32. Marta Harnecker, "Democracy and Revolutionary Movement," in S. Jonas and E. McCaughan, *Latin America Faces the Twenty-First Century*, op. cit., p. 64.

33. Ibid., p. 66. A similarly flawed attempt to retain the conceptual notion of "class dictatorship" as an essential component of the transition to socialism can be found in Richard Harris, *Marxism, Socialim, and Democracy in Latin America* (Boulder: Westview, 1992), particularly in his chapter on the transitional state.

However, notions of "class dictatorship" do not translate as "strength of the majority" when the majority has no autonomous form of representation. Marifeli Pérez Stable and Margaret Randall, both sympathetic to the Cuban revolution's historic goals, have emphasized in their critical assessments of Cuba's political regime that mass organizations such as the Cuban Women's Federation and the Confederation of Cuban Workers are seriously limited in their ability to serve as democratic institutions by their lack of autonomy from the Cuban Communist Party and the state.[34] The critical issue of civil society's autonomy, as a necessary component of democracy, was brought to the fore of left political and theoretical debate by Latin America's various struggles in the 1970s and '80s against military dictatorship and toward democracy. Such ideas have had a difficult time finding vocal advocates within the still restricted intellectual climate of Cuba. However, changing ideas about democracy are gradually beginning to influence even some of Cuba's more orthodox thinkers. For example, Harnecker is now writing a book on the Brazilian Workers Party and collecting testimonies from popularly-elected, left governments in various Latin American cities, because she recognizes that there are important lessons to be learned from those non-orthodox experiences.[35]

The evolving discourse of Fidel Castro himself illustrates the tentative but evident influence of new democratic notions on the still quite statist views of Cuba's orthodox tendency. Castro laments that Gorbachev's reforms, intended to perfect socialism, unintentionally destroyed the very "pillars" of socialism by undermining the authority of the Communist Party and the Soviet state. The orthodox statism of this assessment seems self-evident. Yet, indicating his own openness to necessary political reform, Castro suggests that Gorbachev's error was not having taken a more gradual approach rather than trying to do it all at once.[36] Castro then implicitly accepts one of liberalism's fundamental critiques of the Soviet political model when he identifies Stalin's violations of legality and abuses of power as grave errors.[37] Castro goes on to define democracy in terms that thoroughly mix liberal, nationalist, and Marxist discourse:

---

34. Marifeli Pérez Stable, *The Cuban Revolution. Origins, Course, and Legacy* (New York and Oxford: Oxford Univeristy Press, 1993) and Margaret Randall, *Gathering Rage. The Failure of 20th Century Revolutions to Develop a Feminist Agenda* (New York: Monthly Review Press, 1992)

35. Marta Harnecker, interview with author, Havana, February 9, 1993.

36. Fidel Castro in Tomás Borge, *Un Grano de Maíz. Conversación con Fidel Castro* (Mexico: Fondo de Cultura Económica, 1992), p. 48.

37. Ibid., p. 61.

[D]emocracy, first of all, as Lincoln once defined it, is the government of the people, by the people, and for the people. . . . Democracy implies the defense of all of the rights of the citizens, among them the right to independence, the right to all freedom, the right to national dignity, the right to honor; for me democracy means fraternity among men, true equality among men, equal opportunity for all men, for each human that is born, for each intelligent being that exists.[38]

Castro ends his comments on democracy by saying it can never exist, in these terms, in highly unequal capitalist societies. He criticizes efforts to impose "capitalist bourgeois democracy" on Cuba by calling on the na-tionalist, anti-imperialist credentials of José Martí and Simón Bolívar, who, Castro says, "never conceived of this form of democracy for the countries of Latin America."[39] While Castro's preoccupation with the authority of state and party, and his unequivocal dismissal of "bourgeois democracy," indicate the extent to which his views remain firmly within the more orthodox tendency, his comments also suggest an effort to rec-oncile these views with liberal notions about citizenship rights, liberty, and legality, and to legitimize the reluctance of this partial embrace of liberalism with the still powerfully popular discourse of nationalism.

Within the broadest sectors of Mexican left, because authoritarianism of both left and right has been so thoroughly discredited, orthodox perspectives on democracy and democratization are more visible in *prac-tice* than in conscious intellectual formulation. Such tendencies often reveal themselves within the Mexican left both internally (e.g., top-down, bureaucratic, careerist behavior by some individuals within the PRD) and externally (e.g., occasionally reproducing corporatist relations with the mass movements).

As in Cuba, orthodox views about democracy among the Mexican left also tend to reveal themselves in assessments of the past. In a large gathering of the left in Mexico City in September, 1992, for example, de-fense of the Soviet Union remained firm in some quarters. A once-com-mon justification for the Soviets' undemocratic past was given by Arturo Bonilla following arguments by Andrea Revueltas, daughter of the fa-mous José Revueltas.[40] She asserted that there is much currency in Rosa Luxemberg's critique of Lenin's and Trotsky's fear of democracy, be-cause a viable model of socialism could only be built through mass, democratic participation. In response, Bonilla, another prominent left intellectual, objected to her critical assessment of the Soviet Union, insist-

---

38. Ibid., p. 106.

39. Ibid., pp. 106-107.

40. Andrea Revueltas and Arturo Bonilla, public comments at Foro Luchas Emanicipadoras de Fin de Siglo, Mexico City, September 4, 1992.

ing that the "bureaucratization" of the Soviet regime can be explained by the unfavorable international context in which it emerged.

A small group of former Communists, who opposed the dissolution of the Mexican Socialist Party as part of the formation of the PRD in 1989, are now associated with the journal *Socialismo*, probably the clearest expression of the orthodox perspective within the Mexican left.   Its editors are critical of the PRD for struggling only for democracy but not socialism and call for "democracy that is not reduced to respect for citizen suffrage."[41] In contrast to liberal forces who criticize the PRD for its "politics of rupture," the editors of *Socialismo* are critical of it for not pursuing a genuine "democratic rupture."[42]

Edmundo Jardón Arzate criticizes the Mexican left, and especially the former Communists now inside the PRD, for having abandoned the class struggle. Citing passages from the U.S. *Declaration of Independence* and the French *Declaration of the Rights of Man and of the Citizen* to demonstrate that social classes are not formally recognized in the founding statements of liberal democracy, Jardón says of the former Communist leadership:

> They deceived themselves and us with conceptions and objectives that were not those of the proletariat but rather those of classes and social formations that dominate, as Marx affirmed, the world of production, and they are the ones who dominate at the political level and those who generate the dominant cultural ideas, contributing to the formation of a false consciousness about the class situation, the function of which is not to push the course of history forward, but to detain it, disguising everything, or almost everything, in the 'struggle for democracy.'[43]

As in Cuba, there are ranges of opinion among orthodox leftists in Mexico and an ongoing process of reassessing long-held doctrines. Even among some left activist-intellectuals who, on most issues, have more renovative ideas, there is a certain reluctance to abandon elements of Marxism-Leninism associated with preserving the power of the "revolution" and its organizations. This is perhaps an understandable concern in light of the history of repression and intervention against

---

41. Editorial, "Ruptura y compromiso democráticos," *Socialismo* (Mexico), Año 2, Nú. 5, Jan.-May 1990.

42. Ibid. For more on their critique of the left's emphasis on electoral struggles, see Eduardo Montes, "Izquierda sin brújula," *Socialismo* (Mexico), Año 3, Nú. 7, Feb. 1992.

43. Edmundo Jardón Arzate, "¿Qué pasó con la lucha de clases?" *Socialismo* (Mexico), Año 2, Nú. 5, Jan.-May 1990, p. 56.

revolutionary organizations, movements, and governments. Raúl Alvarez Garín, for example, who, like Cuba's Juan Antonio Blanco is far from orthodox on many questions, insists that "democratic centralism" was not the problem in the past, but rather the lack of individual and social knowledge and education among the rank-and-file.[44]

One of Mexico's most eminent Marxist scholars, Adolfo Sánchez Vásquez, offers another example of this reassessment-in-process. He is critical of the Latin American left for having long negated the value of democracy in the process of legitimately denouncing the limits of formal, political, representative democracy.[45] Yet, like Marta Harnecker, he is reluctant to give up the "dictatorship of the proletariat." Sánchez Vázquez draws a distinction between Marx's conception of the dictatorship of the proletariat, which he finds "compatible with the broadest democracy," and Lenin's conception of "power subject to no law."[46]

Also like Harnecker, Sánchez Vázquez never deals with the contradictions implied by the dictatorship of any "majority," defined in class terms or otherwise, which is inevitably heterogeneous.[47] But in the

---

44. Raúl Alvarez Garín, public comments at Foro Luchas Emanicipadoras de Fin de Siglo, Mexico City, September 4, 1992.

45. Adolfo Sánchez Vásquez, "Democracia, revolución y socialismo," *Socialismo* (Mexico), Año 1, Nú. 3-4, Oct.-Dec. 1989, p. 15.

46. Ibid., p. 16.

47. Although a full assessment of the left's current thinking on the significance of social class is beyond the scope of this book, a few observations can be made based on my interviews. More orthodox thinkers tend to focus almost exclusively on the category of class as the most relevant for understanding and predicting social and political action. Their conception of democracy as defined in terms of the "working class majority" has not significantly taken into account issues of gender, race, ethnicity, and sexuality. More liberal left intellectuals have been far more influenced by feminism, new social movements theories, and other discourses that are critical of overemphasizing social class. However, the liberal tendency is to liquidate the problem by stressing democratic reforms that supposedly protect the rights of all individual citizens, regardless of social identity. The renovative left tends to reject the totalizing nature of orthodox class analysis and recognizes the critical importance of coexisting (and mutually contingent) social identities and demands. However, relatively little headway has been made toward reformulating a viable conception of democracy that effectively addresses both individual citizenship rights and the multiple social demands that arise from heterogeneous, contemporary societies. The Chiapas uprising has greatly spurred the Mexican left's reassessment of indigenous peoples' rights and put the issue of autonomy on the front burner of debates about democracy. In Cuba, there has been less progress in rethinking issues of race, which still tend to be dissolved into unproblematized notions of class and/or nation.

end his assessment of the practical experience of such formulations is critical:

> The exclusion of representative democracy in the name of real democracy, understood as direct participation, eliminates democracy itself, i.e., all forms of democracy. This is the lesson from the historical experience of the October Revolution when it dissolved the Constituent Assembly and transferred all power to the Soviets.[48]

The views of Sánchez Vásquez are more representative of the *direction* of thinking in the Mexican left today than are the more orthodox perspectives cited earlier. In Mexico, where the opposition faces what has been described as "the perfect dictatorship," the negative lessons from the real, historical experiences of Marxism-Leninism have generally been taken to heart. In Cuba, where orthodox left forces still dominate much of the state-party regime, there is greater reluctance to abandon the ideology, political doctrines, and state institutions that have helped them preserve power.

Liberal Perspectives

While orthodox forces in Mexico still think largely in terms of dismantling the bourgeois state and orthodox Cubans concentrate on preserving the socialist state, more liberal-influenced sectors of the left lean toward privileging reform of the political system (or even merely of the government). The liberal perspective often ignores the economic and social power relations deeply embedded within the state, choosing to emphasize the importance of a vaguely defined "civil society" in advancing the process of democratization.[49] In some Latin American na-

---

48. Ibid., p. 17.

49. In a critique of the liberal left's current emphasis on civil society, Jaime Osorio has cautioned that, "The autonomy of civil society vis a vis the state is one step on the path of democratization, but it does not resolve the disparities that exist in terms of the capacity of different social sectors to express their points of view, to make known their visions of the world, and to propose their projects for the country and society." Osorio argues that some left intellectuals, like Norbert Lechner, in misreading Gramsci's ideas about the gradual accumulation of forces within civil society, fail to adequately distinguish between power as it exists in all social relations (e.g., within the family) and *political* power more specifically residing in the state and reflecting particular class interests. See Jaime Osorio, "La Sociedad civil y el asunto del poder," manuscript (Mexico), January 1995.

tions, still shaken from the traumatic experiences of military rule and bloody repression of the left, liberal left perspectives today often share with neoconservatives a preoccupation with governability and "pacted" transitions.

A more restricted conception of democracy became particularly influential among some sectors of the left in the Southern Cone during the difficult transitions back to civilian rule in the 1980s. In Argentina, leftist scholar Juan Carlos Portantiero at one point urged a radical departure from traditional left thinking by suggesting that "democracy as an objective is independent from the socioeconomic order which contains it."[50] In Brazil, Guillermo O'Donnell was focussing on how best to assure a smooth transition to civilian rule through elite-negotiated pacts between military soft liners and civilian political moderates.[51] In Chile, Norbert Lechner urged the left to abandon old ideas about political change through revolution and instead to help construct a new order through respect for parliamentary institutions and political realism about "what is possible."[52] Chilean scholar Jaime Osorio, who has lived in Mexico since his exile following the overthrow of the Salvador Allende government in 1973, cites various factors to explain the ascendency of this perspective among sectors of the left in the Southern Cone. Osorio's explanations include the severe societal ruptures and trauma represented by the military coups of the 1960s and 1970s and the new importance of privately-financed institutional spaces which have helped shape the conservative direction of research.[53]

---

50. Juan Carlos Portantiero, quoted in Ronaldo Munck, *Latin America. The Transition to Democracy* (London: Zed Books, 1989), p. 11 Those comments were first published in 1986. It is worth noting that by 1989, following several years of neoliberal politics under Argentina's new civilian regimes, Portantiero was writing about the need to democratize the economy and to "broaden classical representative democracy with institutions of direct democracy, with referendums, plebicites, recalls, and popular initiatives." See Juan Carlos Portantiero, "La múltiple transformación del Estado latinoamericano," *Nueva Sociedad* (Venezuela) #104, November-December 1989, pp. 88-94. Apparently the experience of living under resctricted democracy, however much an improvement over military dictatorship, encouraged Portantiero to reconsider some of his earlier, more classically liberal formulations about democracy.

51. See Guillermo O'Donnell, Philippe C. Schmitter, and Laurence Whitehead, eds., *Transitions from Authoriatarian Rule* (Baltimore: Johns Hopkins University Press, 1986).

52. See Norbert Lechner, *La Conflictiva y Nunca Acabada Construcción del Orden Deseado* (Santiago: FLACSO, 1984); and N. Lechner, *La Democratización en el Contexto de una Cultura Pos-Moderna* (Santiago: FLACSO, 1986).

53. Jaime Osorio, "Los Nuevos Sociólogos," manuscript (Mexico) 1992.

The views of these liberal left intellectuals are generally consistent with the historic ideology of liberalism as a politics of reform designed to stabilize capitalism and assure governability through the political and institutional incorporation of broader sectors of the citizenry. In some cases, this approach has led to left forces being elected to government only to find themselves administering the economic crisis and implementing neoliberal restructuring schemes (e.g., the Siles Suazo government in Bolivia, Socialists in the Patricio Aylwin government in Chile, and now, apparently, the Fernando Henrique Cardoso government in Brazil).

Thus, liberal perspectives within the left tend to define democracy primarily with regard to the political system, often leaving aside either the more permanent structures of state power or issues of democratic participation outside the formal political sphere. Democratization has come to be defined by the liberal left largely in terms of procedural, juridical, and institutional reforms to enhance citizen representation and/or participation in the existing political regime, regardless of whether one is currently in the opposition (e.g., more liberal voices within the Mexican PRD and "Democratic Socialists" in Cuba) or in power (e.g., leftists in Mexico's Carlos Salinas government and reform-minded Cuban Communists).

Among the Mexican left, liberal thinking is more dominant in political discourse than it is, as we shall see in chapters five and six, in perspectives about state-market relations (where concerns about preserving national autonomy in the face of North American economic integration have moderated liberalizing influences). The Mexican left was far more incorporated into Latin American debates about democratic transitions than were their Cuban counterparts. Some of the Southern Cone intellectuals who have moved their discourse on democracy toward more restricted, liberal formulations worked in Mexico for many years and therefore exert more influence there than they do in Cuba. For many on the Mexican left, democratization of Mexico has become defined almost exclusively in traditional liberal terms of civil rights and a fair electoral system. Take, for example, the "basic requirements of democracy" offered by Jorge Castañeda: "electoral competition for power, with free choice, fairness, and at least a moderately level playing field."[54]

Some of the intellectuals interviewed in Mexico expressed a certain complacency about accepting the limitations of liberal democracy. For example, one former Central Committee member of the now defunct Mexican Communist Party told me, "Within the process of economic modernization, there are political advances: military regimes were bro-

---

54. Jorge Castañeda, *Utopia Unarmed*, op cit., p. 327.

ken. The worthy aspect of liberalism is that economic modernization is accompanied by political modernization."[55] Such notions are occasionally offered as common wisdom by Mexican leftists, even though Mexico's recent record of economic liberalization and political authoritarianism would seem evidence to the contrary. Indeed, a significant number of leftists, after years spent in the opposition battling the state-party regime, accepted positions in the Carlos Salinas government and laud the very limited political reforms undertaken by the PRI.[56]

José Woldenberg, associated with the revolutionary nationalist current of Mexico's post-1968 left, argues that real headway has been made toward democratization of Mexico, despite what he considers the "impatience" some leftists express for the slowness of reform. Woldenberg has claimed that, as a result of a series of political reforms since the mid-1970s, Mexican elections are becoming what "the texts on democratic theory say: formulas for competition among diverse options that recognize and accept that the capacity to govern or legislate depends on citizen support gained at the polls."[57]

His predictions to the contrary, the August 1994 elections were marked by extensive fraud, irregularities, and a slanted playing field that allowed the PRI to claim a less-than-credible victory.[58] Woldenberg also takes issue with those on the left, like former Communist Party leader Arnoldo Martínez Verdugo and former Communist theoretician Enrique Semo, who insist that democratization of Mexico requires more than a reform of the political system. Woldenberg maintains that reform is in fact all that is needed and says, "I don't know what the fear is in calling this by its name, 'a reform of the Mexican state,' of its institutions, of its

55. Américo Saldívar, interview with author, Mexico City, August 4, 1993.

56. For an account of some twenty prominent Mexican leftists who worked in the Salinas government, see Carlos Acosta Córdova, "Ayer, opositores de izquierda; hoy dirigen y ejecutan programas de Pronasol," *Proceso* (Mexico), No. 827, September 7, 1992, pp. 18-21.

57. José Woldenberg, "Más vale prevenir que lamentar," in Jorge Alcocer, et al., *El Futuro de la Izquierda en México* (Mexico: CEPNA, 1992), pp. 64-65. In a public debate of left intellectuals in Mexico City in July 1992, Woldenberg defended as significant the advances made in reforming Mexico's political system and criticized other participants for not fully appreciating the significance of the changes in the press, parliament, and electoral institutions. J. Woldenberg, "Comentarios Finales," in J. Alcocer, ibid., p. 311.

58. There are many sources documenting the 1994 electoral fraud; see, e.g., "Informe de Alianza Cívica Observación 94: La Calidad de la jornada electoral del 21 de agosto de 1994," special supplement in *La Jornada* (Mexico), September 20, 1994; and "Informe de la Comisión por la Verdad sobre las elecciones federales de 1994," special supplement in *La Jornada* (Mexico), November 5, 1994.

electoral legislation, of the parties' influence, of the significance of elections."[59]

Such liberal notions about democracy may have restricted the vision of the Mexican left, but liberal values also have helped give real content to the left's democratic project, in contrast to the vague generalities that often plagued abstract notions of socialist or proletarian democracy. The PRD's program for "democratization of the state and society," for example, is filled with concrete reform proposals such as two-round voting in presidential and gubernatorial elections, specifics for altering the balance of legislative and executive power, steps for democratizing municipal governments, nonpartisan electoral institutions, guarantees for the press and other mass media, and more.[60] However, as we will see more clearly in the following chapter, renovative forces on the left support such liberal reforms as part of a broader and deeper process of democratization understood as "the socialization of political power."[61]

The more liberal sector of the Mexican left, represented by intellectuals like José Woldenberg, Rolando Cordera, Carlos Tello, and Adolfo Sánchez Rebolledo, also shares the preoccupation with order, continuity, governability, and cautious, pacted transitions which have dominated so much of the debate about democratization in the Southern Cone. Various articles and editorials in the Mexican publications *La Jornada* and *Nexos* during August 1993 made explicit or implicit critiques of what they consider to be the PRD's "politics of rupture." One analysis of this debate claims that the PRD's refusal to negotiate electoral outcomes with the PRI cost the new party the support of several such influential intellectuals.[62] Woldenberg, for example, views the PRD's concept of "democratic revolution" as problematic,[63] and stresses the need for a pacted outcome of the political struggle: "Perhaps one of the greatest challenges facing all of the parties is to construct scenarios so that everyone wins (in different proportions) or so that at least the 'game' is not zero-sum."[64] Along similar lines, Rolando Cordera warns of the exces-

---

59. J. Woldenberg, "Comentarios Finales," op. cit. The contrasting views of Arnoldo Martínez Verdugo and Enrique Semo appear in the same volume (Jorge Alcocer, et al., *El Futuro de la Izquierda en México*, op. cit.)

60. Partido de la Revolución Democrática, "La democratización del Estado y la sociedad," in *Proyecto de Programa del PRD* (pamphlet) (Mexico: Comité Ejecutivo Nacional PRD, 1993).

61. Ibid., p. 3.

62. Jesús Galindo López, "Para (re)pensar al PRD," *etcétera* (Mexico), Nú. 21, June 24, 1993

63. J. Woldenberg, "Comentarios finales," op cit., p. 311.

64. J. Woldenberg, "Más vale prevenir que lamentar," op. cit., p. 65.

sive verbal polarization and lack of will to engage in dialogue that characterizes much of today's political struggle.[65] While he does not directly point a finger at the PRD, he is extremely careful not to criticize the PRI or Salinas, whose program Cordera and Woldenberg have described as "social liberalism" and as a role model for the rest of Latin America.[66]

Following the PRI's claimed victory in various 1994 elections, the debate about pacts and dialogue versus popular mobilization and rupture became increasingly sharp within the PRD itself. The more liberal wing of the party argued that the time was ripe to negotiate better terms for electoral reform, a resolution of existing post-electoral conflicts, and a more pluralistic cast to the Ernesto Zedillo government (elected in 1994).[67] According to columnist Joel Ortega, the party's past strategy of insisting on the illegitimacy of the Salinas presidency and relying on constant mass mobilizations in pursuit of a radical democratization had failed. Ortega was particularly critical of the "instransigence" of Cuauhtémoc Cárdenas and that sector of the PRD he refers to as "ultras." The time had come, he claimed, to negotiate with the government to achieve far more modest goals: "reformist and moderate change."[68] Ortega's position was shared by a significant number of the PRD's liberal wing, as well as by center-left, pro-reform PRI dissidents like Demetrio Sodi de la Tijera, who urged the government and the opposition alike to abandon recriminations and begin a dialogue to find a political resolution of the nation's various conflicts.[69] As we will see in the following chapter, a more renovative wing of the party, closely identified with mass movements and support for the Zapatista rebellion in Chiapas, did not reject dialogue but insisted on the need for constant, ongoing mobiliza-

---

65. Rolando Cordera Campos, "Ecos y recuerdos de la sucesión presidencial," *Nexos* (Mexico), August 1993.

66. Rolando Cordera and José Woldenberg, "La Cumbre Iberoamericana," *Cuaderno de Nexos* (Mexico), August 1993, p. iv.

67. The Zedillo government did end up negotiating a new electoral reform acceptable to the left and right opposition parties (PRD and PAN), but the reforms were subsequently blocked in Congress by PRI hardliners in 1996.

68. Joel Ortega, "Cambiar Ya," *La Jornada* (Mexico), November 6, 1994, and "El cretinismo parlamentario y lo posible," *La Jornada*, November 13, 1994.

69. Demetrio Sodi de la Tijera, "La hora del dialogo," *La Jornada* (Mexico), October 28, 1994. One of the more interesting phenomena taking place within the liberal left has been the increasing radicalization of the discourse of those, like Demetrio Sodi de la Tijera, who are moving away from the PRI toward the opposition, and the increasing liberalization of the discourse of those, like Rolando Cordera and José Woldenberg, who have been moving away from the opposition and toward a sector of the PRI.

tion of popular sectors to secure the fullest possible democratization and avoid co-optation.[70]

To be clear, however, I include many of these liberal-leaning intellectuals within a broadly-defined left because of their continued commitment to social goals not offered by pure free-market, formally political liberalism. Jorge Castañeda, for example, qualifies his rather restricted definition of political democracy with the following warning:

> Poverty and democracy don't mix easily; since the postponement or abrogation of democracy is not an acceptable option [for Latin American democrats], only the elimination of poverty will do. Failing to bring this about is tantamount to democratic suicide: in the midst of destitution and exclusion, and absent any trend toward their eradication, democracy will not survive.[71]

In a perhaps more cynical example, Rolando Cordera, who praised Salinas's "social liberalism," is critical that "the themes of equity, exploitation, self-government of the masses, and social justice are absent from the discourse of the 'democratic revolution.'"[72] Cynical or not, the point is that even Mexico's liberal left remains concerned with the social themes that have historically distinguished the left from pure liberals.

To a far greater extent than the Mexican left, Cuban revolutionaries remained isolated from the liberalization of political discourse about democracy that swept through most of Latin America in the transitions from military to civilian rule. Since the collapse of the Soviet bloc, a degree of economic liberalization has been imposed in Cuba by the severity of its crisis (as following chapters describe). Political liberalization, however, has been less evident. Nonetheless, more liberal notions of democracy are emerging among some of Cuba's left intellectuals as well. This is particularly evident among individuals associated with the social democratic opposition inside Cuba and among some left-leaning Cuban American intellectuals. They have tended to-

---

70. This debate within the Mexican left about whether to directly confront or cooperate with the PRI in the process of political reforms dates back at least to the José López Portillo administration (1976-1982). Several of the revolutionary nationalists who favored collaboration with the regime back then ended up working in the Salinas government. Many of those who refused are now inside the PRD, ironically perhaps, working with the left forces who broke with the PRI during Cuauhtémoc Cárdenas' 1987-88 bid for the presidency.

71. Jorge Castañeda, *Utopia Unarmed*, op. cit., pp. 338-339.

72. Rolando Cordera, interview with author, Mexico City, September 9, 1992.

ward a somewhat idealistic embrace of multiparty electoral politics as a silver bullet to resolve the island's political and economic crises. In oversimplifying the complexity of the problem of power, they have largely ignored the real political and economic threat represented by the U.S.-sponsored, right-wing Cuban American community.[73]

At the same time, among some reform-minded Cuban revolutionaries, an exaggeration of the importance of the political system relative to the state sometimes encourages an emphasis on procedural and institutional reforms to "perfect" the current system without addressing the absolutist nature of the state.[74] These reformers look to liberal traditions as one source of ideas for improving socialist democracy. For example, a Cuban social scientist, who has studied political and social movements in Latin America for many years, observed that, "Liberal thought has been much more profound [than socialist thought] in elaborating the institutional forms needed to realize its project of democracy."[75]

A liberal-leaning political perspective among Cuban revolutionaries, then, emphasizes that existing political institutions have to be reformed, be made real because in the past they have remained only formal. Several people interviewed expressed a belief that the February 1993, secret-ballot, elections for the National Assembly were an important advance in the process of democratization, but cautioned that it remains to be seen whether the new Assembly will become a forum of real debate and decision-making over real policy alternatives.

In Cuba, the rethinking of democracy also involves a historical discussion of the Stalinist model, significant components of which were incorporated into the Cuban political system during the institutionalization of the regime in the 1970s. The influence of liberal ideas can be seen in the reassessment of the Soviet Union by a Cuban scholar, who admits to having only recently recognized the fatal flaws of that system:

---

73. See the Cuban social democratic opposition's "Cuba: Proyecto de Programa Socialista Democrático (Síntesis)" (Havana), December 1991-January 1992. In February 1993, a group of liberal-left Cuban Americans initiated an open letter to President Clinton that, on the one hand, opposed the tightening of the embargo against Cuba and, on the other hand, condemned the lack of "freely contested elections" in Cuba and the Cuban government's "repression and intolerance." Some of the initiators were leftists who actively supported the revolution for many years.

74. See, e.g., Miguel David Limia, "Lo laboral versus lo territorial en la representación estatal cubana (Propuestas para el desarrollo de la democracia)," manuscript (Havana: Instituto de Filosofia, Academia de Ciencias de Cuba, January 1993).

75. Juan Valdés Paz, interview with author, Havana, February 25, 1993.

The limitations of the model in the political sphere were the fusion of the party, state, and government. Rather than reflecting Montesquieu's division of powers, in the USSR all were associated with one center of power, the party. In Cuba, with the Call to the Fourth Party Congress, there was a rejection of this model, theoretically.[76]

Consequently, liberal perspectives in Cuba stress the need for a clearer delineation of legislative powers and oversight. A lifelong Marxist, who is now a sympathizer of the social democratic current in Cuba expressed this concern in the following terms:

> Some mechanism of legislative or parliamentary power seems to me indispensable. There has to be a separation between the parliament, as representative of the popular will, and the government, which leads for a given period of time, so that the government will be obliged to constantly account for its actions. In the dictatorships of the proletariat that existed in the so-called socialist countries of Europe, Asia, and Cuba, that mechanism disappeared. This aspect of bourgeois democracy, even if it may appear a little formal, is necessary, in one form or another, in any socialist model: the obligation of the government and its institutions to account for their actions before a parliament elected by the people or before the people directly.[77]

Liberal-leaning Cuban revolutionaries also call for the professionalization of elected representatives, so that legislators have the time and resources to do more than meet once or twice a year to rubber-stamp policy decisions already made by the state-party's top leadership. As noted above regarding Mexican leftists and as explored further in the following chapters, there is also a renovative current of Cuban intellectuals who support these same liberal reforms but see them as steps toward a still fuller democracy.

More liberal-minded Cuban intellectuals also emphasize the need for pluralism in the revolution, but many still believe it is possible within a single party: "Pluralism does not equal a multiparty system."[78] This is one of the key points that distinguishes liberal forces still loyal to the Communist Party from the social democratic opposition within Cuba, which calls for a multiparty system and represents a more solidly liberal perspective. Vladimiro Roca, son of legendary Communist leader Blas Roca and now an influential figure in Cuba's small social democratic tendency, argues that "a multiparty system is preferable, even if it's

76. Julio A. Díaz Vásquez, interview with author, Havana, March 12, 1993.
77. Cecilio Dimas, interview with author, Havana, February 11, 1993.
78. Aurelio Alonso, interview with author, Havana, February 23, 1993.

imperfect, because it allows itself to be perfected and improved with the participation and the criteria of almost all strata of society."[79]

Cuban intellectuals with more liberal views object to the regime's censorship of literature and film that raise criticisms of the revolution. Several Cubans interviewed were particularly disturbed by the controversy that erupted about the 1991 film by Daniel Díaz Torres, *Alicia en el pueblo de las Maravillas (Alice in Wonder Town)*. A humorous satire of bureaucracy and petty corruption run amuck, the film was branded as counterrevolutionary by the then-powerful politburo ideologue, Carlos Aldana. Several Cubans described the conflict as part of as a high-level power struggle between hard-line and reform-minded individuals within the national leadership. Reformers, including Cultural Minister Armando Hart, reportedly lost that battle, and the film was shown in very limited release.[80] Many Cubans were incensed and an international stir was created. Eventually, in an unrelated scandal, Aldana was removed from power. *Alicia* and director Díaz Torres subsequently were allowed to tour internationally and *Cine Cubano*, magazine of the Cuban Film Institute directed by Castro's old friend Alfredo Guevara, gave extensive coverage to the controversy, presented all points of view and attempted to repair seriously damaged relations between the regime and the film industry and artists.[81] This anecdote perfectly illustrates an astute observation made by Margaret Randall that "The Cuban revolution is extraordinary in its ability to admit mistakes and rectify them; it is slower to permit a critical discourse that encourages real debate and may help prevent such errors from being made."[82]

Abel Prieto, a reform-oriented writer who heads Cuba's Union of Writers and Artists (UNEAC) and now sits on the Politburo, appears to

---

79. Vladimiro Roca, interview with author, Havana, March 1993.

80. Hart was not re-named to the new Politburo approved at the 1991 Party Congress, but he retained his position as minister of culture. The fall-out from the *Alicia* controversy continued in a bitter polemic involving Hart, Cuban novelist Jesús Díaz, and Uruguayan writer Eduardo Galeano. After Díaz made public criticisms of the revolution during a debate in Zurich in 1992, at which Galeano defended the revolution, Hart wrote a public letter denouncing Díaz in the harshest of terms. Some Cubans interviewed attributed Hart's extreme posture to his need to defend his revolutionary credentials after Aldana's criticisms of *Alicia*, which was made with Hart at the helm of Cuba's cultural sector, and his removal from the Politburo. For more on the Díaz-Galeano-Hart polemic, including a reprint of Hart's letter, see *Brecha* (Montevideo), February 5, 1993 and February 26, 1993..

81. See *Cine Cubano*, No. 135, April-May-June 1992.

82. Margaret Randall, *Gathering Rage*, op. cit., p. 138.

encourage space for a more critical discourse, at least within the sphere of culture and the arts. UNEAC's journal, *La Gaceta de Cuba*, for example, has given coverage to young Cuban writers and artists critical of some regime policies.

A case in point is the young writer Senel Paz, whose controversial novella about the troubled friendship that develops between a Communist Party member and a gay artist, *El lobo, el bosque, y el hombre nuevo (The Wolf, the Forest, and the New Man)*, was made into Cuba's most widely publicized feature film of recent years, *Fresa y Chocolate (Strawberry and Chocolate)*. Nominated for a 1994 Academy Award in the United States as best foreign film, *Fresa y Chocolate* honestly addresses themes of social and political intolerance in the revolution. In an interview in *La Gaceta*, Senel Paz spoke about the repression of artists and gays in Cuba in the late 1960s, and warned:

> I hope we have acquired enough experience and wisdom so that such errors, which in no way serve either the country or the Revolution, will not be repeated. But we have to be alert, because there persists in some the criteria that when the situation is normal and relaxed you can give artists free rein, but when things get complicated, like now, we need to be reined in and controlled.[83]

Paz also expressed concern that the regime still seems to understand "tolerance" as something conditioned by the international conjuncture, "rather than as a necessity of art and the Revolution."[84] His concern is well taken. During moments of greater international tension the government has often tended to increase censorship and repression of artists. Even among more liberal-oriented Cuban intellectuals there is considerable sympathy for the argument that the magnitude of the economic crisis and the dangerous international context mitigates against a thorough democratization of the regime. One young Cuban social scientist even went so far as to acknowledge that "I have a more neoconservative position" on the issues of political democratization. "I agree with the Cuban leadership very much in this regard," he said, "because I lived the experience of the USSR and I experienced the chaos and disorder."[85]

Julio Carranza, subdirector of an influential Cuban research institute, summarized the dilemma:

---

83. Senel Paz, interview with Magda Resik, "Escribir es una suerte naufragio," *La Gaceta de Cuba* (Havana), September-October 1992.

84. Ibid.

85. Santiago Pérez, interview with the author, Havana, March 4, 1993.

Cuba needs to respond not only to the economic and social problems, but also in terms of the political aspects of democracy. There is no
agreement on this, but there have been important changes. The Constitutional changes (electoral reform, decentralization of power) are a step
in the direction of resolving the problem of our old Soviet model of
"popular democracy." I don't like the term "perfecting democracy," because there is much more required than simply tinkering with what we
had. But that is difficult in the context of U.S. hostility. We have to be
very careful with any opening that the enemy might take advantage of.
Look what the National Endowment for Democracy did in Nicaragua,
creating a system of organizations that helped bring down the Sandinistas, while representing the interests of the United States.[86]

As did other Cubans interviewed, Carranza said that the debate about
democratization opened up considerably right after the Call for the
Fourth Party Congress was issued in March 1990, but the rapidly dete-
riorating international situation slowed the debate. There were also
"conservative forces," according to Carranza, who took advantage of the
worsening crisis and "wanted to maintain the status quo for their own
political ends."[87] Gail Reed, the only foreign journalist to attend the
party's congress in October 1991, described it as a five-day battle, in
which liberal reforms allowing for direct elections to the National Assembly were won only against fierce opposition.[88]

Efforts to institute liberal reforms of Cuba's political system, let alone
fully democratize it, are indeed hampered by old left orthodoxy of "unity
at all cost." Carollee Bengelsdorf's study of "the problem of democracy
in Cuba" names the importance of unity as "the single most primary
factor influenceing the Cuban revolutionary leadership from its earliest
moments."[89] In Benglesdorf's assessment, "For Fidel Castro, unity stood
above everything else."[90] This apparently continues to be the case. A
telling recent example is the way the first direct elections for the National
Assembly were actually implemented in early 1994. Two weeks before
the scheduled elections, Fidel Castro called on all Cubans to vote for the
entire slate of candidates. Emphasizing the imortance of uniting behind
the whole slate in a time of crisis rather than the significance of using the
electoral process to voice an opinion about the candidates, Castro
redefined the elections as a national referendum on the Cuban

---

86. Julio Carranza, interview with author, Havana, February 18, 1993.

87. Ibid.

88. Gail Reed, ed., *Island in the Storm: The Cuban Communist Party's Fourth
Congress* (Melbourne: Ocean Press).

89. Carollee Bengelsdorf, *The Problem of Democracy in Cuba*, op. cit., p. 73.

90. Ibid.

Revolution.[91] Several of those interviewed were highly critical of this development.

Finally, liberal voices within the Cuban left are inclined to encourage dialogue between the regime and its critics and to warn against any violent rupture. Cecilio Dimas, for example, insists that "any political solution to the current crisis has to involve Fidel Castro." He assured me that the democratic opposition is fully committed to a peaceful, non-disruptive process of democratization.[92] Similarly, Gustavo Arcos, a human rights activist who spent seven years in a Cuban prison in the 1980s, now draws the wrath of Miami's right-wing Cuban community because of his calls for a national dialogue among all Cubans, including the Castro government and the exiles. After many years of trying to leave Cuba, Arcos said in 1990 that he was committed to remaining on the island to contribute to his nation's "transition toward democracy."[93] While the liberal Mexican left's calls for the opposition to negotiate with the PRI raise well-founded concerns about the age-old traps of co-optation and duplicity, the liberal left's calls for dialogue within the Cuban context surely can have only salubrious effects.

The ideas expressed in the interviews and publications just cited do not add up to any coherent, organized liberal tendency within the Cuban left. Rather, they reflect the growing influence of liberal notions about political representation, division of powers, and individual liberties. Cuba clearly does not yet have a reasonably democratic political system, but the terrain of political debate (and to some extent practice) is shifting all the time, as it did in transitions toward relatively more democratic regimes in other Latin American nations, such as Brazil and Chile. Liberal notions about democracy are among the influences on that debate. Yet even the most liberal of left perspectives expressed during the interviews in Cuba, including by the social democratic dissidents, are clearly distinguished from mainstream liberal and neoliberal tendencies elsewhere in Latin America by their commitment to social justice and equality and their belief in the responsibility of the state to help ensure such social goals.

As seen, even in the post-Cold War 1990s, much of the lefts' discourse on democracy still revolves around one or the other of the old

---

91. Margaret Randall (*Gathering Rage*, op. cit.) discusses a parallel example from Nicaragua, where the Sandinistas encouraged supporters to elect the "united slate" for its national directorate in 1991. She elaborates more on the "unity at all cost" danger, particularly as it has affected women. See especially pp. 82-85.

92. Cecilio Dimas, interview with author, Havana, February 11, 1993.

93. *Washington Post*, July 9, 1990.

antimonies: orthodox socialism and liberalism. Marxist-Leninist formulations of political power remain quite strong in Cuba, where they still serve to justify the authoritarianism of the postrevolutionary regime and to preserve the power and privilege of many officials, bureaucrats, and intellectuals. While socialist orthodoxy stands in the way of full democratization in Cuba, it does have the merit of cautioning against an extreme liberalization of politics that could erode the revolution's many social accomplishments. The orthodox left in Mexico is small and marginal. While its sectarianism does not serve further unification of the left opposition, its insistence on the class nature of capitalism and skepticism about the effectiveness of electoral democracy in class societies can also be a healthy reminder of the many obstacles to genuine democracy in neoliberalized Mexico.

Liberal conceptions of democracy have been incorporated into the discourse and program of the vast majority of left forces in Mexico, who have come to appreciate the value of political rights, clean elections, parliamentary struggle, and judicial reforms. Mexico's liberal left tends to settle too easily for limited political reforms and elite-negotiated pacts that do not substantially enhance the democratic participation and power of the popular classes, but they have encouraged the left to take on the often unglamorous task of elaborating and doggedly pursuing political reforms that are slowly but surely opening up Mexico's political system.

Liberal conceptions of democracy are far less influential among Cuba's left intellectuals, but they have begun to inform the way some Cubans think about reforming their own political institutions, balancing executive power with real legislative power, giving more emphasis to secret-ballot elections, encouraging greater pluralism within the Communist Party, promoting dialogue between the regime and dissidents. Though they are relatively few, such liberal voices (both inside and outside the regime) are a healthy and necessary addition to the debate about the political future of the Cuban revolution, even if their focus on institutional reform may fall short of the task of complete democratization of state and society.

The class position of these intellectuals certainly carries some explanatory weight here. The prevalant, orthodox defense of a Leninist conception of power in Cuba is undoubtedly related to a desire to defend the relative class privilege of the intellectuals associated with the regime. The desire of many liberal-left intellectuals in Mexico to promote a cautious, limited liberalization of politics certainly corresponds in part to their class interests, as they represent a technocratic strata of the petty bourgeoisie who are well positioned to play key roles in any pacted, transitional regime. However, class analysis is inadequate to explain the current ideological tendencies within the lefts of these nations. The seventy-four intellectuals interviewed for this study, most of whom share similar, relatively privileged positions within the petty bourgeoisie, self-select themselves into one or the other of three different political currents. Their class interests are strongly mediated by other factors, such as political generational experience (e.g., one's relationship to 1968), participation in social movements, and the structural realities of the semiperiphery. Such factors are key to explaining the existence and relative strength of the third ideological current, the renovative left.

The following chapter examines that renovative left, which seeks to transcend the artificial socialism-liberalism dichotomy by pursuing a vision of democracy informed by both traditions as well as by new practices and thinking produced in the very struggle for democratization.

CHAPTER 4. DEMOCRACY II

Renovative Perspectives on Democracy

Orthodox left conceptions about democracy, such as "dictatorship of the proletariat" and "democratic centralism" persist in Cuba and Mexico, but they have been seriously discredited by the collapse of European socialism and the setbacks of various Third World revolutions. Meanwhile, liberal ideas about restricted political reform have clearly found their way into the discourse of the left in Mexico and Cuba. However, they remain far less influential in these countries than they have been in parts of South America. In fact, a strong theoretical and political challenge to both socialist orthodoxy and liberalism is emerging from a renovative left in Mexico and, to a lesser extent, in Cuba. In part, this is because the social, intellectual, and institutional ruptures that contributed to the new influence of liberal and sometimes even neoliberal ideas among some Southern Cone leftists have not been experienced so thoroughly in Mexico and Cuba.

It is not that renovative left forces do not exist in countries like Argentina and Chile. They do, but their numbers are still relatively small, their influence more marginal, and the national contexts in which they operate, until quite recently, have not been propitious. Regarding Argentina, for example, scholar Donald Hodges has written:

> The single most important factor in restructuring the Argentine Left was the historic defeat of 1976-1982. This sanguinary episode, which decimated the Left, went hand in hand with a system of state terrorism aimed at eradicating Marxist cultural as well as political military subversion. . . . The military dictatorship concentrated on stamping out not only the insurgent Left but also its legal and political structures. In the conviction that armed subversion was nourished by the national Left as well as by the Communist and Trotskyist parties, the armed forces were determined to cripple them.[1]

---

1. Donald C. Hodges, "The Argentine Left Since Perón," in Barry Carr and Steve Ellner, eds., *The Latin American Left. From the Fall of Allende to Perestroika* (Boulder: Westview Press, 1993), pp. 156-157.

The Argentine left is only now beginning to regroup and reassert itself in national politics. In Chile, the left is a stronger presence and sectors of the left have participated in the first postmilitary governments. But the brutality of the dictatorship that followed the September 1973 coup encouraged a cautious, even timid approach by much of the Chilean left which has appeared hesitant to stray beyond liberal reformism. As Brian Loveman wrote about the postdictatorship Chilean left:

> Piecemeal reform has become respectable, democracy essential, pragmatism desirable, and moderation a virtue. The political culture of much of the Chilean Left has been transformed. Prudence—or understandable fear of direct confrontation with Pinochet and the military— permeated public discussion and government initiatives. Fear of 'another September 11, 1973' has been internalized; seeking consensus rather than imposition of revolutionary programs was the new motif.[2]

Despite the authoritarian nature of the state-party regimes in Cuba and Mexico, neither nation has experienced the generalized, violent repression and the sort of brutal ruptures described above. Even though the Cuban and Mexican regimes are in crisis, important components of the political cultures spawned by their revolutions remain more or less intact. There is still a broadly accepted national discourse that continues to emphasize social justice, social equality, and the legitimacy of "revolutionary" ideals. Nationalist and Marxist left traditions have continued to evolve, even if under sometimes difficult circumstances. Likewise, despite the neoliberal restructuring of the Mexican state and the severe fiscal crisis of the Cuban state, public research institutions, universities, and publications continue to be important spaces for Marxist-influenced intellectual production.

The organizations of Cuban civil society certainly lack autonomy from the state, but they have never been targeted for violent, generalized repression. In Mexico, civil society and new popular movements and organizations have experienced a resurgence since the mid-1980s, but even in their newness they reflect much of the historic traditions and ideologies of the nation's nationalist and Marxist lefts. Thus, in many regards, left intellectuals in Mexico and Cuba are in a better position to incorporate newly influential liberal political thinking without abandoning their historic social concerns, thereby contributing to a renovative approach to democratization. On the other hand, the fact of greater continuity with the revolutionary past surely also helps account for the

---

2. Brian Loveman, "The Political Left in Chile, 1973-1990," in B. Carr and S. Ellner, ibid., p. 36.

dogged persistence of more orthodox socialist perspectives among some sectors of the left in Cuba and Mexico, even as it mediates against a full embrace of liberalism.

Brazil, a country which suffered authoritarian military rule and yet today has a large and influential renovative left, might seem to contradict these suggestions about the explanatory significance of Mexico and Cuba having avoided similar ruptures. However, Brazil is more accurately the exception that proves the rule. Emir Sader has observed that, because Brazil's military coup happened in 1964, a decade earlier than those in Argentina, Chile, and Uruguay, there has been a longer period of time for Brazilian society to recover from the trauma and for a new Brazilian left to emerge, organized along new lines.[3] The wounds of rupture have begun to heal, allowing for the birth of a nonliberal, renovative Brazilian left, which generally exhibits even fewer orthodox influences than do the lefts in Mexico and, especially, Cuba. This would suggest that, with time, stronger renovative left currents may emerge in other postmilitary regimes of the Southern Cone, as they are clearly doing in Uruguay.[4]

Indeed, in much of Latin America, in addition to the shared structural realities of the semiperiphery, there are important conjunctural factors in the 1990s that foster renovative efforts to escape the blind alleys of both statist/socialist and liberal orthodoxies. Internationally, the unexpectedly rapid collapse of the Eastern communist regimes helped reveal the surprisingly weak underbelly of societies in which state, regime, and party were difficult to untangle. The neoliberal policies of international finance capital are wreaking havoc everywhere, and the late 1994-early 1995 collapse of the Mexican peso clearly revealed the house-of-cards-like nature of the global "order" such policies have created. Regionally, the pacted, electoral democracies of Latin America quickly have proven themselves incompetent or powerless to resolve the pressing social crises they are supposed to manage. (Witness, e.g., the fall of Venezuela's center-left Carlos Andres Pérez government in the face of angry citizens exhausted from the burden of "shock therapy" and "restructuring" and the rapid rise and fall of Fernando Collor de Mello in Brazil.)

Particularly within Mexico and Cuba, conjunctural developments are encouraging the left toward fresh takes on old political paradigms. As recent PRI administrations have pursued new regimes of accumulation

---

3. Emir Sader, "Brazil: Against the Winds of History," in Susanne Jonas and Edward J. McCaughan, eds., *Latin America Faces the Twenty-First Century. Reconstructing a Social Justice Agenda* (Boulder: Westview, 1994), pp. 104-123.

4. See Luis Stolovich, "Uruguay: The Paradoxes and Perplexities of an Uncommon Left," in S. Jonas and E. McCaughan, ibid., pp. 170-184.

and domination that directly undermine the historic social pact on which the postrevolutionary Mexican state was built, the left has found itself better able to distinguish between those elements of the old order worth fighting to preserve and those still requiring a "democratic revolution."[5] In Cuba, the abruptness and severity of the regime's post-Soviet Union crisis is helping to shatter old dogmas and create intellectual and political openings for new, though still tentative, thinking about democracy in a socialist society. In both nations, crisis has provoked serious divisions among ruling elites, which in turn have altered the fortunes of renovative thinkers by making new political and material resources available to leftists prepared to challenge the old dogmas. Thus, in addition to the relatively uninterrupted evolution of their postrevolutionary cultures, conjunctural factors also make Mexico and Cuba particularly ripe for new left thinking.

In many regards, the moment is propitious for renovative reassessments of statist and liberal political models alike. Three quotes suggest the possibility as well as the dilemma facing the renovative lefts in their efforts to democratize Cuba and Mexico:

- From Esteban Morales, political economist and director of Cuba's Center for U.S. Studies (CESEU):

The fall of European socialism does not represent so much a crisis of Marxist theory or methodology as a crisis of politics and practice. The excessively ideologized Marxism was related to the lack of democracy and participation, including of social scientists. The experiences in the Soviet Union have led to a serious questioning of democracy in Cuba, a renewed concern with popular participation. We need a new paradigm of democracy, which is especially difficult now given the renewed hegemony of the liberal democratic paradigm.[6]

- From Cristina Laurell, a leading intellectual figure in Mexico's PRD:

Within neoliberalism, democracy is viewed with real suspicion, because it implies the ability of people to organize and fight for their interests and to force the state or government to accept compromises that infringe on the market. Democracy is a process of construction, in which

---

5. For an analysis of this process, see Edward J. McCaughan, "Mexico's Long Crisis: Toward New Regimes of Accumulation and Domination," *Latin American Perspectives*, Issue 78, Vol. 20, No. 3, Summer 1993.

6. Esteban Morales, interview with author, Havana, February 15, 1993.

people gain experience, skills and confidence to resolve their own problems.[7]

• From Jorge Ibarra, an eminent Cuban historian:

Changes in the world have provoked changes in the concept of political power in socialism. But this discussion always revolves around two axes: one, market democracy with multiple parties, and, two, a single-party state. This is *not* the issue. The question is whether it is possible for the distinct classes to exert influence on political power through all of the existing institutions. To what extent can the people govern—that is the issue. This implies a far more radical revision of the concept of democracy than that implied by adopting a bourgeois, multiparty system.[8]

Such dissatisfaction with the old paradigms is leading to the emergence of a renovative tendency in both Cuba and Mexico. The term "renovators" is meant to signify those leftists who still emphasize social goals and social, even collectivist, political and economic visions, and who are critical of both statist-socialist and liberal approaches. A renovative perspective tends to understand democratization in terms of the state, political regime, government, and civil society. Renovators are inclined neither to expand the concept of democracy so broadly as to be virtually synonymous with Marx's utopian communism, and thus meaningless in any practical sense, nor to restrict democracy to purely formal political rights that likewise become nearly meaningless in the real world of political, economic, and social inequality.

A good part of the intellectual and political task of renovators is to break the old socialism-liberalism dichotomy and to reassert the compatibility of social equality, individual liberty, and democratic rule. The emerging renovative perspective on democracy entails doing away with the false association between collectivist, social goals and centralized state power. Renovators also face overcoming the fear that democracy will always be used against the left by its enemies, and that the pluralism and heterogeneity of "really existing society" inevitably threaten the political unity and cohesion required to tackle society's enormous tasks. Renovators seek a "socialization of power" freed from the authoritarian constraints of past statist and vanguardist conceptions.[9]

---

7. Asa Cristina Laurell, public comments at Foro Luchas Emanicipadoras de Fin de Siglo, Mexico City, September 4, 1992.

8. Jorge Ibarra, interview with author, Havana, February 21, 1993.

9. An important example of a renovative efforts to redefine power, broaden the conception of democracy to gender rights as political rights, and to tackle the

The renovative left appears to be a still small yet influential minority in Cuba, but I think their numbers will grow as the broader Latin American left debate about democracy is incorporated into Cuba's political scenario.[10] In Mexico, renovators represent a more substantial sector of the left but cannot be considered dominant. In any event, beyond their actual numbers in either country, the renovative tendency includes many highly respected left intellectuals who are in a position to influence debates about the future of democratization.

Cuban Renovators

Among Cuban revolutionaries, a renovative perspective on democracy emphasizes that the key issue is *participation* in decision-making at all levels of society, and that such participation has been very limited since the early 1960s. Fernando Martínez Heredia was once affiliated with the University of Havana's Philosophy Department and the unorthodox Marxist journal, *Pensamiento Crítico*, both of which were closed down by the regime in 1971 for their controversial perspectives. Like a number of other Cuban intellectuals from that circle, he is now among the more renovative voices in Cuba. According to Martínez Heredia, during what is considered as the second stage of the revolution (the period of institutionalization and Sovietization in the mid-1970s), Cuba's legislative system of Poder Popular was very successful at the local level, but "in general the political system was weighed down by ritualistic formalism, a conservative expression that tried to take over society as well."[11] Martínez Heredia describes it as a period of intolerance, during which critics were silenced and debate among revolutionaries was eliminated, a period from which Cuba's political system and civil society have never fully recovered. Despite the importance and achievements of Cuban mass organizations, Martínez Heredia says their tendencies to-

---

old problem of imposed unity is offered by Margaret Randall's account of a women's conference held in Managua, Nicaragua in January 1992, the final document of which was called "For Unity in Diversity." See M. Randall, *Gathering Rage. The Failure of 20th Century Revolutions to Develop a Feminist Agenda* (New York: Montly Review Press, 1992), pp. 66-68.

10. For an interesting example of how the Latin American lefts' thinking on democracy is being incorporated by renovative thinkers in Cuba, see Alberto Alvarez, "América Latina: Crisis y Democratización," *Cuadernos de Nuestra América* (Cuba), Vol. IX, No. 19, July-Dec. 1992.

11. Fernando Martínez Heredia, "Cuba: Problemas de la liberación, la democracia, el socialismo," paper presented at the Latin American Congress of Sociology, Havana, April, 1991.

ward authoritarianism and paternalism have prevented civil society from becoming more than an appendage of the political system.[12]

Other criticisms of Cuba's political system from a renovative perspective are far more fierce, but hardly liberal, as suggested by the following words of a still-loyal party militant and scholar who considers herself among "the pure flames of the revolution" (referring to the circle of intellectuals once associated with *Pensamiento Crítico*):

> The Party is the only institutional space here. Small groups, like the one around [social democratic dissident] Elizardo Sánchez, have created a little space. Young intellectuals in the mid-1980s began to create a new space outside the party that was not oriented toward Miami—in theater, sculpture, and to some extent the social sciences. But then the Party moved in and closed that space, co-opting some and leading others to move to Mexico. The Party is very verticalist, authoritarian, statist, and militarist. One is ever less able to participate.
>
> But, personally, I don't believe in representative democracy. I don't like the term democracy, but we're stuck with it. I would simply prefer to talk about "participation," because that is what it is really about: "Do I or do I not participate in all decisions about power?" I agree with Pablo González Casanova's concept of participatory democracy.[13]

As this quote might suggest, Cuban renovators see institutional innovation, like the recent emergence of Non-Governmental Organizations, as important, because it opens up new spaces outside of the state and the party for democratic participation in society. Several Cubans interviewed expressed optimism about the potential contribution to Cuba's democratization of the new "Consejos Populares" (popular councils). According to Sergio Baroni, a renovative urban planner:

> The Consejo Popular is the most important development in terms of democracy. The Councils are organized at the electoral precinct level. Each precinct chooses a representative to the Council for the daily government of the community. The Council deals with problems like housing and street repairs and water service, the problems of daily life. There are 93 Councils in Havana, each representing about 20,000 people. Each council has a paid professional, elected by the neighborhood and important work places. Each month the representative has to give an accounting before the electorate.[14]

---

12. Ibid.

13. Anonymous source, interview with author, Havana, March 1, 1993.

14. Sergio Baroni, interview with author, Havana, February 26, 1993.

One interviewee saw the popular councils as a key mediating link between the state and civil society: "They can be seen either as the government organizations closest to the masses, or as the community organization vested with the greatest governmental powers."[15]

These new institutions could help "deepen" (not "perfect") democracy in Cuba, *if* they are able to assert their autonomy from the state party, a problem renovators identify as key to having limited the effectiveness of governmental bodies and mass organizations in Cuba. Baroni told me:

> The basic idea of Poder Popular here was for society to control the state and government. But it is part of the state and has never been able to exert adequate control over government. That's one of the biggest tasks of socialist society: how society controls the state. And there are elements of liberal traditions that are important to look at in that regard.[16]

A telling example of the problematic relationship between state and civil society in Cuba is that of the Cuban Women's Federation. Ostensibly one of Cuba's most important mass organizations created to represent women's interests, it has never enjoyed any real autonomy from the Communist Party and recently has come under serious criticisms for not adequately representing Cuban women.[17] Several people interviewed mentioned a recently established network of women's centers throughout Havana as a potentially important effort to respond more democratically and effectively to women's particular needs during the current crisis with more decentralized, local institutions. Now it remains to be seen whether the Communist Party will allow these new centers any effective autonomy and, just as importantly, whether Cuban women will demand and exercise control over them. While Cuban women made many gains in terms of health, education, and occupational mobility following the revolution, the lack of autonomous women's movements, such as exist in Mexico and elsewhere, has limited feminism's influence. It was striking, for example, that many of the Cuban women interviewed expressed quite orthodox perspectives about democracy, while almost all of the Mexican women interviewed were among the most renovative thinkers.

---

15. Fernando Barral, interview with author, Havana, February 18, 1993.

16. Sergio Baroni, interview with author, Havana, February 26, 1993.

17. On the Cuban Women's Federation's origins and relationship to the ruling party, see Marifeli Pérez Stable, *The Cuban Revolution. Origins, Course, and Legacy* (Oxford: Oxford University Press, 1993), espcially Chapters 5 and 6. For more anecdotal but no less persuasive evidence of constraints on the Cuban women's movements, see Margaret Randall, *Gathering Rage*, op. cit., particularly Chapter 4.

In addition to the emergence of autonomous social movements and organizations, one seemingly obvious change in the Cuban political system that would address the problem of the Communist Party's domination of all politics would be the adoption of a multiparty system. However, for the moment, voicing support for a multiparty regime is one of the lines that separates "counterrevolutionary" socialists from "revolutionary" socialists. In my interviews, only the social democratic dissidents were prepared to declare themselves against the single-party model. This does not mean that renovators are not concerned with issues of pluralism, dissent, debate, and alternative programs, but for the moment they call only for democratization, perhaps even reconceptualization, of the single party. It is difficult to determine whether this position is based on principle or on a strategic assessment of the best way to push forward democratization without risking complete political marginalization.

One illustrative formulation of this position, voiced by a number of renovators, calls upon the discourse of independence hero José Martí, who urged the formation of a unified party of the nation in the late 1800s to achieve independence from Spain. Rafael Hernández, a prominent figure at the Centro de Estudios Sobre America (CEA) who is well regarded in U.S. academic circles, says that the biggest challenge facing the Cuban Communist Party is to become a "party of the nation," with space for different currents of thought. In Hernández's view, whether or not Cuba will need more than one party in the future depends on how well that challenge is met.[18] Outside of Cuba, this may seem a mild assessment, but within the context of the current political conjuncture, even to suggest that the future may require more than the historic party of the revolution is a bold idea. The call to first attempt a genuine "party of the nation" is a somewhat persuasive position given the legacy of Cuban political culture, which allows all political stripes to summon up the image of Martí. Even a more liberal-minded sympathizer of the social democratic dissidents acknowledged that a single party could conceivably accommodate pluralism, if it were organized along the lines envisioned by Martí, whose party, the dissident asserted, "truly brought together a wide range of social sectors."[19] But then Martí was not talking about a single party to govern Cuba, simply one that would unite the nation against its colonial rulers.

Haroldo Dilla, a political scientist at CEA, does not want the critical issue of pluralism side-tracked by debates about multiparty systems,

---

18. Rafael Hernández, "Mirar a Cuba. Notas para una discusión." Draft manuscript (Havana, August, 1992).

19. Cecilio Dimas, interview with author, Havana, February 11, 1993.

which he says "confuse the present with the future." Dilla says the bigger problem is to overcome the assumption that pluralism undermines unity, because unity has been distorted to mean a monolithic unanimity. The solution is to be found in what he describes as a simultaneous decentralization *and* socialization of power, "the ideal matrix for correcting what has been a deficit in Cuban politics: the maturation of pluralism understood as the recognition of the diversity and autonomy of the participant subjects, and consequently of *conflict* as a moment in the creation of consensus."[20] Admitting the necessity of conflict is something that distinguishes this renovative perspective from the more orthodox Cuban views on dissent within hegemony described in the previous chapter.

From a renovative perspective, then, the issue of democratization cannot be reduced to a particular conception of political pluralism defined in terms of multiparty politics. Nor is it understood to be simply about elections. Rather, democratization is about increasing the degree of real power people have over the decisions that affect their lives. A prominent but heretical party intellectual recalled:

> After the 1960s, the capitalist ruling classes were in shock because their children rebelled. Samuel Huntington presented an analysis of the danger that people were taking democracy seriously, that the system was overloaded with demands that couldn't be satisfied. So it was necessary to lower expectations, which is what has happened since the 60s. In the 60s, democracy was associated with "power" and power was in the streets—black power, Chicano power, etc. Now democracy is all about elections. It's a big myth.
>
> What could Cuban democracy be? I don't want Cuban socialist democracy to be what Huntington suggests. Elections are a trap. The question in Cuba now is how much power will the people elected to the National Assembly [in February 1993] really have. The elections weren't really the issue. Now, are we going to pass real shares of power from the centralized, self-appointed bureaucracy to the popularly elected representatives? Will elected delegates be able to give orders to Ministers of State? What will be the balance of power between the self-appointed bureaucracy and the popularly elected delegates?[21]

Cuban renovators also reject the argument made by some that a Chinese model might be viable for Cuba, i.e., economic liberalization

---

20. Haroldo Dilla Alfonso, "Cuba: La Crisis y la rearticulación del consenso político (Notas para un debate socialista)," manuscript (Havana, December 1992), pp. 22-23. An English translation of a version of this paper is Haroldo Dilla Alfonso, "Cuba Between Utopia and the World Market: Notes for a Socialist Debate," *Latin American Perspectives*, 21:4 (Fall 1994), pp. 46-59.

21. Anonymous source, interview with author, Havana, March 4, 1993.

without democratization (a formula gaining adherents within the Cuban regime, as the following chapter demonstrates). Juan Valdés Paz, another social scientist from the *Pensamiento Crítico* circle, explained:

> There are some frankly liberal tendencies within the national debate. The first manifestation of liberalism is to deny the relationship between the economy and politics, to want to implement economic liberalization and think it will have no political effects. Another example are the proposals for economic decentralization without accompanying democratization. These proposals are fundamentally about the enterprises and the economic bureaucracy, not about greater democratization and popular control.
>
> There are also socialist forces arguing to liberalize the economy out of necessity but to compensate for the effects with greater democratization and social control by the masses over all spheres. You can't compensate for the risks involved in the necessary economic liberalization without a radical project of democratization.[22]

Along similar lines, Haroldo Dilla concedes that liberalization of the economy may be necessary but certainly not sufficient and perhaps even counterproductive if liberal economic reforms "are not accompanied by policies designed to strengthen the spaces for participation and popular control."[23] Dilla regards the liberal values of "liberty" and "individuality" as "organic to any genuine democracy," but he rejects liberalism "as a theoretical body and a sociopolitical practice designed to legitimate and reproduce capitalist accumulation."[24]

Like Dilla, Valdés Paz also concedes the value of liberal democratic experiences as part of the historical legacy that the left must draw upon:

> Regarding democracy, there's a substantive question and an institutional question. The substantive question—what is democracy?—still has to be elaborated by the left. There are three requisites: more equality, more liberty, and more participation. Socialist democracy has to offer more of all three and in all spheres of society. Bourgeois democracy is restricted to the political system. Real socialism tried to rationalize the lack of democracy by pointing to the economic sphere.
>
> In terms of the institutional question, liberal thought has been much more profound in elaborating the institutional forms to realize its project of democracy. The left, socialist thought, can't pretend that on either the substantive or the institutional question we have to start from zero. The left has to start from the insufficient but necessary historical

22. Juan Valdés Paz, interview with author, Havana, February 25, 1993.
23. Haroldo Dilla Alfonso, op cit. p. 3.
24. Ibid., footnote 3.

discussion of democracy, and we have to transcend (in the Marxist sense), not reinvent, what has come before. The parliament may be an insufficient mechanism, but improvement has to be based on this experience.

This is not to say that in the struggle for power and in defense of power, it won't be necessary to have restrictions. But we can't try to make such restrictions virtues. For example, the lack of multiple parties in Cuba, the lack of adequate space for minority opinions, etc.—these can all be explained but they cannot be seen as virtues.[25]

As the last comment about "necessary restrictions" implies, in Cuba even the most renovative views on democratization are conditioned by two factors. First, there are the dangers inherent in any severe moment of crisis: "There is a serious contradiction between the popular participation demanded by the people and the discipline required by the current crisis."[26] Secondly there is what most Cubans perceive to be an overwhelmingly hostile international environment: "Socialist democracy is viable in Cuba to the extent we can survive as a nation."[27] Those dangers strengthen the position of the more conservative forces who resist any democratization of the system. According to several people interviewed, the sudden disintegration of the Soviet Union seriously narrowed the democratic opening that had begun prior to the October 1991 Party Congress:

> Preservation of the state and of political power became the overriding question, which is not to deny that there are conservative forces who might try to use the situation to strengthen their own positions. But there are also *fuerzas aperturistas* [forces supporting an opening up of the system] who have had to fight to make sure that the emergency is not used as an excuse to make no changes at all, even the minimal changes necessary to remain faithful to the revolution's commitments. That's the scenario at the moment: minimum changes that are necessary to preserve the commitment.[28]

The construction of a participatory and pluralistic democracy appears as a *condition* for patriotic resistance and for the articulation of consensus around a path filled with obstacles and sacrifices. . . . Probably the clearest message that we have received from the collapse of Eastern European bureaucratic socialism is the need to reinterpret the relationship between democracy and governability in a socialist con-

25. Juan Valdés Paz, interview with author, Havana, February 25, 1993.
26. Niurka Pérez, interview with author, Havana, March 1, 1993.
27. Jorge Ibarra, interview with author, Havana, February 21, 1993.
28. Juan Valdés Paz, interview with author, Havana, February 25, 1993.

text, in which only lengthening and accelerating the pace of constructing democracy is capable of assuring the stability and governability of
the system.[29]

Just how far the democracy debate has evolved in Cuba is evidenced by
such calls, from loyal revolutionaries, to recognize that democratization
is a *condition* for resolving the crisis and rescuing socialism, not a goal to
be postponed for some undetermined future. There is not a reasonable
democratic political system in Cuba today, but the opinions cited here
suggest that there are influential voices calling for a process of democratization consistent with goals of social equality and justice.

Mexican Renovators

The renovative Mexican left's emerging view of state-society relations is informed both by the extensive critique of authoritarian statism
of the PRI and the old Communist regimes and by neoliberalism's devastation of the welfare state. For all its limitations, Mexico's version of the
welfare state was won only as a result of popular struggle and did provide an important social net for large sectors of the poor majority. Jaime
Tamayo's comments suggest the renovative left's concern with balancing
the lessons of these experiences:

> In Latin America, we have to give careful thought to how the state
> recedes and how civil society is strengthened. We have to think about
> how we can allow society to strengthen itself without necessarily reduc-
> ing the state, which might simply reproduce a social disarticulation
> rather than strengthening civil society, given the historical weakness of
> civil society and social classes here.[30]

Pablo González Casanova is particularly concerned about the dismantling of the Mexican state during the past ten to fifteen years of neoliberal
restructuring, and he has outlined in very concrete terms the extent to
which the state has been stripped of the most elemental resources needed
to address the social crisis facing Mexico.[31] This is a particularly
alarming fact when combined with Raquel Sosa's assessment that the
more dramatic results of political and economic restructuring throughout

---

29. Haroldo Dilla Alfono, op. cit. p. 20.

30. Jaime Tamayo, interview with author, Guadalajara, August 20, 1992.

31. Pablo González Casanova, "México: ¿Hacia una democracia sin
opciones?" in Jorge Alonso, et al., eds., *El Nuevo Estado Mexicano. IV. Estado y
Sociedad* (Mexico: Nueva Imagen, 1992).

Latin America in the 1980s were not the emergence of democratic regimes but rather generalized unemployment, underemployment, extreme poverty, marginalization, and the exclusion of the majority from any link with "the system."[32]

Given such conditions, the debate among renovative left intellectuals in Mexico is not so much about whether to further weaken or re-strengthen the state as much as it is about the nature of the state and the quality of its relations with civil society. Raúl Alvarez Garín, a leader of the 1968 student movement who has served as a federal deputy for the PRD, says frankly, "We need more state and less government."[33] This view earns him criticisms from some leftists for being excessively statist and authoritarian. Perhaps, but listen more carefully to what he imagines the Mexican state might be:

> There are many more autonomous protagonists today than in the past and there is more possibility for self-directed organizations that understand their tasks and challenges. We need more autonomous state institutions, more self-governed, like the Universities, which have a high level of autonomy and self-government in Mexico. This should also be true for the Social Security Institute and other state institutions.
>
> To make sure they don't become places for doing private business, they need a management structure that is clearly defined and understood. We need institutions that are more directly accountable to the people, because their leadership is elected, but also more influenced by qualified professionals. I am insisting on the issue of professional qualifications because of the problem of political interference in the state bureaucracy.[34]

Cristina Laurell has begun to elaborate more fully how the democratization and professionalization of public health and education in Mexico

---

32. Raquel Sosa Elízaga, "Sujetos dominantes y sujetos alternativos en América Latina de fines del siglo XX," *Memoria* (Mexico), December 1993, pp. 43-45.

33. Raúl Alvarez Garín, interview with author, Mexico City, August 27, 1992.

34. Ibid. As an example, he offers the problems of garbage collection in Mexico City, which require technical solutions. The problems remain unsolved, Alvarez argues, not because garbage collectors work for the state but because political corruption and incompetence leads the government to contracting eight different private companies to carry out studies of different aspects of the problem without any integration or coordination. The problems would be more effectively approached, Alvarez suggests, with a more autonomous and more democratic management structure for garbage collection combined with technical professionalization of state employees.

offer a more effective *and economically efficient* alternative to the neoliberal privatization schemes now under way.[35] Along a similar vein, Pablo Gómez, a former general secretary of the Unified Socialist Party of Mexico (PSUM) and now part of the national leadership of the PRD, argues that democratization of public productive enterprises is what resolves the problems of statism. He sees the central problem in Russia today being not the slowness of economic liberalization but lack of democracy: "They have replaced one absolutist state with another." Moreover, he continues, they've been able to do so because there is not a democratic movement from below as there is in Mexico. Like Alvarez Garín, Gómez is very concerned about the technological innovation Mexico requires to enter the "postindustrial world," but he stresses that technical innovation requires democracy, the key element missing in the former Soviet Union and the key element missing in Mexico.[36]

In the renovative view, then, the problem is not "too much or too little state." Rather, the task is the democratization and professionalization of state institutions and the concomitant democratization and education of civil society, to allow for citizen participation and self-government informed by skills and knowledge. Reflecting this perspective, González Casanova told a gathering of Mexico's left that it had two important weaknesses to overcome in the immediate future: first, the left and progressives cannot think only in terms of electoral struggle or in terms of governing, but of democracy in civil society, democracy of *"los de abajo"*; secondly, the struggle for hegemony must be understood not just in terms of propaganda but in terms of political education and culture.[37]

A significant practical example of a Mexican social movement that has attempted to respond to both of González Casanova's challenges is the Worker-Peasant-Student Coalition of the Isthmus (COCEI). The COCEI is Zapotec in its ethnic identity and rooted in the Isthmus of Tehuantepec's long history of indigenous struggles for autonomy; but it is also strongly influenced by the cross-fertilization of Marxist class analy-

---

35. See Asa Cristina Laurell, "For An Alternative Social Policy: The Production of Social Services," in S. Jonas and E. McCaughan, *Latin America Faces the Twenty-First Century*, op cit. Her study is also available in Spanish in Eduardo González, et al., *México: la búsqueda de alternativas* (Mexico: Ediciones de Cultura Popular, Facultad de Economía, UNAM, 1990).

36. Pablo Gómez, interview with author, Mexico City, August 19, 1992. Arnoldo Martínez Verdugo (interview with author, Mexico City, September 1, 1992) sees Russia's current problems differently than Gómez, saying it is now a democratic country with the freedom to organize political parties, etc.; the problem, in his view, is the social regime.

37. Pablo González Casanova, comments made at the Foro Luchas Emanicipadoras de Fin de Siglo, Mexico City, September 4, 1992.

sis and social movement activism characteristic of Mexico's generation of 1968 leftists. The Oaxacan-based organization was founded in the early 1970s, won the municipal elections in the city of Juchitán in 1981, was removed from office by army and police forces in 1983, then made a controversial decision to participate in a coalition city government with the PRI from 1986 to 1989, after which COCEI again won Juchitán's municipal elections in 1989 and 1992. Despite its impressive electoral successes, however, COCEI has never limited itself to the electoral arena. It has continued to use mass mobilization tactics around workplace and agricultural issues and has engaged in sophisticated cultural politics that have drawn upon local artists and writers. "COCEI supporters" one observer has noted, "do not prefer procedural democracy, which occurs in some situations, to other forms of participation and decision-making characteristic of the organization."[38] Víctor de la Cruz, a poet and COCEI activist, provides an example of how Zapotec tradition has influenced the movement's efforts to redefine a democracy of *"los de abajo"*:

> For COCEI, the Juchitecos [residents of Juchitán] are not equal citizens under the law as in bourgeois-liberal ideology. Treating the unequal equally is an inequality. For COCEI, the Juchitecos are *bichi'*, brothers. . . . One should not exploit, rob, or kill a brother.
> Citizens, because they are legally equal, must be treated as equals even though this permits the exploitation of some and the enrichment of others. . . . But a brother must be helped to go forward, to grow, to construct his house or educate his children. That is why we hold tightly to didxazá [the Zapotec language], because its experience in the past offers us solutions and points of departure toward the future and toward a type of modernity that is less unjust.[39]

Thus, in Mexico renovative voices on the left insist that meaningful democracy must be more than liberal, electoral democracy. In doing so, they also face the challenges that radical democratization poses for governability, as the COCEI's difficult experiences with local government illustrate. As we saw in the previous chapter's discussion of liberal tendencies within the left, the PRD's call for a "democratic revolution" has exposed it to charges of promoting a dangerous rupture, of refusing to negotiate a pacted transition with the PRI, and of not taking seriously the

---

38. Jeffrey W. Rubin, "COCEI Against the State: A Political History of Juchitán," in Howard Campbell, et al. (eds.), *Zapotec Struggles. Histories, Politics, and Representations from Juchitán, Oaxaca* (Washington, D.C.: Smithsonian Institution Press, 1993), pp. 167-168.

39. Víctor de la Cruz, "Brothers or Citizens: Two Languages, Two Political Projects in the Isthmus," in Howard Campbell, et al., ibid., p. 248.

issue of governability. These questions are far more complicated for renovative voices than the sometimes facile criticisms from the liberal left might suggest.

Alejandro Alvarez, an economic advisor to the PRD, asserted in 1992, for instance, that "no one in the PRD is willing to negotiate with the PRI at whatever cost."[40] Far from an irresponsible, maximalist position, however, Alvarez, a leading figure in the now dissolved Punto Crítico, views such mistrust of negotiating power as a rational response to Mexico's history of corporatist control. The essence of corporatism, according to Alvarez, is that the PRI tells you what your share of power will be.

> And if you accept what they offer just once, you're screwed for life. Instead, we've said, "No, we get whatever is reflected in the vote. If that's only five mangy cats, fine, but we keep what we won and we don't negotiate." The rule has to be, first we count the votes and then we know how many people we represent, not that you come and tell us how many.[41]

Nevertheless, recall from the discussion of the liberal left that in late 1994 and early 1995, sectors of the PRD were, in fact, calling for a "dialogue" with the PRI government to negotiate a resolution of various postelection conflicts in Chiapas, Vera Cruz, and Tabasco. Such calls for negotiation with the government caused prolonged, occasionally rancorous debate within the PRD. Urban popular leader Marco Rascón was one of the most vocal critics of the liberal left's strategy. He argued that their calls for dialogue with the new Zedillo government were not accompanied by a program of action that responded to the demands of Mexico's many social movements and that they were designed to marginalize Cuauhtémoc Cárdenas and other more radical PRD leadership. According to Rascón:

> The war in Chiapas pushed forward the social struggle and the electoral struggle, creating legitimate conditions for radicalizing both. In this context, the PRD has two basic options: become a party that is part of the crisis of the political and economic system, or transform itself into an organizing party that represents, in the political sphere,

---

40. Alejandro Alvarez, interview with author, Mexico City, August 28, 1992.

41. Ibid. Asa Cristina Laurell, a leading figure in the PRD, says that the party has won some support for its principled stand but has also paid a very high price in terms of repression and fraud. A.C. Laurell, "Democratic Challenges in Mexico," paper presented at the XVIII International Congress of the Latin American Studies Association, Atlanta, March 1994, p. 8.

social, programmatic demands [and offers] an alternative to . . . the co-government of the PRI and the PAN. A pacted transition means that all parties, including the government, are willing, and that is not the case. Consequently, it is necessary to generate organized, social and political force.[42]

Adolfo Gilly, closely allied with Cárdenas, claimed that the debate inside the PRD was being presented in terms of a false antinomy: "No one opposes dialogue; politics is also dialogue. What many of us oppose is beginning a dialogue about a future and improbable (yet one more?) electoral reform with the same people who have not met any of their commitments" from the previously negotiated reforms.[43] Many renovative voices within the PRD, perhaps the majority of the party, shared such concerns and said, "yes to dialogue, but with mobilizations," in order to strengthen the party's negotiating position and assure that its mass constituency would not be excluded from the process.[44]

In maintaining a skepticism about negotiating with the state-party regime and insisting on mobilization outside the formal political realm, it is not that the renovators are unconcerned with governability and the need to construct a broad national pact. However, they view these issues in terms that are quite different from the historical experience of elite-negotiated, pacted transitions to restricted, electoral regimes in countries like Venezuela, Colombia, or Chile.[45] The need for a pact that can assure governability is a concern of clearly nonliberal figures like Raúl Alvarez Garín and Pablo González Casanova. Alvarez Garín worries that the PRD's program is not sufficiently developed on "the issue of governability, neither in regard to the party's popular base, with its demands for dramatic material changes should the PRD win, nor in regard

---

42. Marco Rascón, "1995: Año del vuelo de la serpiente," *La Jornada* (Mexico), January 3, 1995; also see M. Rascón, "Otra Década Perdida," *La Jornada,* January 17, 1995.

43. Adolfo Gilly, "El PRD en su hora crítica," *La Jornada* (Mexico), January 20, 1995.

44. Rosa Icela Rodríguez, "En una semana se definirá el PRD acerca del diálogo," *La Jornada* (Mexico), December 4, 1994.

45. See, e.g., Daniel H. Levine, "Venezuela Since 1958: The Consolidation of Democratic Politics," in J. Linz and A. Stepan, eds., *The Breakdown of Democratic Regimes: Latin America* (Baltimore: Johns Hopkins, 1978); Terry Karl, "Petroleum and Political Pacts: The Transition to Democracy in Venezuela," in G. O'Donnell, et al., *Transitions from Authoritarian Rule* (Baltimore: Johns Hopkins, 1986); Alexander W. Wilde, "Conversations Among Gentlemen: Oligarchical Democracy in Colombia," in J. Linz and A. Stepan, op. cit.; Arturo Valenzuela, *The Breakdown of Democratic Regimes: Chile* (Baltimore: Johns Hopkins, 1978).

to the oligarchy."[46] But he is also optimistic about the prospects for forg-
ing a national alliance, essential for governing, that is far broader than
that now represented by the PRD:

> There are many forces to be counted on in Mexico. I have great
> confidence in the whole nationalist sector of the PRI, the PAN, and the
> PRD. A PRD government will have to be a government of integration.
> There are some developments along these lines, like the Accord for
> Democracy, which brings together people from all the parties, who re-
> spect one another. It is important to transcend ideologies and establish
> a base on which there is recognition of one another's qualifications,
> skills, and knowledge.[47]

González Casanova is concerned that neither the opposition nor the
government currently offers a national and social project that has economic force and political viability.[48] The problem, he advises, is not
simply one of extreme positions held by government and opposition, but
also of the limited options available to any progressive or popular government, especially given the state's erosion by neoliberal restructuring,
in confronting the real destabilizing power of transnational capital and
U.S. ruling circles.

In addition to developing the technical proposals needed for an alternative economic and social policy, González Casanova says the opposition needs to deal with the issues of politics and power required for

---

46. Raúl Alvarez Garín, interview with author, Mexico City, August 6, 1993.
The issue of Mexico's military clearly comes into play in discussions of
governability. Asa Cristina Laurell (interview with author, Mexico City, August
6, 1992) says the army was very divided during the 1988 presidential election,
with the lower ranks favoring Cuauhtémoc Cárdenas. Laurell says Salinas
subsequently gave the armed forces substantial wage increases and took other
measures to secure their loyalty, while Cárdenas tries to appeal to the army's
nationalism by stressing the sell-out nature of Salinas' reforms. Raúl Benítez
(interview with author, Mexico City, August 11, 1992), who has studied the
military in Mexico and Central America, says Cárdenas's efforts have been
ineffective and that the Mexican military is very anti-Cárdenas, associating him
and the PRD with the model that failed in the former Soviet Union and is now in
crisis in Cuba. Sergio de la Peña (interview with author, Mexico City, August 16,
1992) fears there would be a coup if the PRD should win the presidency, because
"the military is at the heart of the state"; minimally, he argues, the PRD would
be unable to govern.

47. Raúl Alvarez Garín, interview with author, Mexico City, August 27,
1992.

48. Pablo González Casanova, "México: ¿Hacia una democracia sin
opciones?" op cit., p. 267.

viable implementation: "What struggles—of resistance, defense or offense—are required to apply a distinct economic policy, and [to secure] a real and universal democracy, that is, electoral and social, and not just for a few Mexicans but for the majority of Mexicans?"[49] Achieving a "democracy with options," rather than simply another elected government forced to carry out the same neoliberal programs, requires "an accumulative *política de masas*, reflecting an increasingly democratic, popular, and national organization and consciousness."[50] The sort of "national social pact" envisioned in this concept cannot be negotiated by elites. Nor are there any new "October Revolutions" in González Casanova's scenario; it would be a gradual but not necessarily rupture-free process.

Yet, within this long-term scenario, González Casanova is equally concerned that the opposition and government find *immediate*, mutually agreeable reforms to avoid the destabilization and ungovernability threatened by the social fallout of neoliberalism. The opposition, he suggests, finds itself in a particularly difficult situation, given the real possibility that ruling forces may reject even a minimal pact.[51] Arnoldo Martínez Verdugo, former general secretary of the Communist Party and a leading figure in the PRD, says the reluctance of the PRI to accept any reforms "has to do with problems inherent in the form of the state-party," a characterization he uses for the old Soviet Communist Party as well as the PRI. "These are institutions which find it very difficult to reform themselves, because what's being defended is not just the form of power but power itself."[52] Nevertheless, "effective suffrage," argues González Casanova, while not the panacea imagined by more liberal forces, could be the basis for a "constituent agreement" that would provide the conditions in which the long-term political struggles could evolve more fruitfully.[53] That is a position shared by Martínez Verdugo and other renovative left forces in the PRD.

The type of national pact conjured up by the comments of Alvarez Garín and González Casanova, and the *"política de masas"* required to build it, distinguish their views both from the elite-negotiated pacts accepted by more liberal left forces and from the revolutionary class struggle discourse of more orthodox left. Likewise, the idea of "effective suffrage" as the necessary first step in a more long-term and more radical

---

49. Ibid., p. 278.

50. Ibid., p. 280.

51. Ibid. p. 289.

52. Arnoldo Martínez Verdugo, interview with author, Mexico City, September 1, 1992.

53. González Casanova, "Mexico: ¿Hacia una democracia sin opciones?" op cit., p. 281.

process of democratization, is different from the liberal left's glorification of electoral democracies and the orthodox left's dismissal of "reformism."

"Fair elections is the first priority on the political agenda," insists Cristina Laurell, who, like Alejandro Alvarez and Raúl Alvarez, was part of the Punto Crítico leadership for many years.[54] She says fair elections are a demand taken up by many nonpartisan, civic organizations, which suggests "the emergence of a nascent identity as citizens with rights and capacity to act."[55] However, she continues with a qualification that distances her views from more liberal left voices:

> [T]he building of democracy in Mexico goes beyond granting fair elec-
> tions that by themselves do not automatically grant a participatory
> process capable of overcoming the social crisis. The challenges are ex-
> tremely complex because the dismantling of a state-party regime poses
> the urgent necessity to found new relations and institutions that sub-
> stantiate the democratization of society. It implies, in that sense, a
> democratic revolution.
>
> What is at stake is the creation of conditions that make possible the
> organized participation of people in decisions that concern their lives,
> be it through political parties, unions, producer organizations, neigh-
> borhood associations, professional or student societies, etc. This
> implies initially the elimination of corporatist control over mass
> organizations, particularly the unions, and the abolition of the spectrum
> of repressive practices used against independent organizations.[56]

"Unlike in many places in the Latin America, the response in Mexico to authoritarianism—both that of the Latin American dictatorships and that of the socialist countries—has not been simply to demand formal democracy," says Marco Rascón, a prominent leader of Mexico City's Asamblea de Barrios neighborhoods organization. "There is an impor-tant social content to democracy in Mexico, based on the contents of the Mexican revolution and *cardenismo*."[57] Patricia Ruiz, a PRD activist and grass-roots organizer, adds that "this fact distinguishes the left project here very clearly from neoliberal democracy."[58]

The rebellion that began in Chiapas on January 1, 1994, has helped erode the influence of traditional liberal conceptions of political democ-racy (and how to achieve it), and has encouraged the renovative cur-rent's attempts to reconcile the struggle for political rights with the

---

54. Asa Cristina Laurell, "Democratic Challenges in Mexico," op. cit. p. 10.
55. Ibid., p. 9.
56. Ibid., pp. 11-12.
57. Marco Rascón, interview with author, August 14, 1992.
58. Patricia Ruiz, interview with author, August 14, 1992.

struggle for social rights.[59] Carlos Monsiváis has said that democracy is "inconceivable" in the context of massive poverty. He credits the Chiapas rebellion, which forced the nation to recognize the social conditions of its indigenous peoples, and the "moral" content of Subcomandante Marcos's discourse with having returned the issues of "poverty and inequality" to the top of Mexico's agenda.[60]

Elvira Concheiro, an economist formerly from the Mexican Communist Party and now active in the PRD, believes that, "The PRD, because of its origins in social movements, cannot fall into a glorification of electoral democracy as an end in itself, because the social demands of those movements are real."[61] The role of popular and social movements and their relationship to the PRD was one of the most common concerns addressed by the renovative left in discussing emerging ideas about democracy for this book. Many of those interviewed spoke to the PRD's acute awareness of the historical legacy of the PRI's corporatist control of labor and peasant organizations, a legacy ironically dating back to Lázaro Cárdenas, father of the PRD's most prominent leader. "Cuauhtémoc Cárdenas has the potential to forge a huge, powerful mass party," according to Pablo González Casanova, "but only if the PRD learns to allow the masses to keep organizing themselves and only if the party establishes a respectful relationship with them."[62] Assessments of how successful the PRD has been in that regard vary. Cristina Laurell says,

> The PRD is trying hard not to recreate corporatism. That's why it is organized on a federal, territorial basis rather than on a sectorial basis (even though this weakens the possibilities of workers, peasants, and Indians being represented in the leadership). Along the same lines, the party was organized as a party of citizens, not of organizations.[63]

---

59. The Zapatista rebellion in Chiapas has sparked a flurry of publications; two of the best English-language sources on the ELZN movement are John Ross, *Rebellion From the Roots: Indian Uprising in Chiapas* (Monroe, Maine: Common Courage Press, 1995) and Subcomandante Marcos, *Shadows of Tender Fury: The Letters and Communiques of Subcomandante Marcos and the Zapatista Army of National Liberation* (New York: Monthly Review Press, 1995). A useful collection in Spanish, which focuses on the discursive aspects of the rebellion, is Raul Trejo Delarbe (ed.), *Chiapas: La Guerra de las Ideas* (Mexico: Editorial Diana, 1994).

60. Carlos Monsiváis, quoted in *La Jornada* (Mexico), February 4, 1994.

61. Elvira Concheiro, interview with author, Mexico City, August 5, 1993.

62. Pablo González Casanova, interview with author, Mexico City, August 23, 1991.

63. Cristina Laurell, interview with author, Mexico City, August 6, 1992. The same concerns about territorial versus sectorial representation were raised by Cubans as well, and considerable attention is being given by some in Cuba to

The problem is not just one of territorial versus sectorial representation, however. According to PRD activist Nuria Fernández, the party lacks "a strategic leadership to insist on the participation of the leaders of social sectors." Instead, she and others observe, there are internal party struggles over who will be the PRD candidates for the Senate and House of Deputies, positions which are very highly paid in Mexico.[64] The result is to sidetrack more important political issues, such as having the party's elected national legislators reflect the social movements that make up its base, and the need to build a much broader popular national alliance.

Political differences and tendencies within the PRD clearly complicate the process of defining new approaches to building party-movement relations that are healthy, respectful and mutually beneficial. Some within the party reportedly take a traditional corporatist approach to relations with the movements, while others are experimenting with direct democracy.[65] According to Julio Moguel, a former Maoist now active in the PRD, one sector (mainly former PRIistas and Communists) emphasizes strictly citizen-based democratic struggles, while another sector (Maoists and Asamblea de Barrios leadership) is more clearly identified with particular social movements and sectors.[66] Others argue that the PRD's near total absorption with the electoral arena has kept it from addressing the demands of the indigenous and environmental movements.[67]

Despite the difficulties, there is real potential for a new relationship between party and popular organizations, and many point to the PRD's relationship with Mexico City's Asamblea de Barrios neighborhood organizations and to various local movements and organizations in states like Chiapas, Veracruz, and Tabasco as examples. The promise of "*neocardenismo*," as Jaime Tamayo describes the movement that gave

---

sectorial representation in the Poder Popular structure (See Miguel Limia, "Lo laboral versus lo territorial," op cit.). Perhaps a more fruitful innovation that would address representation of minority sectors is the "cumulative voting" scheme proposed by Lani Guinier to enhance "proportional representation" for minority communities in the United States. See Lani Guinier, *The Tyranny of the Majority* (Free Press, 1994).

64. Nuria Fernández, interview with author, Mexico City, August 5, 1993. The problem she says, is not so much with the top leadership (Cárdenas and Porfirio Muñoz Ledo) but "with long-time left cadre who feel they've spent a lifetime struggling and sacrificing and now deserve the perks and privileges afforded by entry into the political class, which are substantial."

65. Alejandro Alvarez, interview with author, Mexico City, August 28, 1992.

66. Julio Moguel, interview with author, Mexico City, August 18, 1992.

67. Enrique de la Garza Toledo, an intellectual and labor activist, interview with author, Mexico City, August 10, 1993.

birth to the PRD, is "in the autonomy of social and popular movements." Historical *cardenismo*, says Tamayo, "became increasingly corporatist but it also included the experience of civil society organizing itself, finding its own voice," and the existence of many autonomous social and popular movements in Mexico since the mid-1980s has helped the advance toward democracy. But, warns Tamayo, "the old authoritarian political culture, of the PRI and of the left, continues to reproduce itself, even within the social movements themselves."[68]

In any event, the fact that there is marked concern and debate about the tension between liberal notions of individual citizen-based politics and the need to incorporate the social demands of popular movements is part of what distinguishes the renovative left from the more liberal and orthodox tendencies in Mexico. From the renovative perspective, "the struggle for the democratization of our country is," in the words of former Communist Elvira Concheiro, "the process of socializing power in the long run."[69] How to move from step one—free elections and political rights—to the full socialization of power, presents a formidable strategic challenge to the renovative left.

Recent political developments in the Mexican states of Chiapas and Tabasco offer interesting examples of how these challenges are being met in practice. Mass movements, closely identified with but broader than the PRD, mobilized in support of gubernatorial candidates in 1994: Armando Avendaño in Chiapas and Andrés Manuel López Obrador in Tabasco. In both elections, the PRI claimed victory, but, citing substantial evidence of fraud, the PRD candidates and their movements refused to concede defeat. The Chiapas movement declared Avendaño to be *"gobernador en rebelión"* (governor in rebellion), and López Obrador was recognized by his constituents as *"gobernador popular"* (the people's governor) in Tabasco. Mass mobilizations continued for months following the elections. Supporters refused to pay taxes and participated in the efforts of these "parallel governments" to create concrete programs and institutions independent of the officially recognized PRI governors (e.g., alternative health clinics, schools, centers for fruit and vegetable distribution, and employment services).

These can be seen as examples of the broad left opposition's attempts to "socialize power" outside the confines of the formal political system. In a telling example of how the renovative left's conception of political

---

68. Jaime Tamayo, interview with author, Guadalajara, August 20, 1992. Also see Jaime Tamayo, "Neoliberalism Encounters *Neocardenismo*," in J. Foweraker and A. Craig, eds., *Popular Movements and Political Change in Mexico* (Boulder and London: Lynne Rienner Publishers, 1990).

69. Elvira Concheiro, interview with author, Mexico City, August 5, 1993.

power and democracy is changing in the course of such struggles, PRD gubernatorial candidate Manuel López Obrador said, "The idea is not that I should govern at any cost. I am not fighting for the governorship but for democracy."[70] Similarly, in a complete departure from historic guerilla movements whose main purpose was to seize state power, Zapatista leader Marcos has stated repeatedly that he hopes the mass movement for "democracy, freedom, and justice" is so successful as to leave his army without a job. These are not movements about political power in the traditional understandings of either the orthodox or the liberal lefts, but about a "socialization of power," a notion yet to be fully defined in theory and practice. For many in the Mexican left today, this is the essence of their "democratic revolution."

Finally, is there an inherent contradiction in the PRD's support of liberal political reforms and its call for a "revolution," even a democratic one? Likewise, is there a conflict between the PRD's defense of the 1917 Constitution (the legal framework of what became a highly authoritarian, corporatist, and centralized state) and the pursuit of a democratic revolution? Are these contradictions adequately resolved by notions of the "unfinished," "frozen," or "betrayed" Mexican revolution, which has been a theme in the left for many years? José Woldenberg sees absolutely no place for a "revolution" in this process.[71] Jorge Castañeda is certain that the era of revolution is over.[72] Yet Pablo González Casanova has called the Chiapas rebellion the "first revolution of the twenty-first century,"[73] and Mexico's most viable left opposition calls itself the party of the "democratic revolution."

The ambivalence of the concept, "democratic revolution," is not unlike the ambivalence of Gramsci's ideas about hegemony and accumulation of forces. Gramsci's discourse has allowed social democratic forces to move gradually toward a more cautious emphasis on order and con-

---

70. Andrés Manuel López Obrador, quoted in *La Jornada* (Mexico), February 23, 1995. López Obrador was subsequently elected president of the national PRD in 1996. Cuauhtémoc Cárdenas has been quoted making similar statements, such as, "I am not for being president by force. That is not my objective. My objective is that we change the country's situation, that we enter a period in which we can effectively participate in the decisions that regulate the political, economic, social, and cultural life of the country." See Pascal Beltrán del Río, "Las cifras electorales son tan falsas como las de 1988 . . .", *Proceso* (Mexico), September 5, 1994, p. 7.

71. José Woldenberg, "Comentarios Finales," op. cit.

72. Jorge Castañeda, *Utopia Unarmed*, op. cit.

73. Pablo González Casanova, quoted in *La Jornada* (Mexico), February 10, 1995.

tinuity over accumulated change and rupture.[74] Yet more radical left interpreters have seen in Gramsci an alternative to revolution defined as the abrupt, usually armed seizure of state power, but nonetheless as a revolutionary alternative.[75] In this view, Gramsci's notion of "national-popular collective will" as a process of building a bloc of social forces under the hegemony of the popular classes is a gradual but revolutionary process.[76] The latter interpretation informs the renovative Mexican left's thinking on the relationship between reform of the political system and eventual radical transformation of the state and society. Arnoldo Córdova, for example, one of the few leading intellectuals associated with the revolutionary nationalist MAP in the 1970s who is now in the PRD, concedes that efforts to democratize the political system from within the system can tend to strengthen the state, because such participation manifests one's adhesion to the system. But, he argues, that is not the only truth, because the struggle for democratization of the political system can also strengthen those forces who want to radically transform society. As those forces gradually gain influence:

> There is always a moment when the state can go no further in this direction. At that moment, it becomes impossible for the state to continue

---

74. See Jaime Osorio, "Los nuevos sociólogos," op. cit.

75. The January 1994 armed uprising in Chiapas, Mexico, has reopened discussion about armed struggle as an instrument of social and political change but not necessarily about the prospects for a revolutionary seizure of state power. Jorge Castañeda, in comments at the March 1994 Latin American Studies Association meetings in Atlanta, distinguished between armed struggle as a method of struggle versus a certain idea of revolution as sudden, radical transformation of society. He described the Zapatistas in Chiapas as "armed reformists par excellence," calling for land, dignity and fair elections. Even before the Chiapas uprising, Raquel Sosa noted that Latin America's extremely polarized societies still provide conditions for the emergence of new guerrilla movements, but predicted they would have a less precise ideological perspective than in the past about long-term social change. See Raquel Sosa Elízaga, "Sujetos dominantes y sujetos alternativos en la América Latina de fines del siglo," op. cit. Cuauhtémoc Cárdenas has stated that "the demands of the Zapatistas are the same we have fought for beginning years ago" (San Francisco Chronicle, May, 17, 1994), again suggesting that the reappearance of armed struggle in Mexico does not substantially alter the reassessment about the nature of revolutionary or reformist change, as much as about the forms of struggle available to the opposition.

76. For a useful discussion of the relevance of Gramsci's ideas to left thought in Latin America, see William Rowe and Vivian Schelling, *Memory and Modernity. Popular Culture in Latin America* (London: Verso, 1991), especially Chapter 3 on "Popular Culture and Politics."

to strengthen itself and, instead, what occurs is that the state weakens until it ceases to carry out its functions as the foundation of the ruling social system.[77]

Understanding power as resting not simply on force of arms but also on popular consensus, Córdova defines the struggle for democracy as "a struggle for the consensus of the majority of society that can have no objective other than the revolutionary transformation of society itself."[78]

To summarize, renovative left thinkers in Cuba and Mexico are drawing upon but attempting to transcend both liberal and Marxist conceptions of democracy. From liberalism, they have taken such traditions as the importance of political rights, the rule of law, and elected, representative, parliamentary institutions. Political reforms, such as proposals for two-round voting in Mexico or for paid, professional representatives in Cuba, are recognized by renovators as important but insufficient steps toward democratization of their respective political systems. Drawing from the Marxist tradition, renovators in both countries still understand democracy as a process of "socializing power." While acknowledging that political democracy cannot be conflated with the idea of a socialist economy, as orthodox leftists still tend to do, renovators believe that democracy cannot be fully meaningful without a concomitant redistribution of wealth and greater popular control over the economy. Thus ideas about workers self-management and various co-ownership schemes as well as democratization and professionalization of state enterprises are considered by renovators alongside reforms of the political system.

For the renovative left, democratization must take place within the state, political regime, government, and civil society. Renovators tend to talk less about reducing the state than they do about democratizing and professionalizing state institutions, which they believe also require providing state employees and their public clients with the information and skills necessary to assume democratic control. Renovators also give considerable attention to strengthening the autonomy of civil society vis a vis the state and the parties of the left. Thus in Cuba, we heard references to the importance of new NGOs, women's centers, and local popular councils as spaces potentially more independent of the Communist Party. In Mexico, the renovative left is particularly concerned with how to build a left party that politically represents but does not replace or overshadow the network of myriad social movements and organizations.

---

77. Arnoldo Córdova, *La Nación y La Constitución. La Lucha por la Democracia en México* (Mexico: Claves Latinoamericanas, 1989), p. 386.

78. Ibid., p. 387.

The renovative left in Cuba and Mexico is exploring how to balance and/or combine territorial and sectorial schemes of representation (within political parties and within legislative bodies) that reflect and protect both individual citizen rights and the social rights of particular groups.

Finally, while renovative struggles for democracy demonstrate the renewed attention given by the Latin American left to liberal political reforms, they are not confined to the formally political sphere. In Cuba, where the state-party still thoroughly dominates the nation's political system, significant examples of renovative influences on democratization are often found in the cultural sphere, or in academic research centers, churches, and various NGOs. In Mexico, the examples of how the struggle for democratization transcends the formal political sphere are more visible and dramatic; there, the renovative left's efforts to redefine democracy range from actions to increase the power of urban community organizations, to attempts to build "parallel governments" in Chiapas and Tabasco, to the multifaceted struggle of the Zapotecs in Oaxaca, to a massive, national movement in support of a peaceful resolution of the armed Zapatista movement's multiple demands. The lefts in Cuba and Mexico both enjoy certain advantages over those in postmilitary countries like Chile and Argentina in terms of the continuity of socially-oriented political cultures, but the presence of many, strong social movements and popular organizations in Mexico make that country par-ticularly conducive to a renovated left discourse on democracy. Cuban renovators remain considerably hamstrung by the strong authoritarian tendencies of the Cuban Commnist Party. Nevertheless, I share Carollee Bengelsdorf's assessment that the present crisis in Cuba holds promise as well as danger: "A vacuum has opened up: the old, imposed, rigid theoretical models are being discarded and experimentation with new ideas, methodologies and approaches has become, increasing, the order of the day."[79]

A Postscript on Democracy and Leadership:
Fidel, Fidel, ¿qué tiene Fidel?

No doubt readers have noted an obvious omission in the previous summary of the left's rethinking of democracy: no word about prevailing opinions in either country of Fidel Castro's role or about the Mexican left's current view of the Cuban revolution. In the 1960s, a popular Latin

---

79. Carollee Bengelsdorf, *The Problem of Democracy in Cuba: Between Vision and Reality* (New York and Oxford: Oxford University Press, 1994), p. 175.

American protest song humorously asked, in so many words, What it is about Fidel that makes the *Americanos* crazy? The implicit answer was that the U.S. government's extreme reaction to Fidel Castro was not altogether explainable in rational terms. I found myself up against a similar dilemma in trying to interpret and categorize the attitudes of progressive Cuban and Mexican intellectuals toward Castro. The question of his historic role and current leadership is so thoroughly saturated with emotions and symbolism as to defy any neat correlation with the orthodox statist, liberal, and renovative tendencies outlined above. Similarly, the Mexican left's relationship to the Cuban revolution is invested with all the love-hate tensions of any two siblings raised in a dysfunctional family.

An additional problem in interpreting the interviews from Cuba is that the somewhat strained political climate does not lend itself to soliciting views about Castro that are not self-censored. Because I could not take most verbal or written statements about Castro at face value, I determined that it was fruitless to attempt any meaningfully systematic interpretation of these issues. There are simply too many layers of possible meaning to negotiate. Nevertheless, a few observations are worth making.

First, although it was somewhat contradictory, I often found among Cuban intellectuals a more vigorous or explicit defense of Fidel Castro's leadership among pro-democracy liberal and renovative voices than I did among the more authoritarian, orthodox thinkers. This was particularly evident in comments by various intellectuals who had directly experienced censorship and scorn by the regime when the Philosophy Department and *Pensamiento Crítico* were closed down in 1971. Remembering how Castro used to drop by unannounced for coffee and political debate with that circle of intellectuals in the 1960s, one man told me he would be eternally grateful to Fidel Castro, who, he said, personally made sure that the intellectuals targeted for harsh criticism by Castro's younger brother Raúl in 1971 were allowed to continue "working for the revolution," rather than being jailed or completely marginalized.

A woman from the same circle told me of her total disagreement with the official call for voters to elect the entire slate of candidates nominated for the National Assembly in the February 1993 elections. The demand to vote for the united slate, she said, "represents the dominant authoritarian and verticalist nature of the party." She entered the polling booth determined to vote only for those candidates she considered worthy to represent her. But at the last moment, she could not disobey Castro's plea for a united vote. She did as her leadership had ordered, she told me, and then "went home and cried for three days." She tried to explain: "I have followed Fidel since I was a 16-year-old girl in 1956, when my grandfather, a Mambí,[80] told me Fidel was going to save the country. I would rather die for the revolution than betray Fidel." Such anecdotes illustrate the extent to which personal political loyalties, forged over decades of struggle, and the authority of genuine charismatic leadership, which so fascinated Max Weber precisely because it defied a purely rational understanding, dominate Cuban political culture. These factors make it nearly impossible to offer an "objective" assessment of the Cuban left's view of Castro today. That same old protest song from the 1960s also said, "The Americanos say Fidel is a communist./ Well, if Fidel is a communist, add me to the list." Loyalty to Fidel then had relatively little to do with commitment to a particular ideology, and I suspect the same is true now.

On a less personal level, Rafael Hernández, who strongly supports a decentralization and democratization of Cuba, defends the record of Castro's leadership and says it is indispensable at the critical moment facing the nation:

> To steer the boat through these turbulent waters requires not only appropriate ideas about democracy and economic policy. It requires a real authority that will allow needed relief, as well as readjustments; continuity of the social revolution's achievements and goals, as well as a bloodless rupture with old schemes; the necessary delegation of power to allow for a viable transition to a more decentralized and democratic system, as well as reformed structures, economic and juridical reorganization, and more efficient mechanisms. Who can lead this process in a manner that is the least costly and above all the least dangerous for the country's stability? Obviously, Fidel Castro.[81]

There are many possible interpretations of such a statement. Perhaps what we see is what we get: a political assessment that Castro is the "best man" for the job, based on his track record and the authority he still commands. Or, perhaps it is an effort to legitimate and strengthen democratic demands, and avoid political marginalization, by proclaiming loyalty to Fidel. Given Castro's historic role within the party as political arbiter and mediator more than ideologue, both interpretations could be correct. Even Cecilio Dimas, for example, an intellectual considerably alienated from the regime and sympathetic to the views of the social democratic dissidents, insists that "any political solution to the current crisis must involve Fidel Castro." He even ventured that Castro's

---

80. The *mambises* were the guerrillas of the Liberation Army led by Antonio Maceo during the Ten Years' War against Spain, 1868-1878.

81. Rafael Hernández, "Mirar a Cuba. Notas para una discusión." Draft manuscript, Havana (August 1992).

renowned pragmatism might well eventually place him on the side of reformers, "if he is convinced that is the least disruptive solution" to the current crisis.[82]

As to why more orthodox forces seemed less inclined to invoke or defend Castro's leadership, there are at least three plausible explanations. First, orthodox socialist intellectuals may feel secure in their association with the still dominant tendency within the party, assume that their views carry Castro's authority, and thus feel less compelled to legitimize their ideas by invoking his name. Secondly, several people I interviewed told me that many upper- and middle-level party functionaries and state bureaucrats were still angry at Castro for doing away with some of their perks and privileges during the period of rectification in the late 1980s. Thus they may be in no mood to praise him. A third possible explanation for these findings is that some of the support for Castro among liberals and renovators may be due to a belief that he is preferable to any currently visible alternative, whereas the orthodox forces may see themselves as the most likely alternative and hence be less concerned about losing Castro.

The Mexican left's current attitudes toward Castro and the Cuban revolution are somewhat easier to assess but are also complex. More liberal left voices, such as those frequently published in the journals *Nexos* and *Plural*, are predictably critical of Cuba's record on political rights and intolerance of dissident views.[83] More orthodox publications, such as *Socialismo* (edited by former Communists critical of what they consider to be the PRD's reformism) and *Nuestro Tiempo* (often described as a Mexican version of the U.S. Marxist journal *Monthly Review*) remain staunch defenders of Fidel Castro and the Cuban revolution, which they see as the most democratic nation in Latin America. There are no big surprises there, but within the loose renovative tendency, perspectives range wildly from former Communist Pablo Gómez's scathing critique of the Cuban revolution's "senility"[84] to Pablo González Casanova's belief that "Cuba is becoming ever more democratic."[85] An emotionally heated debate about Cuba among various Mexican artists and intellectuals

---

82. Cecilio Dimas, interview with author, Havana, February 11, 1993.

83. See, for example, the July 1992 issue of *Plural*, edited by Jaime Labastida, which focussed on Cuba and unleashed a bitter exchange between Labastida and the leadership of UNEAC, Cuba's writers and artists association. Much of the debate was published in the Mexican daily, *Excelsior*, and in UNEAC's *La Gaceta de Cuba* (November-December 1992).

84. Pablo Gómez, "¿Sinilidad de la Revolución?", serialized in *La Jornada* (Mexico), Feb. 2 through February 18, 1990.

85. Pablo González Casanova, "Thinking About Cuba," in S. Jonas and E. McCaughan, *Latin America Faces the Twenty-first Century*, op cit.

raged in the pages of *La Jornada* in July 1993, provoked by a humorous but sharp critique of Cuba in the paper's cartoon supplement *El Ahuzote*. That there is debate about Cuba in the Mexican left is itself significant because for many years any criticism of the revolution that successfully thumbed its nose at "Tío Sam" was considered heretical. This change suggests an increasing appreciation for pluralism among progressive forces.

However, the debates remain full of contradictions, ambiguity, and ambivalence. This is understandable in light of the tremendous intellectual, political, and symbolic importance that the Cuban revolution and Fidel Castro have had for the Latin American left, and indeed for broad sectors of Latin American society. Why does Fidel still make the *Americanos* crazy? Because whenever he visits any country in Latin America, where democracy has arguably become a very generalized and highly valued goal, he is greeted by masses who enthusiastically applaud his defiance of U.S. power and arrogance. This is true in Africa as well. In South Africa during Nelson Mandela's inauguration, while U.S. Vice President Al Gore and First Lady Hillary Clinton carefully avoided being seen on the same side of the room with Fidel Castro, crowds of Black South Africans cheered his presence.

The question of personal political leadership is an important element in the left's reassessment of democracy, particularly given the legacy of Lenin, Stalin, and Latin America's own traditions of *caudillismo* and *caciquismo*. There is certainly considerable sensitivity, if not yet clarity, about the issue among the Mexican left. While some charge Cuauhtémoc Cárdenas is just one more authoritarian *caudillo*, others speak of him in reverent terms.[86] Cárdenas is certainly not a charismatic leader, but his persona is tremendously magnified by some of Mexico's most enduring historical myths: son of the nation's most beloved president and named after the Aztec leader who defended his nation against the Spanish conquerors. One PRD intellectual from the Maoist tendency provided an example of this phenomenon, telling me there is a sector within the PRD that pushes a more radical vision of direct, mass democracy and yet

---

86. A significant dispute at the PRD's congress in summer 1993 was about how the party's candidates for the 1994 congressional elections would be chosen. According to Cristina Laurell (interview with author, Mexico City, August 1, 1993), after a heated debate, the majority agreed that Cuauhtémoc Cárdenas would be allowed to name 50 percent of the candidates (the other 50 percent to be chosen by the party's state bodies). The argument was that this would allow the PRD leadership maximum flexibility in building broader national alliances by offering to support PRI dissidents or local leaders who may not be in the party. The minority argued that this was undemocratic and *caudillista*. The issue is clearly not a simple one.

expresses not concern about Cárdenas's great personal power within the party:

> A party militant can curse any number of personalist, paternalistic, authoritarian *caciques* or *caudillos*, but you don't touch Cárdenas. There's not necessarily a logical connection between one's political position and one's action on this question. It's partly that Cárdenas is not seen as human. He *is* the history of Mexico. He's the part of the country you have inside you. He is your flag. It's a very unusual thing, like having a treasure. This is more a question for psychologists.[87]

Alongside such reverence of individual leaders, there are examples in Mexico of new attitudes and practices clearly aimed at breaking with the culture of *caudillismo*. Note, for example, that both Super Barrio (a popular leader among Mexico City's poor neighborhoods movement who dresses like a cartoon super hero) and the Zapatistas' Subcomandante Marcos are masked, anonymous leaders. Their personal identities are not widely known and considered largely irrelevant.[88] Do they perhaps represent new symbols of the still-necessary *function* of leadership absent the personalization of leadership? Are they reflective of efforts on the left to assert a new relationship between leader and rank-and-file? Clearly, in assessing the left's evolving understanding of democracy, the questions of leadership and of the particular role of figures like Fidel Castro and Cuauhtémoc Cárdenas deserve far greater attention than I am able to give them here. But indications are that, on the issue of leadership too, changes are in the air.

---

87. Julio Moguel, interview with author, Mexico City, August 18, 1992.

88. In February 1995, the Mexican government announced with theatrical fanfare that it had learned the true identity of Marcos. Government spokesmen appeared confident that revealing Marcos to be a former university professor would strike a psychological blow against the rebels. Public reaction was hardly what the Zedillo government hoped for. One columnist wryly commented that the news was the equivalent of announcing that Superman was really Clark Kent, and tens of thousands of demonstrators chanted *"Todos Somos Marcos"* ("We Are All Marcos") in repeated mobilizations throughout the nation.

CHAPTER 5. SOCIALISM I

State vs. Market

Throughout the twentieth century, debates raged within the left over the nature of socialism. Some of the most persistent questions were directed at the role of the state: Had the Soviet Union restored a form of state capitalism? Wasn't democratic control of the means of production more important than formal state ownership? Wasn't worker self-management rather than bureaucratic central planning the key to socialism? Was socialist agriculture better served by distributing private plots of land to the peasantry, by organizing the countryside into collectives, or by establishing large, state farms? All too often these debates became hopelessly imprisoned in a rigid opposition of state versus market. When all was said and done, the assumption remained among broad sectors of the left that socialism was closely associated with, if not precisely defined by, state control of the economy.[1]

For the Latin American left, this association was further reinforced by the tradition of nationalist developmentalism, which elevated nationalization of key economic sectors to a *sine qua non* of national sovereignty and development. In the words of Rafael Galván, Mexico's late labor leader and ideologue of revolutionary nationalism: "We grow and advance through our history [by] nationalizing."[2] The identification of socialism with state-run economy took on added weight for the Latin American left following Cuba's 1968 "revolutionary offensive," which

---

1. These observations are by no means meant to suggest that Marx's own writings justify such a statist conception of socialism. Opposing sides of the many debates on these issues were taken by people who considered themselves Marxist and justified their position by citing one or another of Marx's texts. Many Marxisms have emerged in the 150 years since the *Communist Manifesto* was written. The intention here is not to uncover the "true" Marxism, but to suggest that amid all the variations there emerged a pervasive tendency to associate socialism with state control.

2. Rafael Galván, quoted in Barry Carr, *The Mexican Left, the Popular Movements, and the Politics of Austerity* (San Diego: Center for U.S.-Mexican Studies, University of California, San Diego, 1986), p. 12.

extended state ownership of the economy to even the smallest consumer services, "from the woman running a hamburger stand to the guy selling snow cones on the street corner."[3] Despite important debates about the nature of socialism that continued among left intellectuals in Latin America and elsewhere, the overwhelming historical weight of the Soviet bloc, reinforced by the experience of Third World socialism and nationalism, tended to obscure alternative notions of a nonstatist, socialist economy. As Marta Harnecker, one of Latin America's best-known Leninists, observed:

> If, indeed, no one declared that their model was the model of Eastern European socialism, that was nonetheless the model in many respects. We cannot deny that for the left, socialism was best when the means of production were the most nationalized and most owned by the state, and when the party was the only party. This was the left's vision until just a short time ago.[4]

Then, in the 1980s, as the neoconservative "revolutions" of U.S. President Ronald Reagan and British Prime Minister Margaret Thatcher restored classical economists Adam Smith and David Ricardo to the high priesthood of global political economy, neoliberalism's ascendancy seemed to rule out anything other than the most radical versions of "free market" capitalism. Even Keynesianism, let alone Marxism, became a dirty word associated with the "failed" state interventionism of the past. In Latin America, the debt crisis and "lost decade" of the 1980s further established neoliberalism as the only acceptable economic model. International financial institutions used the severity of the region's economic crisis to dictate policies favoring privatization, deregulation, social service cutbacks, wage controls, and prioritization of exports over the internal market. The neoliberal ideological offensive was remarkably successful in laying blame for Latin America's economic woes at the doorstep of nationalist state economic regulation.

Already reeling from the astonishingly rapid ascent of radical "free marketism," the socialist and nationalist lefts were then dealt an additional blow with the quick disintegration and collapse of the state socialist regimes in Eastern Europe and the Soviet Union. As the dust settled from the Cold War, winners and losers seemed all too apparent. Jorge

---

3. Juan Antonio Blanco, quoted in Medea Benjamin, "Cuba: Talking About Revolution. Conversations with Juan Antonio Blanco" (manuscript, 1993).

4. Marta Harnecker, "Democracy and Revolutionary Movement," in Susanne Jonas and Edward J. McCaughan (eds.), *Latin America Faces the Twenty-First Century. Reconstructing a Social Justice Agenda* (Boulder: Westview, 1994), p. 75.

Castañeda began his important assessment of the current state of the Latin American left with an unequivocal assertion:

> The Cold War is over and Communism and the socialist bloc have collapsed. The United States and capitalism have won, and in few areas of the globe is that victory so clear-cut, sweet, and spectacular as in Latin America.[5]

Over the cacophony of celebratory assertions about capitalism's now indisputable, natural superiority, the voices of those wanting to challenge neoliberal orthodoxy with reminders of historical fact were hard-pressed to make themselves heard. "Facts, schmacts," seemed the smug reply of dogmatic free-marketeers, who conveniently ignored the massive state intervention (in the form of military spending and public bail-outs of failing industries and financial institutions) that characterized the Reagan and Bush administrations in the United States. The left found itself confronted with what Franz Hinkelammert calls "a metaphysical antistatism."

> This antistatism dominates the current debate about the state and has become a *leitmotif* of today's worldview. It appeared first in the neo-liberal theories about the economy and society and has become today a kind of common sense of public opinion the world over. It even appears in the socialist countries and dominates a majority of the international institutions that make policy decisions.[6]

Caught between the rise of neoliberalism and the collapse of state socialism, the left experienced a serious paradigm crisis. For most of the century, the left's project had given overwhelming theoretical and strategic importance to the state as the central protagonist in the construction of a noncapitalist alternative. Certainly, sectors of the lefts in Europe and the United States had already incorporated antistatist perspectives into their discourse by the 1970s and early 1980s. These lefts had been influenced significantly by the antiauthoritarian critiques of 1968, as well as by feminism, "new social movements" theories that stressed the importance of civil society, and emerging postmodern analyses of a

---

5. Jorge Castañeda, *Utopia Unarmed. The Latin American Left After the Cold War* (New York: Alfred A. Knopf, 1993), p. 3.

6. Franz Hinkelammert, "Our Project for the New Society in Latin America: The Regulating Role of the State and Problems of Self-Regulation in the Market," in S. Jonas and E. J. McCaughan, *Latin America Faces the Twenty-First Century,* op. cit., p. 13. Also see Hinkelammert, "La simetría del neo-liberalismo y el estatismo," *Envío* (Nicaragua), No. 123, February 1992, pp. 33-48.

fragmented world and decentered subjects. All of these ideological currents made themselves felt within the Latin American lefts as well, but did not contribute to a more generalized antistatism, as they had in Europe and the United States. This difference is partially explained by the distinct structural realities of the semiperiphery, where considerable importance is still attributed to the state in (a) mediating national sovereignty vis a vis the United States and transnational capital, and (b) providing a social welfare safety net in societies where large sectors of the population live in extreme poverty. Nevertheless, at the century's close, antistatism was riding the crest of the wave of capitalism's triumph over socialism, even within the Latin American lefts.

The Impact in Cuba and Mexico

Ironically, as left political forces gained strength and influence in some Latin American countries, many left intellectuals seemed at a loss to offer a clear economic alternative to unattractive neoliberal prescriptions. As Sergio de la Peña, a leading theoretician of the former Mexican Communist Party and now an economic adviser to the PRD, put it:

> There has been an important redefinition of the ideological points of reference available to the left. Socialism (above all, the European practices and experiences) and the various schools of the whole Marxist current offered alternative visions. They also represented real options, in the sense of socialist states that could offer aid, financing, military support. With this whole set of options now taken apart, there has been created a huge theoretical, ideological, conceptual vacuum, a vacuum of political projects.[7]

For the Cuban revolution, clearly the crisis was more than ideological. Some eighty-five percent of Cuba's trade was with the socialist bloc that proceeded to self-destruct almost overnight. Juan Antonio Blanco offers some statistical evidence of the impact:

> The figures are dramatic. In 1989 we imported about 13 million tons of oil from the Soviet Union; in 1992 we could only import 6 million tons. In 1989 we imported around $8.4 billion dollars worth of goods; by 1992 our import capacity plunged to $2.2 billion. By 1992 we had only 30 percent of the resources for the sugar harvest that we had in 1989, so

---

7. Sergio de la Peña, interview with author, Mexico City, August 16, 1992.

sugar production has been dropping sharply. . . . Imagine what would happen to Mexico if suddenly all trade with the United States ceased.[8]

Mexico, of course, did not suddenly lose all of its international economic relations; in fact, after nearly a decade of deep neoliberal restructuring, it was on the verge of signing the North American Free Trade Agreement. But for much of Mexico's left opposition, the paradigm crisis prompted by such dramatic global changes was significant. Elvira Concheiro, an economist active in the PRD, and formerly a leading figure in the defunct Mexican Communist Party, described the impact on Mexico's left:

> The majority of the left has taken refuge in pragmatism. Much of the debate that was developing since the early 1980s has been more or less suspended. The left hasn't redefined socialism. Socialism remains a point of reference, but little more. Some of the left has also lost all confidence in its own discourse. Nevertheless, I have a sense that we've finally passed the first stage of shock and are moving toward more reflection.[9]

A similar loss of confidence among Cuban intellectuals was noted by criminologist Margarita Viera:

> Cuba copied so much from the Soviet Union in every sphere; the Soviets were elevated to idealized, near perfect beings. This led Cubans to deny their own abilities, to lose self-confidence and to lose touch with their own historical roots. Only in the past couple of years have Cuban intellectuals begun to regain their sense of self-confidence and to remember their potential.[10]

In negotiating their way through the paradigm crisis of the left's historical, state-centered socialist and nationalist projects, Cuban and Mexi-

---

8. Juan Antonio Blanco quoted in Medea Benjamin, op. cit., pp. 22-23.

9. Elvira Concheiro, interview with author, Mexico City, August 5, 1993.

10. Margarita Viera, interview with author, Havana, March 13, 1993. Franz Hinkelammert has made a more general observation about the Third World left losing confidence to propose an alternative in the aftermath of socialism's collapse and neoliberalism's rise; see his "La crisis de socialismo y el Tercer Mundo," *Tareas* (Panama), No. 78, May-August 1991, p.99. Ciro Mayén similarly notes that for several years the left was somewhat paralyzed in the face of neoliberalism's ascendancy and socialism's collapse, but suggests that the defeat of George Bush was an important turning point in opening up space to challenge neoliberalism; see his "Una alternativa de reforma económica," *Memoria* (Mexico), No. 57, August 1993.

can intellectuals bring with them quite different assets and liabilities. Cuba's left intellectuals, largely incorporated into the state-party regime, enjoy the advantages of power (resources, real influence over policy, practical application of their ideas), but they also suffer the disadvantages of incumbency (the caution and pragmatism imposed by the desire to preserve power and ensure governability). The great majority of Mexico's left intellectuals are in opposition to their state-party regime and enjoy almost inverse fortunes: their status as opposition frees them of some of the constraints imposed by governing and robs them of the resources and real power to implement many of their ideas.

Conjunctural circumstances also weigh differently in each country. The severity of Cuba's economic crisis has helped shatter dominant orthodoxy, creating divisions among ruling elites, and allowing fresh voices to be heard. That same reality, however, simultaneously demands inordinate attention to daily crisis management at the expense of long-range strategic thinking and planning. Mexico's left managed to avoid the more extreme despair and paralysis that afflicted left forces elsewhere because the worldwide crisis of socialism coincided in Mexico with the emergence of the most powerful left coalition since the 1930s. Divisions within the long-ruling PRI, the Cuauhtémoc Cárdenas campaign in 1988, and the subsequent unification of large sectors of the left and popular movements in the PRD provided new energy, purpose, and historically-rooted national identity. At the same time, the sudden real possibility of replacing the state-party regime with a broad-based, democratic government through grassroots electoral struggle tended to direct the attentions of left intellectuals away from the reformulation of long-term alternatives to capitalism and toward the practical requirements of day-to-day electoral politics.

With these differences in mind, however, the responses to the strategic and conjunctural crises facing left intellectuals in both Cuba and Mexico can be grouped into the same three dominant perspectives identified in the previous chapters on democracy. As we will now examine, some leftists retreated into socialist *orthodoxy* and some accepted (if not fully embraced) *liberal* economic paradigms. And, as we will see in the following chapter, others attempted to *renovate* the historical values of socialism within the realities of late twentieth-century capitalism.

Orthodox Perspectives

In Mexico, orthodox socialists are a small, fairly marginal tendency, though the statism of revolutionary nationalism remains influential.

Socialist orthodoxy remains strong in Cuba, though its former hegemony has been substantially eroded by the urgency of resolving the economic crisis, even at the cost of economic liberalization. Orthodox perspectives, both explicitly socialist and statist-nationalist, reveal themselves in their defense of the past and in their prescriptions for the left's program. Orthodox socialists also continue to use the classic discourse of Marxism-Leninism.

As an example of the orthodox Mexican left's assessment of the past, the highly regarded Marxist economist Fernando Carmona told me that the crisis of real socialism was in essence the crisis of Stalinism, an assessment which too easily dismisses other issues of the Soviet model's extreme statism.[11] Similarly, when Soviet-style socialism was criticized at a left forum in Mexico City in the summer of 1992, another well-known Marxist intellectual quickly offered the familiar defense that the Bolshevik party had been up against a hostile international environment, which facilitated bureaucratization, and that economic backwardness had demanded industrialization *"a marchas forzadas."*[12]

There is a similar tendency to gloss over past errors among the most ardent nationalist intellectuals as well. Ifigenia Martínez, for example, a prominent economist formerly with the PRI's left wing and now a leading figure in the PRD, strongly disagrees with those who claim that the nationalist policies of strong state participation in the economy and import-substitution were failures:

> The Mexican government became both an investor and a banker, and its policies were protectionist, in order to develop the national forces of production. Mexico then maintained a growth rate in the GNP of seven percent annually for more than 40 years. I wouldn't call that a failure. The problem with the [Lázaro] Cárdenas model is that Cárdenas left office in 1940.
>
> Since then the process of industrialization and development in Mexico created an entrepreneurial class which really hasn't responded to national interests. In 1982 there was what I call a silent coup d'etat. A new class came to power, the financial class, which changed the goals.
>
> Under the neoliberal model, the most important goal was to avoid the collapse of the international private banking industry. That's when the decision was made that the number one priority of all economic policy would be payment of the debt. The crisis was a crisis of state

---

11. Fernando Carmona, interview with author, Mexico City, August 25, 1992.

12. Arturo Bonilla, comments made in response to Andrea Revueltas, at "Foro las luchas emancipadoras de fin de siglo," Mexico City, September 4, 1992.

financing. It's not true that it was a crisis of state-led import sub-
stitution.[13]

Martínez's instinct to blame traitorous, self-interested actors and shy
away from a critique of the state-centered model itself offers distinct
echoes of those Marxists who look no further than Stalin's authoritarianism in assessing the failures of Soviet socialism.

Regarding the left's present and future, orthodox socialists in Mexico
tend to be critical of their former Communist comrades who "renounced
the socialist program" in order to join the PRD (a party they consider to
be hopelessly pragmatic and electoralist), arguing that the main task of
the socialist current in Mexico is to "formulate the program of Mexican
socialism and thereby lay the basis for reconstructing the party of Mexican socialism."[14] Orthodox socialists tend to retain vanguardist formulations of what a left political party should be, even if its goal is no longer
to seize state power:

> [Socialist parties] should be small minorities, with very well trained,
> solid and active cadre, and their revolutionary perspective is not to take
> power, as parties, but rather to politically educate the [working] classes
> through the class struggle.[15]

This perspective has kept the orthodox socialist intellectuals largely
marginalized from Mexico's principal opposition movement.

Orthodox socialists also uphold more traditional conceptions of socialism and are hesitant to consider the possible benefits of private enterprise or a mixed economy within a future socialist society.[16] Eduardo

---

13. Ifigenia Martínez, interview with author, Mexico City, August 27, 1992.
For a fuller elaboration of her analysis, see her series of articles on the Mexican
economy in *Siempre* (Mexico), No. 2034, June 17, 1992; No. 2035, June 24, 1992;
No 2036, July 1, 1992; No. 2037, July 8, 1992; No. 2038, July 15, 1992; No. 2039,
July 22, 1992; No. 2041, August 5, 1992; and No. 2045, September 2, 1992.

14. Eduardo Montes, "Tenemos historia y futuro," *Socialismo* (Mexico), Vol.
1, Nos. 3-4, October-December 1989, pp. 11-12. With the goal of forming a new
socialist party, a group of about 200 socialists met in November 1993; the
purpose of the meeting was outlined by Eduardo Montes in "Debate Socialista,"
La Jornada (Mexico), August 7, 1993.

15. Octavio Rodríguez Araujo, "El socialismo no está en crisis," *Socialismo*
(Mexico), Vol. 1, Nos. 3-4, October-December 1989, p. 31.

16. For an articulate presentation by a U.S. scholar of an orthodox
perspective on the transition to socialism in Latin America, see Richard L. Harris,
Marxism, Socialism, and Democracy in Latin America (Boulder: Westview Press,
1992). Harris discusses the transition to socialism as including the destruction of

Montes, a former Mexican Communist and editor of the journal *Social-ismo*, believes that the essential features of socialism outlined by Marx, Engels, and Lenin, are as valid today as ever; among those features, he particularly notes "the abolition of private ownership" in favor of "the social ownership" of the "large means of production."[17] Finally, ortho-dox perspectives in Mexico adhere to the formal discourse of the Marx-ist-Leninist classics, showing little inclination to incorporate liberal for-mulations or the language of the post-Marxist, poststructuralist schools of thought.[18]

Cuban orthodoxy reveals the same hesitancy to understand past failures of socialism in terms of the state-centered model, rather than in terms of specific policy errors or institutional weaknesses. However, unlike the Mexican socialists' focus on Stalin, orthodox thinkers in Cuba give more attention to the errors of perestroika. Castro's view of the So-viet Union's collapse is telling: it self-destructed, he argues, as a result of leadership errors. Specifically, according to Castro, perestroika "unintentionally" destroyed the authority of the party, one of the "pillars" of socialism, and with it the state.[19] Ramiro Abreú, a Central America specialist in the Central Com-mittee's international relations de-partment, offers a similar assessment:

> Can we talk about a failure of the planned economies? We would have to ask which institutions really failed. Perestroika and related phenom-ena led to the collapse because of conceptual errors, not because of planning. Russian perestroika proved to be a way to get to capitalism through socialism.[20]

Orthodox thinkers in Cuba tend to blame Soviet experimentation with market mechanisms rather than its authoritarianism or statism: "One of the greatest deformations of Soviet socialism was its attempt to manage market relations with different forms of property."[21]

---

the capitalist state, establishment of a class dictatorship (pp. 192-93), and the expropriation of "all large capital" (p. 212).

17. Eduardo Montes, "Tenemos historia y futuro," op. cit., pp. 8-9.

18. For examples of the current usage of classic Marxist discourse by left intellectuals in Mexico, see Adolfo Sánchez Vázquez, "Democracia, revolución y socialismo," *Socialismo* (Mexico), Vol. 1, Nos. 3-4, October-December 1989; Adolfo Sánchez Vázquez, "El valor del socialismo," manuscript, August 1992; and Edur Arregui Koba, "Cuatro Crisis Socialistas," manuscript, n.d.

19. Fidel Castro quoted in Tomás Borge, *Un Grano de Maíz. Conversación con Fidel Castro* (Mexico: Fondo de Cultura Económica, 1992), pp. 46-48.

20. Ramiro Abreú, interview with author, Havana, March 8, 1993.

21. Germán Sánchez, interview with author, Havana, March 10, 1993.

Cuban orthodoxy also reveals a complacency with the Cuban revolution's clearly notable achievements and to blame the U.S. embargo and adverse international conditions for its shortcomings. A young, orthodox Cuban economist lectured me: "You have to be very careful when you start to criticize a state that has been able to meet the basic needs of the people and provide a level of education, health care, and social security that doesn't exist in some developed countries."[22] In Castro's famous "Socialism or Death" speech, delivered as the Eastern Communist regimes proceeded to fall one after the other, he insisted that the problems of Cuban socialism were largely a result of the hostile international environment in which it was built.[23]

Orthodox intellectuals in Cuba fiercely oppose private property and even most non-state forms of social property and only begrudgingly and very cautiously accept the need to introduce some market-oriented reforms. "Capitalist reforms" cannot solve the problems of socialism, Castro said just a fews year back,[24] and socialist property cannot mean simply the ownership of certain means of production by a collective of workers; socialism must mean "the ownership by all the people of all the means of production."[25]

Central Committee member and ideologue Darío Machado similarly warns, "We cannot defend a united project if our people are divided, and private property divides them."[26] Another intellectual and Central Committee functionary rejects (like Castro) even the notion of collective property, because "we need to preserve the revolution's advances in terms of ownership in favor of all the people."[27]

The ideological rigidity of these positions, however, is being rapidly undermined by Cuba's urgent need to reinsert itself into the world market and attract foreign capital. Even these orthodox thinkers are beginning to resign themselves to some compromises toward liberal reforms. While Machado asserts that social property is one of the main principles of Cuban socialism, he now refers to a "variation of social property, which is the mixed enterprise, combining capitalist property and social property to meet the necessity of having to insert our national economy

---

22. Gladys Hernández, interview with author, Havana, March 2, 1993.

23. Fidel Castro, *Socialism or Death* (Havana: José Martí Publishing House, 1989).

24. Ibid.

25. Fidel Castro, "La crisis del socialismo en Europa y su impacto en la Revolución Cubana," *El Caribe Contemporáneo* (Mexico), No. 21, July-December 1990, p. 83.

26. Darío Machado, interview with author, Havana, February 17, 1993.

27. Germán Sánchez, interview with author, Havana, March 10, 1993.

into a world economy regulated by the market."[28] Two Cuban economists make similar arguments:

> It's not objective or prudent to ignore the usefulness of market relations. But that doesn't mean it makes sense to begin a process of destatization, which would lead to chaos. Instead, we're trying to promote new forms of mixed enterprises, which doesn't represent a decapitalization of the state.[29]

> We lack entrepreneurial skills; our companies are not prepared to compete on the market. But this doesn't necessarily mean changing our state forms of property. We are now making some very flexible moves toward mixed forms of property in areas that can generate hard currency, but the intention is not to change the form of property.[30]

Despite the reluctance expressed by many influential orthodox intellectuals and officials, however, in practice liberal economic reforms are now well under way in Cuba, and liberal ideology is making itself felt. Some orthodox socialists attempt to accommodate, and perhaps even legitimate, such changes in terms of the left's historical discourse. Marta Harnecker, for example, notes that Lenin's views on the relationship between socialism and state-owned property evolved in practice:

> It is clear that in his classic work, *State and Revolution*, . . . [Lenin] thought that once the state passed into the hands of the proletariat, social property would be identified with state property. . . . Later, because of the practical experience of the first proletarian revolution and of the unforeseen new realities that emerged in the construction of socialism, Lenin's analysis of the role of the state became more nuanced. He began to distinguish between "state-ization" and socialization of the means of production. Later, during the New Economic Policy, he began to place ever greater value on cooperative organization.[31]

---

28. Darío Machado, interview with author, Havana, February 17, 1993. Further elaboration of Machado's views on "social ownership of the fundamental means of production" as essential to socialism can be found in his "El proceso de rectificación y la ideología de la Revolución Cubana," manuscript, 1993.

29. Gladys Hernández, interview with author, Havana, March 2, 1993.

30. Elena Alvarez, interview with author, Havana, March 5, 1993.

31. Marta Harnecker, "Democracy and Revolutionary Movement," op cit., p. 68.

Other Cuban intellectuals appear inclined to adopt liberal discourse and reforms on their own terms, without the blessings of Marx or his Lenin.

Liberal Perspectives

Liberal influence on left intellectuals in both Cuba and Mexico can be seen primarily in two tendencies: first, acceptance of certain economic "laws" about market competition, efficiency, and growth and, second, resignation to the idea of politics being subordinated to economics. What distinguishes such liberal perspectives from radical neoliberalism, and allows them to be contained within the discourses of the left, is the conviction of their proponents that national economies can be rationally reformed within the context of global capitalism while still pursuing the goals of greater social equality. In understanding how these liberal tendencies are expressed within the particular circumstances of the Cuban revolution and the Mexican left, it is worth keeping in mind the sound observation of Cuban social scientist Aurelio Alonso:

> The rest of the Latin American left has to re-find its way on the basis of societies that have been liberalized to the max. Cuba, on the other hand, has been state-ized to the max. The rest of the Latin American left needs a process of de-liberalization. Cuba needs the inverse.[32]

Some Cuban Communists explicitly accept the inevitability of economic liberalism, as the following statements illustrate: "There is now only one world economy and there has been a generalization of the rules of supply and demand."[33] "We clearly have to consider the use of market relations and non-state forms of property, not only because of the failures of the East and of Latin American developmentalism, but in consideration of the Cuban model itself—to increase efficiency and productivity."[34] Another Cuban Communist offered the consistency of prices on the black market, in contrast to the variation in prices in the state-run stores, as evidence that the market sets prices very precisely.[35]

Not surprisingly, Cuba's social democratic dissidents, many of whom were Communists themselves for many years, support economic liberalization: "Of course the market produces social differences, but the

---

32. Aurelio Alonso, interview with author, Havana, February 23, 1993.

33. Julio Carranza, interview with author, Havana, February 18, 1993.

34. Santiago Pérez, interview with author, Havana, March 4, 1993.

35. Rafael Hernández, interview with author, Havana, February 21, 1993. Several other Cubans interviewed drew upon their frustrating experiences as consumers to explain their growing support of economic liberalization.

other way hasn't worked, and at least the market would produce greater wealth. Social justice can't be achieved without wealth."[36] Vladimiro Roca, son of the late Communist leader Blas Roca and a leading figure in the social democratic opposition in Cuba, most clearly expresses the liberal acceptance of economic "laws":

> The so-called socialist countries, including Cuba, ignored the objective laws governing the economy. Those are the law of value and the law of supply and demand. They also ignore the principle of economic efficiency. The role of the state in the economy should be reduced in order to achieve high levels of economic efficiency needed to achieve appreciable levels of economic growth necessary to overcome the current crisis as quickly as possible. The realities of the past decade demonstrate that if we ignore the laws governing the economy and put man's will over such laws, economic and social involutions are produced throughout society.[37]

What is the rationale for including such clearly liberal perspectives within a study of the "left"? Simply that the primary objective of the people expressing these ideas remains a society in which social justice prevails, and they have come to believe that economic liberalism offers some advantages toward that end. Moreover, like traditional liberal-left reformers, they still hold firm to the belief that the state must play a key role in assuring social justice, through regulation, fiscal policies, and income redistribution. Communist intellectual Julio Carranza describes the role of the state in terms of (1) protecting the interests of the low-income population, preventing extreme inequality, guaranteeing social equality; (2) stimulating strategic sectors of the economy; and (3) defending the interest of the nation against foreign enemies. How, I asked, is that different from the role of the Keynesian state? He replied:

> The difference is that Keynesian policies seek to increase demand and redistribute wealth to serve capital accumulation for capital accumulation's sake, to serve capital. In Cuba, redistribution of wealth to increase demand is not to expand capital but to increase the well-being of the population. That's the key goal; increasing capital is a route to that goal.[38]

Along similar lines, I asked social democrat Cecilio Dimas, who described the role of the state as being to "make sure no one becomes ex-

---

36. Cecilio Dimas, interview with author, Havana, February 11, 1993.
37. Vladimiro Roca, interview with author, Havana, March 1993.
38. Julio Carranza, interview with author, Havana, February 18, 1993.

cessively rich," to explain the essence of a socialist economy. He answered:

> What distinguishes a socialist society from a capitalist society is the control exercised by the state, which will never allow for huge inequalities to be produced, and would permit a much higher level of social justice than the capitalist countries.[39]

The similarity of the responses from Carranza and Dimas suggests the extent to which liberal-minded Communists share more in common with dissident social democrats, in terms of economic policy, than they do with the orthodox members of their own party. The most significant dividing line between "loyal" Communists and "counterrevolutionary" social democrats, as discussed in a previous chapter, is their stand on the single-party system. Indeed, some Cuban Communists who hold liberal views on economic reform are quite orthodox in their views about democratizing the political system. Santiago Pérez, for example, who supports liberal reforms to make the economy more efficient, only half-jokingly told me, "I have a more neoconservative position" on the issues of political democracy.[40]

The real influence of economic (as opposed to political) liberalism in Cuba is found less in discourse than in rapidly changing practice. As of the 1991 Communist Party Congress, the Cuban leadership was still rejecting proposals to reopen the farmers markets, a popular but short-lived experiment with market reform in the early 1980s that allowed private farmers to sell their produce in city markets.[41] In winter 1993, though many of the forty-some Cubans I interviewed supported the idea of reopening the farmers markets, no one believed such a reform would be implemented any time soon. Some cited political resistance from orthodox hardliners, and others said that Cuba's resource scarcity and excess liquidity made such markets unworkable for the time being. Nevertheless, after another year-and-a-half of economic crisis and severe scarcity, in September 1994, Raúl Castro announced the reopening of markets in which agricultural producers could sell, at prices "freely" determined by supply and demand, any produce remaining after contracts with state

---

39. Cecilio Dimas, interview with author, Havana, February 11, 1993.

40. Santiago Pérez, interview with author, Havana, March 4, 1993.

41. Gail Reed, *Island in the Storm. The Cuban Communist Party's Fourth Congress* (Melbourne: Ocean Press, 1992), p. 130. The official reason given for closing the markets was that middlemen were becoming overnight millionaires, but some Cuban observers suggest that the farmers markets' success posed too much of a threat to overall state control, economically and politically.

institutions had been met.[42] Then in October 1994, the Cuban leadership gave the go-ahead for the establishment of similar markets for "industrial and artisanal" products.[43] The new markets were justified in terms of the need to stimulate production and increase supplies available to the country's frustrated consumers.

Another rapidly evolving element of economic reform is the opening up to foreign investment, in an attempt both to attract much needed capital and to facilitate competitive production for export. By late 1994, there were reportedly 165 mixed enterprises (partnerships between Cuban state companies and foreign private or state capital from thirty-eight different countries), operating in twenty-six different sectors of the economy, but primarily in tourism and oil.[44] In October of 1994, Vice President Carlos Lage, one of the government's chief economic architects, announced that all of the island's productive sectors would be opened to foreign capital, including sugar and real estate. Lage noted that the opening to foreign capital and the establishment of the new agricultural and industrial/artisanal markets were seen as a "useful complement" to economic planning. He insisted that Cuba "is not carrying out a capitalist development strategy, but rather a flexible strategy capable of assimilating many processes within the socialist system."[45] Despite Lage's qualifier, the extent to which Cuban Communists were backing away from a "socialism or death" suicide pact was underscored in October 1994 when Fidel Castro himself reportedly admitted in an interview on French television that the conditions for developing socialism do

42. Josetxo Zaldúa, "Anuncia Raúl Castro la próxima liberación del mercado agropecuario," *La Jornada* (Mexico), September 18, 1994; Josetxo Zaldúa, "Operarán desde octubre en Cuba los mercados agropecuarios," *La Jornada* (Mexico), September 22, 1994.

43. Josetxo Zaldúa, "Luz verde en la isla al mercado libre de productos industriales y artesanales," *La Jornada* (Mexico), October 27, 1994.

44. *La Jornada* (Mexico), October 31, 1994.

45. Ibid. For the transcript of an extensive interview with Carlos Lage about Cuba's current economic strategy, broadcast on Cuban television in November 1992, see *Granma* (Cuba), November 10, 1992, and November 14, 1992. Another key intellectual player in Cuba's economic reforms is economist José Luis Rodríguez, currently the government's minister of the economy and vice president of the Council of Ministers; for some of his views, see his "La inversión extranjera en Cuba: mitos y realidades," *Boletin de Información Económica Cubana* (Cuba), Vol. 1, No. 5, May 1992; "Las relaciones económicas entre Cuba y la antingua URSS: 1959-1990," *Boletin de Información Económica Cubana* (Cuba), Vol. 1, No. 7, June 1992; and "Los cambios en la política económica y los resultados de la economía cubana en el contexto del nuevo orden mundial (1986-1989)", manuscript, April 1990.

not currently exist and Cuba is obliged to adapt to the reality of today's world.[46]

Economic liberalization in Cuba still faces serious political and ideological obstacles, however, as a tug-of-war within the party continues. Immediately following the series of new liberal reforms cited above, Cuba's official newspaper, *Granma*, criticized a "loss of revolutionary language" among Cubans, and warned that, despite the necessary economic reforms, "we cannot negate the essence of the revolution." Alongside the editorial appeared a statement from Lage again clarifying that Cuba's economic strategy does not mean a transition to capitalism.[47] A few days later Lage announced that there would be no privatization of stores, cafeterias, and restaurants, nor even a cooperativization of such commercial services, although there were persistent rumors to the contrary.[48]

Despite orthodox opposition to the growing influence of liberal economic paradigms, the urgency of the economic crisis is clearly pushing Cuban Communists in that direction. However, as seen in the previous chapters on democracy, economic liberalization has not been accompanied by much *political* liberalization. If anything, with reports that Raúl Castro (never known for his democratic instincts) and "his loyalists in the military" are increasingly taking charge of Cuba's economic reforms,[49] there is some reason to heed Vladimiro Roca's warning that, "what distinguishes the Cuban government's policies from *neo*liberalism is that while the governments of Latin America and other countries apply these policies with the opposition of the workers, the Cuban government applies them with no opposition whatsoever."[50]

If liberal ideas about economic reform are gaining influence among Cuban revolutionaries, they are viewed quite cautiously by most of the Mexican left and are wholeheartedly embraced by only a few, mainly those left intellectuals associated with the Carlos Salinas administration (1989-1994). This observation might appear contradictory at first, particularly in light of the extensive influence of liberal political discourse among the Mexican left noted in the preceding chapter. But keep in mind Aurelio Alonso's observation that, except for Cuba, the Latin American left confronts societies that have been "liberalized to the max." After more than a decade of neoliberal economic restructuring by the

---

46. Josetxo Zaldúa, "Recibiríamos a Clinton con espíritu abierto: Fidel Castro," *La Jornada* (Mexico), October 21, 1994.

47. *La Jornada* (Mexico), November 6, 1994.

48. *La Jornada* (Mexico), November 10, 1994.

49. Cathy Booth, "Fidel's Brother Sets Up Shop," *Time* (English-language, Mexico edition), November 14, 1994, pp. 18-19.

50. Vladimiro Roca, interview with author, Havana, March 1993.

state-party regime, the majority of Mexico's left intellectuals are more impressed by economic liberalization's devastating social consequences than by its success at curbing inflation and reducing the budget deficit.

Nevertheless, there are some influential, liberal-leaning voices within the Mexican left on the question of economic alternatives. Rolando Cordera, for example, readily acknowledges that even neoliberalism has its merits:

> What neoliberal discourse offers, in the end, is consistency. And, as a result of that consistency, it provides the opportunity for many pragmatic options. This is very disconcerting for the left, which doesn't understand the possible variants of neoliberalism that have been applied.[51]

Among those variants is the Mexican model, which Cordera has supported. While most of the left attacks the economic reforms of the last three PRI presidents as radically neoliberal, Cordera and fellow former-nationalist José Woldenberg have praised them as a model of "social liberalism" that could be adopted by other Latin American governments.[52] Cordera is now self-critical of some of his former views on the state, which were in the tradition of Mexico's revolutionary nationalism, and concedes that he and others had ignored some of capitalism's basic lessons: "We didn't have clarity about the importance of the market, that the market summarizes social relations, and that it is one of society's mechanisms for communication, for which no substitutes have been found."[53]

Similar reassessments of liberalism's economic paradigms have been undertaken by former Mexican Communists as well. Américo Saldívar, for example, argues that "we need real economic growth based on a rational economic model in order to have social programs. If that model is capitalist, O.K., so be it."[54] Like Cordera, Saldívar believes that neoliberalism has its merits. In June 1993 he gave a speech in Poland in which he reviewed the record of neoliberal reforms in Mexico and suggested they could serve as an example for Eastern Europe's transition to a market economy. A "preliminary assessment" of Mexico's privatization pro-

---

51. Rolando Cordera, interview with author, Mexico City, September 2, 1992.

52. Rolando Cordera and José Woldenberg, "La Cumbre Iberoamericana," *Cuaderno de Nexos* (Mexico), August 1993, p. iv.

53. Rolando Cordera, interview with author, Mexico City, September 2, 1992. For a fuller elaboration of Cordera's reassessment of the role of state and market, see his "El Estado y el desarrollo: revisiones y reafirmaciones," *Problemas del Desarrollo* (Mexico), Vol. XXII, January-March 1991.

54. Américo Saldívar, interview with author, Mexico City, August 4, 1993.

gram would have to consider it a "success," he summarized, since it "eliminated excessive protectionism and indiscriminate subsidies."[55]

Again the reader might reasonably ask, why are such perspectives considered here as part of the left? Because these same intellectuals remain committed to social justice and a more equitable society and, in one way or another, even retain "socialism" as an important point of reference. Cordera says that socialism remains on the agenda,[56] as does Woldenberg, who adds, "above all in poor countries that are profoundly unequal and semiauthoritarian/semidemocratic, like ours."[57] Saldívar talks in terms of "a new pluralist socialist paradigm, very diverse and varied according to the particularities of each country."[58] Yet in practice, Cordera and Woldenberg supported the Salinas government's neoliberal restructuring, while Saldívar has advised colleagues in the former socialist bloc nations on how to apply Mexico's experiences to Eastern Europe. This contradiction is partially explained by the extent to which their new appreciation for economic liberalism has led to political resignation before the partly real, partly imagined power of global capitalism.

The accelerated internationalization of capital over the past twenty years, together with the disappearance of the socialist bloc, has encouraged some leftists to attribute a near divine omnipotence to global capitalism. In arguing that the PRD's economic program has to take into account three "inevitable restrictions" (adjustment, competitiveness, and globalization), Ciro Mayén asserts that "globalization is for everyone, without escape, *the religion.*"[59] An even more extreme example of the degree to which neoliberalism has contributed to reified conceptions about the global economy is found in the center-left journal *Nexos*:

> The rules of the global economy, whether we like them or not, are the rules by which we have to live. . . . The rules of the game of the international economy are clear as water: everything to assure that the

---

55. Américo Saldívar, "Realidad y límites del neoliberalismo mexicano," *Memoria* (Mexico) No. 57, August 1993, p. 48.

56. Rolando Cordera, "Notas sobre los socialistas, la izquierda y la perspectiva económica," in Jorge Alcocer, et al., *El Futuro de la Izquierda en México* (Mexico City: CEPNA, 1992), p. 171.

57. José Woldenberg, "Mesa Redonda. La Izquierda frente al siglo xxi: proyetos y utopías," in Jorge Alcocer, et al., ibid., p. 289.

58. Américo Saldívar, "Democracia y marxismo," Memoria (Mexico) No. 30, July-August 1990, p. 159. For his analysis of the failures and crisis of socialism in the USSR and Eastern Europe, see A. Saldívar, *El Ocaso del socialismo* (Mexico City: Siglo XXI, 1990)

59. Ciro Mayén, "Una alternativa de reforma económica," *Memoria* (Mexico), No. 57, August 1993, pp. 44-45 (my emphasis).

economy functions, and nothing more. The economy stands above all else and its success is the common goal that we all must pursue.[60]

While such prostration before the allegedly absolute powers of the global economy is not typical of the Mexican left, the views expressed do illustrate a more common attitude of resignation to the idea that economics has triumphed definitively over politics. As Saldívar admitted,

> Until very recently, I was convinced that there was no alternative to neoliberalism, that it was an error to oppose the market. Theoretically, of course there are always alternatives, but practically speaking, are there political and social forces to push another alternative?[61]

As seen in Chapters Three and Four, liberal political conceptions about restricted forms of democracy have been especially influential among leftists in South American nations recently emerging from decades of brutal military dictatorships. Some of those leftists, once fully committed to socialism, similarly have now accepted liberal (or even neoliberal) economic doctrines. "Socialism has gone out of fashion in the Southern Cone," wrote historian Peter Winn a few years back:

> Years of military repression have left their mark upon the left and its largely working-class supporters, teaching them the dangers of socialist dreams or revolutionary demands. This military tutelage has been internalized, its lessons learned perhaps too well. Few are ready to tempt the same fate again. The regressive impact of the military's social and economic policies and the loss of jobs as a result of economic modernization and capitalist crisis have been equally traumatic. As a consequence, leftist political and labor leaders are now willing to settle for far less than their pre-coup programs, while workers have lowered their sights to securing a steady job and a living wage.[62]

Thus in Chile, socialist Carlos Ominami Pascual served as minister of the economy in the first post-Pinochet, civilian government. In that function, he administered the continued neoliberal restructuring of the Chilean economy, arguing that democratization depended on economic "modernization," which he defined in terms of greater economic disci-

---

60. Luis Rubio, "La política mexicana vs. la economía global," *Nexos* (Mexico), September 1994, pp. 71-75.

61. Américo Saldívar, interview with author, Mexico City, August 4, 1993.

62. Peter Winn, "Socialism Fades Out of Fashion," *The Nation* (New York), June 26, 1989, pp. 882-883.

pline, productivity, competition, and entrepreneurial spirit.[63] Likewise, in Brazil, President Fernando Henrique Cardoso, one of Latin America's most distinguished left intellectuals and a founder of the radical "dependency school" of thought in the 1960s, is currently following similar neoliberal prescriptions for privatization, reduced social spending, and wage controls. In Brazil, at least, it is not the case, as Saldívar suggested above, that "the political and social forces to push another alternative" do not exist. As noted in Chapter Four, time and other factors have allowed a renovated left to emerge with far greater strength in Brazil than in other Southern Cone nations. If anything, Cardoso was elected with the support of the center and right precisely because a more radical, nonliberal alternative was presented by Lula da Silva and the Workers Party (PT). Cardoso could have counted on a mass constituency to pursue an economic program aimed at reducing Brazil's infamously extreme social inequality, but he has either become convinced of the merits and inevitability of the neoliberal economic model or is sufficienctly fearful of another military coup to challenge the status quo more forcefully.

In Cuba and Mexico, despite liberal influences on the lefts' economic thinking, and despite the persistence of old socialist orthodoxy among some, the left appears to have been less inclined to invoke the current neoliberal mantra or to accept the oft-repeated assertions that there are no alternatives to radical "free market" policies. In Mexico, in fact, there is a very broad left opposition that believes the political and social forces exist to pursue an alternative, and there are intellectuals working to elaborate such an alternative. Likewise, many of Cuba's left intellectuals remain convinced that their society can still produce a more humane, more democratic, more just, and more Cuban version of socialism. The perspectives of these renovative thinkers are examined in the following chapter.

---

63. Carlos Ominami Pascual, "La via chilena a la democracia," *Mundo* (Mexico), June 1990, pp. 29-32. Ignacio Walker argues that the Chilean left has become increasingly influenced by more conservative European social democracy, largely in response to "the traumatic impact of authoritarianism." I. Walker, "Democratic Socialism in Comparative Perspective," *Comparative Politics*, Vol. 23, No. 4, July 1991, pp. 439-458.

CHAPTER 6. SOCIALISM II

Renovative Perspectives on Economic Alternatives

In the process of trying to renovate socialist and nationalist values of the past, there are left forces in Latin America that accept the necessity of incorporating lessons from liberalism and the experience of market economies, but that are disinclined to attribute metaphysical powers to the market, as do some of the more liberalized leftists. The liberal left's resolute faith in the market shares something in common with socialist orthodoxy's unqualified rejection of the market: both ignore the fact that "markets themselves are deeply embedded in social relations."[1] One cannot expect the market to function independently of capitalism's class inequalities, nor can one dismiss the potential importance of market forces within noncapitalist societies marked by different social relations. The renovative left's attitude is reflected in the suggestion of Brazil's Francisco Weffort that, "Socialists should marry democracy out of love, but their union with the market need be no more than a 'marriage of convenience.'"[2]

What distinguishes renovators from their orthodox or liberal-leaning comrades is not necessarily their commitment to something called "socialism." In Cuba, exponents of all three perspectives, including those in the "democratic socialist" dissident current, explicitly identify themselves as socialists. In Mexico, as seen in the previous chapter, while orthodox voices urge the left to drawup the blue prints for Mexican socialism immediately, liberal-left intellectuals refer vaguely to socialism while sometimes objectively supporting neoliberalism. Mexican renovators, meanwhile, include both socialists and non-

---

1. Robert Wuthnow, *Communities of Discourse* (Cambridge: Harvard University Press, 1989), p. 565.

2. Francisco Weffort quoted in Jorge Castañeda, *Utopia Unarmed* (New York: Alfred A. Knopf, 1993), p. 432.

socialists. There are many renovative thinkers in Mexico (including former Communists, Trotskyists, Maoists, and independent socialists) who continue to give substantial attention to reconstructing a new socialist paradigm.[3] At the same time, there are nationalists among the renovative tendency, like Cuauhtémoc Cárdenas, whose radical discourse on democracy and popular participation in economic planning distinguish him from orthodox and liberal leftists.[4]

---

3. Among some of the interesting new thinking about socialism among the Mexican left, see: Jorge Alonso, "Alternativas para un socialismo posible," manuscript, n.d.; Jorge Alonso, "En busca de una alternativa con equidad," *Memoria* (Mexico) No. 62, February 1994; Sol Arguedas, "Reflexiones acerca del futuro del socialismo," *Tareas* (Panamá) No. 80, January-April 1992; Elvira Concheiro, "La herencia recuperada por los comunistas," *Memoria* (Mexico) No. 61, December 1993; Sergio de la Peña, "La crítica a los críticos de la izquierda," *Memoria* (Mexico) No. 53, April 1993; Sergio de la Peña, "Tareas pendientes del socialismo," *Mundo* (Mexico), February 1991; Adolfo Gilly, "Socialismo," *La Jornada* (Mexico), February 15, 1991; Pablo González Casanova, "El proyecto socialista hoy," manuscript, 1991; Pablo González Casanova, "La crisis del mundo actual y las ciencias sociales en América Latina," manuscript, September 7, 1990; Arnoldo Martínez Verdugo, "La crisis del socialismo y el aniversario del PCM," *Memoria* (Mexico) No. 29, January-February 1990; Arnoldo Martínez Verdugo, "La renuncia del Gorbachov y el fin de la perestroika," *Memoria* (Mexico) No. 38, January 1992; Jacqueline Ochoa Méndez, "La izquierda mexicana ante la crisis del socialismo real," *El Cotidiano* (Mexico), September-October 1990; Lucio Oliver, "Estado y sociedad en la redefinición socialista," *Memoria* (Mexico) No. 60, November 1993; Lucio Oliver Costilla, "Marxismo y sociología en América Latina," *Memoria* (Mexico) No. 32, January-February 1991; Eduardo Ruíz Contardo, "Falsedades capitalistas, errores y vigencia del socialismo," *Estudios Latinoamericanos* (Mexico) No. 82, January-June 1990; Raquel Sosa Elízaga, "Los cambios en el Este y América Latina," *Memoria* (Mexico) No. 32, January-February 1991. In 1994, following the Chiapas uprising and in light of the 100th anniversary of Peruvian Marxist José Carlos Mariátegui's birth, Mexican intellectuals have also shown renewed interest in the relevance of his writings for a renovated indigenous, Latin American socialism; see, e.g., Joaquín Sánchez MacGregor, "Socialismo indoamericano," *La Jornada Semanal* (Mexico), September 25, 1994; and a collection of papers presented at an October 1994 colloquium on "Mariátegui and the Latin American Left," published in *Memoria* (Mexico) No. 72, November 1994.

4. Cuauhtémoc Cárdenas's views have been published in many forums. Three English-language translations are: Jesús Galindo López, "A Conversation with Cuauhtémoc Cárdenas," *Journal of International Affairs*, Vol. 43, No. 2, Winter 1990; Andrew Reding, "The Democratic Current: A New Era in Mexican Politics," *World Policy Journal*, Vol. 5, No. 2, Spring 1988; Cuauhtémoc Cárdenas, "The Continental Development and Trade Initiative," in S. Jonas and E.

What most clearly distinguish the renovators from defenders of socialist orthodoxy are their acceptance of the limited options available in the aftermath of capitalism's recent triumphs, their sense of obligation to offer realistic immediate alternatives to alleviate the suffering of large sectors of society, and their willingness to consider ideas from liberal political economy in constructing that alternative. What most clearly distinguish them from the liberal-leaning left are their beliefs that an immediate alternative to neoliberal restructuring and a long-term alternative to capitalism are necessary and possible, and that political struggle in pursuit of social goals has not been overridden by reified notions of some all-powerful "global economy." Moreover, renovators, unlike liberals, emphasize democratization as the most important response to failed statist models of the past.

Finally, time and again in interviews, renovative Mexicans and Cubans dismissed as pure ideology neoliberalism's claims about the market's magic and the state's evils, noting the active role of the state in imposing neoliberal policies. Renovators insist that market and state alike are historical constructions whose balance reflects the correlation of social and political forces and the social pact operative in a given society at a given moment. Within these parameters, renovative ideas take on different forms or emphases in the distinct contexts of Cuba's state-centered socialism and the neoliberal regimes in most of Latin America.

Jorge Castañeda accurately summarizes the outlines of the limited, short- to medium-term, economic alternative offered by the most viable currents of the Latin American left in the 1990s, including Mexico's PRD:

> This alternative involved more debt relief and less debt service—a difference of degree, although with qualitatively distinct effects. It included more social spending—education, health, housing, sewage, drinking water, etc.—and a far greater sense of social justice—but again, within limits imposed by the scarcity of resources. It advocated less privatization and more honest, accountable administration by a necessary state-owned sector of the economy—again, a significant nuance but a nuance nonetheless. It implied less trade opening and of a more selective nature, but certainly did not mean a return to full protectionism, which had never really existed in the first place. It signified a larger and more important role for the state in the economy, but of a different state—democratic, accountable, honest—and less dependence on the private sector, local or foreign. It required a new relationship with the business community, as removed from the baiting and hostility of the traditional left as it was from the pandering of the right. It also

McCaughan, eds., *Latin America Faces the Twenty-First Century. Reconstructing a Social Justice Agenda* (Boulder: Westview Press, 1994).

demanded a new understanding with the United States, distant from the tensions of the old left and the subordination of the new right.[5]

Hardly a program for revolutionary socialism, but, as Alejandro Alvarez (a Mexican economist considerably to the left of Castañeda and still committed to a noncapitalist alternative) explained, given the extent of neoliberal restructuring in Mexico, "one has to acknowledge that a mixed economy would be a phenomenal advance. The movement to the right has taken us so far that this is now our starting point."[6] At least in terms of middle-run strategy, this is a perspective shared by most renovators as well as many liberal-left reformers.

As the 1994 presidential elections in Mexico neared, left intellectuals associated with the PRD expended considerable effort in elaborating the specifics of such an economic alternative for Mexico, making up for several years in which much of the left seemed so unsure of its ability to challenge neoliberal dogma.[7] Rather than a simplistic rejection of state in favor of market, a middle-run economic alternative is sought based on concrete examples in contemporary history where the market was effectively regulated and influenced by strategic state action. Castañeda, from a more liberal-reformist perspective, imagines some combination of Germany's "Rhineland" model and the Japanese model (both of which involve significant state involvement), as a variant of "social market capitalism."[8] More clearly anticapitalist intellectuals like Pablo Gómez

---

5. Jorge Castañeda, *Utopia Unarmed*, op. cit., p. 248.

6. Alejandro Alvarez, interview with author, Mexico City, August 28, 1992.

7. Examples of such efforts include the following articles in *Coyuntura* (Mexico) No. 47, April 1994: Arturo Huerta G., "Crecimiento sostenido con equidad y baja inflación," Ifigenia Martínez, "Desarrollo agropecuario y suficiencia alimentaria," Felipe Zermeño, "Crisis agrícola y desarrollo económico"; the following articles in *Coyuntura* (Mexico) Nos. 50/51, July/August 1994: Asa Cristina Laurell, et al, "Reforma de las políticas de salud en defensa de la vida," María Fernanda Campa-Uranga, "Nuestro concepto de desarrollo sustentable," Ifigenia Martínez, "El sistema nacional de planeación democrática," Saúl Escobar Toledo, "Diez propuestas sobre planeación democrática"; as well as, Arturo Huerta G., "Estabilidad, crecimiento económico y equidad," *Memoria* (Mexico) No. 70, September 1994; Fernando Carmona, "¿Es posible un capitalismo mexicano distinto?" *Memoria* (Mexico) No. 62, January 1994; Fernando Carmona, "Sí hay un programa económico contra la crisis," *Memoria* (Mexico) No. 69, August 1994; Jorge A. Calderón Salazar, "Política económica para la transición a la democracia," *Memoria* (Mexico) No. 66, May 1994; Mario J. Zepeda Martínez, "Mexico 1994: la lucha por el futuro económico," *Memoria* (Mexico) No. 62, January 1994; Antonio Gershenson, "Una política económica para México," *La Jornada* (Mexico), September 20, 1994.

8. Jorge Castañeda, *Utopia Unarmed*, op cit., particularly the final chapter.

and Raúl Alvarez Garín point to France as an effective example of strategic state intervention.[9] Alvarez Garín, whose training as an engineer predisposes him to practical solutions, also sees some viable alternatives in Cuba, despite its excessive statism; he suggests an agricultural program for Mexico (inspired by Cuba's resident family doctor program), whereby a trained technician/adviser would live and work within the communities of peasants and small farmers to help solve the urgent problems. It would be a centrally organized and funded state program, but its implementation would be decentralized and involve the active participation of the peasantry.[10]

An illustrative example of how the tension between liberal and statist perspectives is being played out in practice among Mexican renovators is a process of debate that occurred within the PRD over the party's economic program. Two proposals were presented to the party's July 1993 congress, one slightly more market-oriented and one slightly more state-oriented, but both of them justifying their approach in terms of the best way to promote the *national* interests of social justice, equality, and sovereignty. The more liberal proposal described the state's role as being to intervene in order to correct or balance relative prices (i.e., raising minimum wages, lowering interest rates, reducing excessive financial profits), in order for the various social actors to meet in the market place on fairer terms in pursuit of their social interests. The second, somewhat more statist proposal argued that:

> the fundamental economic responsibilities of the state are [to assure] sufficient jobs, the productivity and stability needed for solid development, the fairness needed for a development with social justice, and the competitiveness needed for sovereign development.[11]

Neither proposal was acceptable to the majority of the PRD congress, which decided to hold a subsequent national meeting to hammer out the differences. Through such debates and struggle, the renovative sector of the Mexican left has gone a long way to present a socially progressive alternative to radical free-market capitalism that also meets the obligation of any responsible left opposition to offer a program that is *viable* in the here and now.

The fact that the broad outline of this emerging alternative has the support of former communists, independent socialists, nationalists, and

---

9. Their ideas about the French model are explained more fully in Chapter Eight.

10. Raúl Alvarez Garín, interview with author, Mexico City, August 6, 1993.

11. *Proyecto de Programa de la Revolución Democrática. Comunica* No. 31 (Mexico: Comité Ejecutivo Nacional del PRD, July 1993).

social democrats should not obscure the importance of a qualifier offered by Alejandro Alvarez: "Is this our maximum aspiration? Of course not."[12] For the short- to medium-range future, a version of what Castañeda refers to as "social market" capitalism unifies a very broadly-defined left, but there are differences among these intellectuals about the continued relevance of a noncapitalist, perhaps socialist utopia that are potentially very important for the long-range evolution of a renovative alternative.

Castañeda, for instance, is convinced that revolutionary socialism is dead in the water and that even the most far-reaching of the left's alternatives cannot transcend the parameters of capitalism: "the so-called minimum program . . . and the maximum program become indistinguishable [and] the rest are nuances: how much transformation of a democratic, market-based society inserted in the world economy does one want?"[13] This perspective is consistent with traditional liberalism, understood as the politics of constant, rational, and more inclusionary reform of capitalism.[14] But others disagree with this approach. Jorge Alonso, for example, insists that the alternative needed in Latin America is not to be found in choosing between different models of capitalism.[15]

Although there is broad agreement on the short- to medium-run changes needed, the differences between liberal and renovative left visions of the eventual outcome of economic reforms are potentially quite significant. Two artists may both be dissatisfied with the color of the blue paint on their palette and both may determine to improve the color by carefully adding small amounts of yellow. The first artist may stop after only a few drops of yellow, satisfied with the brightened but still visibly blue paint. The second artist may continue to add drops of yellow, knowing that what she wants is not simply a different shade of blue but green. Though both artists were dissatisfied with the original blue and both agreed upon the initial approach to changing the nature of the paint, at some point the gradual process of transformation, continued by the second artist, results in a qualitatively different color. Blue is not green, unless you are colorblind. Reformed capitalism is not socialism.

Renovative leftists like Jorge Alonso, Alejandro Alvarez, and Cristina Laurell agree with the reforms outlined by Castañeda, but they remain convinced of the importance of socialism, even as a perhaps very distant

---

12. Alejandro Alvarez, interview with author, Mexico City, August 28, 1992.

13. Jorge Castañeda, *Utopia Unarmed*, op. cit., pp. 153-54.

14. On the politics of liberalism and its demise, see Immanuel Wallerstein, "The Collapse of Liberalism," in R. Miliband and L. Pantich (eds.), *Socialist Register 1992* (London: Merline, 1992).

15. Jorge Alonso, "Alternativas para un socialismo posible," manuscript, n.d.

utopia, as a guide to the nature and extent of reforms to be pursued today. Alvarez explains his thinking on this issue:

> The idea of a socialist economy, as a free association of producers, still makes sense. But events suggest that we're still a ways from this! Right now we need an alternative for a transition period, of at least some ten years. In that period, we need to strengthen the process of participation, democratization, collective action, political education. Some of the tasks aren't even so spectacular. For example, in Mexico City, with our brutal levels of pollution, there are many fairly simple, rational steps to be taken, simply to put things in some order. And on the basis of those steps, we can begin to move toward the more profound changes.
>
> I'm not saying socialism is deferred forever, simply that the situation we are in means that the only way to get to socialism is on the basis of beginning to address the problems that confront us daily. So the abstract, ideological, programmatic formulation of socialism will have little importance.[16]

In Cristina Laurell's words, "we need to return to the basics of socialism—justice, equality, liberty—and seek practical ways to pursue those ends in current conditions."[17] In a presentation on "the defense of social rights" at a left forum in Mexico City, Laurell provided a sense of how today's struggles for social reforms also plant seeds for a society organized around noncapitalist social values. She argued that neoliberalism opposes the very idea of social rights (such as those enshrined in the Mexican Constitution: work, wage, health, education, housing), because they interfere with the "free market." Therefore, the struggle for social rights has a particular strategic value. The left's alternative project, according to Laurell, must "view the economy as a means of providing social rights and benefits." Social rights must be considered as universal, that is, not dependent on "a particular insertion in society, such as waged labor," and the state must be seen as having the obligation to guarantee social rights to all members of society. "This is a project of social solidarity, when people demand that all be guaranteed their social rights."[18] Laurell, a medical doctor and sociologist who has served as editor of the PRD's journal, *Coyuntura,* has elaborated these arguments in very practical proposals (attentive to problems of curbing inflation and

---

16. Alejandro Alvarez, interview with author, Mexico City, August 28, 1992.

17. Cristina Laurell, "Por la defensa y expansión de los derechos sociales," oral presentation at "Foro las luchas emancipadoras de fin de siglo," Mexico City, September 4, 1992.

18. Ibid.

allowing for profits) to reorganize Mexico's production of social services, particularly in the areas of health care and education.[19]

While the PRD's economic program corresponds closely to the limited reforms outlined above in Castañeda's summary, the language of the program's various platforms reveal clearly the socialist and Marxist ideals that inform its long-term vision. A draft of the PRD's platform on "The World of Work," for example, contains the following passage:

> [Our] vision of change recognizes labor, and not money, as the source of social progress and as an element unifying those—the absolute majority—whose efforts guarantee society's existence and who constitute the world of work. The PRD's aspiration is to represent this world and upon its base construct a free and egalitarian homeland.[20]

Implied in the ideas of renovators, who are still inspired by socialist ideals, is a Gramscian-like process of change, whereby the noncapitalist values of the broad social forces represented by the left gradually gain influence, until the accumulation of forces is such that a new hegemony has been established. Some renovative socialists emphasize traditions rooted in Mexican history that make such a process imaginable within the nation's political culture. In her defense of social rights, Laurell notes that the principle of "social solidarity" is deeply rooted in Mexican history.[21] Social movements chronicler and theorist Jaime Tamayo points to Mexico's unique collective *ejido* system of land tenure:

> There are certain traditions, even certain communities in Mexico, which while far from what we could call modern or citizen-based, represent a form of socialism or include elements of socialism. The *ejido*, for example, was made with the *campesino*, not against the *campesino*, in contrast to the forced collectivization of Soviet agriculture. Here there still exist very strong collective conceptions of community, including some in which there is a dis-individualization of those who make them up. These perhaps offer an opportunity to salvage and update elements of a Mexican socialist left project. *Neocardenismo* includes some such elements.[22]

---

19. See Asa Cristina Laurell, "For An Alternative Social Policy: The Production of Public Services in Mexico," in S. Jonas and E. McCaughan, *Latin America Faces the Twenty-First Century*, op cit.

20. "El Mundo del Trabajo," draft platform of the PRD Program, manuscript, August 1992.

21. Cristina Laurell, "Por la defensa y expansión de los derechos sociales," op cit.

22. Jaime Tamayo, interview with author, Guadalajara, August 20, 1992.

A practical example of such efforts can be seen in the struggles of the Zapotec community in the Isthmus of Tehuantepec in Oaxaca to recover their traditional, collecitvely-held land and to retain the principle of reciprocity that has long informed social relations. Manuel López Mateos, who has been active in the cultural projects of the Worker-Peasant-Student Coalition of the Isthmus (COCEI), explained:

> The defense of our culture signifies the defense of a way of organizing social relations. This defense is based on the recovery and joint exploitation of our communal resources, on fair interchange of the products of labor, and on control of the negotiating instruments to make the decisions that affect us.[23]

For the renovators, the key is how to build upon such traditions and institutions, through democratic, political struggle. In the process, the movement hopes that the values of solidarity, reciprocity, equality and democracy become so thoroughly embedded in the institutions of state, economy and society as to constitute a qualitatively different system.[24] Even Castañeda, who rejects the possibility of revolution and of a socialist future, admits that what may begin as "hodgepodge" reforms can turn into "a full-fledged paradigm."[25]

---

23. Manuel López Mateos, "When Radio Become the Voice of the People," in Howard Campbell, et al. (eds.), *Zapotec Struggles. Histories, Politics, and Representations from Juchitán, Oaxaca* (Washington, D.C.: Smithsonian Institution Press, 1993), p. 259. In the same volume, Sergio Zermeño ("COCEI: Narodniks of Southern Mexico?", p. 194) questions the potential of COCEI "to link cultural heritage with development."

24. Bjorn Hettne develops the notion of altnerative, intermediate economic institutions and practices as key to constructing a different model of development in the Third World. He argues that, historically, economic relations have involved a combination of reciprocity, market exchanges, and redistribution, and that under capitalism, reciprocity largely disappeared except within the household and some communities. Hettne suggests that the proliferation of acvtivity within the so-called informal economy in the Third World may represent, in part, a resurrection of reciprocity as the basis of economic activity in response to the failures of market exchange and redistribution. See Bjorn Hettne, *Development Theory and the Three Worlds* (Longman Development Studies: Halsted Press, 1990). Indeed there are numerous examples from various social movements in Mexico, such as the COCEI in Oaxaca and Asamblea de Barrios in Mexico City, of grassroots efforts to construct such alternative, intermediate institutions and practices organized around reciprocity.

25. Jorge Castañeda, *Utopia Unarmed*, op cit., p. 428.

While today's renovative Mexican left emphasizes national traditions as key to any new left paradigm, several Mexican intellectuals expressed belief that any eventual qualitative change representing a clearly noncapitalist alternative will also involve world-scale transformations, even if immediate reforms begin at the national level. "The great transition has to be international," according to PRD activist Nuria Fernández; "it can't be country by country."[26] Samir Amin has described how world capitalism emerged not full-blown, but gradually, appearing first in the interstices of the old feudal order until it consolidated as a world-system.[27] Fernández imagines something similar: "The internationalization of the relations of production is also a slow, gradual emergence of a new mode of production."[28] As an example, she cites the way in which the incorporation of women into the waged work force world-wide has contributed to changing modes of sexuality.[29]

Sergio de la Peña offers a similar vision:

> In developing an alternative project, we have to think very long-term. But I am certain that for environmental, material, social, and other reasons, capitalism cannot continue operating as it does now, creating this level of polarization. It is simply not possible. I imagine that the way we can reformulate a truly world project, which at the same time has its national additions and forms, will be through some kind of a world pact of all humanity, in which, for starters, the spaces and forms of competition would have to be limited. And perhaps, as capitalism adjusts to these limitations, it may even give rise to the elements of some new, future form of socialism, a minimal form of socialism.[30]

So Mexico's renovative left continues to inspire and sustain itself with long-term visions of a new, socialist-oriented world-system, while engaging the wearying daily struggles to preserve what little remains of a never very generous, Third World welfare state, which is increasingly whittled away by neoliberal restructuring. Meanwhile, Cuban renovators try to figure out how to find a niche for their nation in today's brutal capitalist world-system without subjecting their society to a process of desocialization and renewed class differentiation.

Cuba's renovative intellectuals find themselves in a particularly difficult situation. While supporting some aspects of the regime's economic liberalization (e.g., more flexibility in the use of market mechanisms,

---

26. Nuria Fernández, interview with author, Mexico City, August 5, 1993.

27. Samir Amin, *Eurocentrism* (New York: Monthly Review Press, 1989).

28. Nuria Fernández, interview with author, op. cit.

29. Ibid.

30. Sergio de la Peña, interview with author, Mexico City, August 16, 1992.

decentralization of management, reopening of the farmers markets, gradual broadening of the spaces for small, private initiative), they are critical of the social consequences of a state-controlled liberalization that is not accompanied by fuller democratization. Yet, as a fairly small minority of Cuban revolutionaries, renovators must make their voices heard against the authoritarianism of still-dominant political orthodoxy.

Unlike their orthodox counterparts, renovative Cuban revolutionaries are pleased with the regime's increased flexibility toward the market, because, as Mexican renovators, they regard the state-market antinomy as artificial. Various comments reflect this view: "The planned economy/free market dichotomy is false and debates about the 'free market' are absurd."[31] "No socialist system can pretend to eliminate the market; all it can do is try to set its contours."[32] "Market relations predate capitalism; the market is not antisocial in its essence. Socialism has to use markets, but planning is the necessary element."[33] "The market is perhaps the greatest discovery of humanity. We need some combination of planning and market."[34]

On the need to combine market mechanisms with planning and state intervention, then, there is broad agreement among renovators and the economic liberals in Cuba. What separates the sheep from the goats, so to speak, is the nature of the "state intervention" half of this combination. Here Cuban renovators and economic liberals part ways. Renovators are concerned with democratizing the social and political dimensions of the state's role in the economy, which leads them into controversial reform ideas involving nonstate forms of property and genuine workers' control. "There is no form of property that is incompatible with planning," argues political economist Esteban Morales. "The problem isn't the form of property but the correlation of various forms of property. The negotiating capacity of the state doesn't conflict with private property or mixed enterprises."[35] In fact, however, it is precisely the possibility that the state-party regime will lose its control over the process of economic

---

31. Juan Antonio Blanco, interview with author, Havana, February 3, 1993.

32. Aurelio Alonso, interview with author, Havana, February 23, 1993.

33. Miguel Limia, interview with author, Havana, February 19, 1993.

34. Esteban Morales, interview with author, Havana, March 10, 1993.

35. Esteban Morales, interview with author, Havana, February 15, 1993. Another renovative take on the issue of ownership in Cuba was offered by philosopher Miguel Limia, which also implicitly addresses concerns about democratic control: "Our socialist relations of property are not very socialist in the strict sense. Socialist property has to bring the producers closer to the means of production and their administration." Interview with author, Havana, February 19, 1993.

restructuring that makes those now in charge of the reforms wary about some of the renovators' ideas.

The issues of genuine worker participation, autonomy, and control are central to the renovators' answer to Cuba's extreme statism. Urban planner Sergio Baroni suggests:

> We need more autonomous, worker-controlled administration. Workers collectives are the direction to go. The inefficiency of state-run enterprises is basically that the worker is a completely anonymous cog, as in Marx's concept of alienation. The worker has no sense of the result of his work in the huge, state production facilities.[36]

Juan Antonio Blanco shares this assessment: "What's the problem with a state-isized economy? The absence of collective creativity and will. But that doesn't mean the state sector should completely disappear."[37] The choices are not between planning and market, between all state or all private property, Blanco insists. The question is, "How can the state indirectly plan the economy?" He continues:

> What should the state administer directly and who should administer what the state doesn't? The state is better than the private sector in administering education, health, transportation. But when the state administers everything, it leads to inefficiency and corruption. That's a valid observation for Mexico and for Cuba.[38]

Baroni's and Blanco's observations may seem fairly innocuous, but among the Cuban leadership who are directing the current economic liberalization, to question the dominant role of state property is still considered heresy. Blanco's suggestion that Cuba should consider "franchises, like McDonalds, but with the state as the owner of the company and workers collectives as the owners of the franchise,"[39] is controversial because such reforms are perceived as a threat to the power of state managers and planners.

Aurelio Alonso also recognizes that Cuba's statist society needs a process of liberalization, and that "the liberal space within Marxism has to be discovered."[40] "Real or historical socialism, by turning the state

---

36. Sergio Baroni, interview with author, Havana, February 26, 1993.
37. Juan Antonio Blanco, interview with author, Havana, March 3, 1993.
38. Ibid.
39. Ibid.
40. Aurelio Alonso, interview with author, Havana, February 23, 1993. Alonso continued with his thought, "There are important sources of liberalism

into owner and administrator, hypertrophied the reach of [government] ministers and other state institutions, and replaced the entrepreneur with the functionary."[41] However, Alonso warns that "liberalization must not lead to *desocialization*."[42] The dangers of desocialization may also be a concern among more orthodox socialist thinkers, but it is the renovators in Cuba who propose full democratization as the only real antidote to the fallout of necessary economic liberalization.

In one of the most thoroughly critical, public analyses of Cuba's current crisis from a still-loyal Communist, social scientist Haroldo Dilla is quite explicit about the potential dangers of desocialization and elite control implied in the current liberal economic reforms. He warns that increasing poverty and marginalization affect Cuban society's most vulnerable sectors, specifically women and young people just entering the job market. He notes that Cuban women are employed disproportionately in jobs, such as clerical and bureaucratic posts, which are the first to be eliminated "under the logic of rationalizing employment." Dilla cites statistics showing that women represented 53 percent of the unemployed in Cuba in 1985 and 60 percent in 1990. "It is precisely within this context that it is legitimate to believe that the Cuban women's movement needs a bigger dose of autonomy."[43]

Yet Dilla notes that under the current economic reforms, instead of increased autonomy and democratic participation for women or workers in general, the state's economic managers (and increasingly foreign investors) wield ever greater power. Liberal economic reforms are necessary, Dilla agrees, but they are not sufficient, and are even counterproductive, "if they are not accompanied by policies designed to strengthen the spaces of popular participation and control."[44] To increase participation, Dilla is not prepared to settle for the labor-management schemes of

---

other than Adam Smith. There is Rousseau and Montesquieue, both of whom have to be included in the liberal traditions rediscovered by Marxism."

41. Aurelio Alonso, "La economía Cubana: El reto de un ajuste sin desocialización," manuscript, 1993, p. 17.

42. Aurelio Alonso, interview, op cit. (emphasis mine).

43. Haroldo Dilla Alfonso, "Cuba: La Crisis y la rearticulación del consenso político (Notas para un debate socialista)," manuscript, 1993, pp. 27-28. An English translation of this paper is Haroldo Dilla Alfonso, "Cuba Between Utopia and the World Market: Notes for a Socialist Debate," *Latin American Perspectives*, 21:4, pp. 46-59 (Fall 1994). Criminologist Margarita Viera (interview with author, Havana, March 13, 1994) expressed a related concern about the desocializing effects of the current economic adjustments, noting that unemployment could lead to a deactivization of work centers and thus to people losing a key point of reference and social/political integration.

44. Haroldo Dilla Alfonso, Ibid., p. 2.

the Japanese and Western Europeans, which he notes have received increased attention in Cuba (especially in certain military industries). Without an extensive process of democratization and increased participation of workers in decision-making, Dilla worries that Cuba could reach a point where,

> Every morning Cuban workers would sing the company's hymn with sincere enthusiasm, but without in anyway leading to the construction of a participatory democracy in which everyone involved—and not just the technocratic, entrepreneurial elites—enjoy effective participation in making the most relevant decisions.[45]

Juan Valdés Paz states the position clearly: "Economic liberalization and radical democratization is the only combination that can save the socialist revolution in Cuba."[46] Referring to the process of broad public debate preceding the 1991 Party Congress, Valdés Paz observed, "The great majority of the proposals from the people called for both things: economic liberalization and democratization. That shows the great wisdom of the masses. Greater participation by society in all systems."[47]

While most debate about the crisis of Cuban socialism focuses on these issues of state-market relations, forms of property, democratic participation in the work place and in policy-making, renovators are also concerned by what they call the revolution's "ethical crisis," a crisis not directly resolvable through technical economic solutions or political democratization. Juan Antonio Blanco describes it as a conflict between an "ethic of being" and an "ethic of having."[48] Similarly, Julio Carranza, who is generally quite liberal on economic issues, talks about the need for cultural change whereby "self-realization does not happen through consumerism."[49] It is a crisis with a particular national manifestation in Cuba, but Blanco understands it in global terms, and his words recall Mexican renovator Sergio de la Peña's message, cited earlier, about the need for a new world pact of humanity. According to Blanco:

---

45. Ibid., pp. 25-26.

46. Juan Valdés Paz, interview with author, Havana, February 25, 1993. For more of Valdés Paz's thinking on these issues, see his "The Socialist Transition in Cuba: Continuity and Change in the 1990s," *Social Justice*, 22:3, pp. 92-110 (Fall 1995),and "La izquierda hoy en América Latina," manuscript, n.d.

47. Juan Valdés Paz, interview with author, Havana, February 25, 1993.

48. Juan Antonio Blanco quoted in Medea Benjamin, "Cuba: Talking About Revolution" (manuscript, 1993), p. 76.

49. Julio Carranza, oral presentation to a small, left forum in San Francisco, October 4, 1992.

Two distinct concepts, civilization and culture, have been confused, collapsed into one another. Civilization is the process of human beings relating to nature via technology. Culture is the process of humans relating to other humans within the context of a particular civilization. The promise under socialism was to achieve civilization without the inhumanity of capitalist culture. Today both socialist and capitalist cultures are in crisis. Cultures based on exploitation and domination have reached their limit, because we have achieved the ability to destroy the planet. We must move to a new alternative culture that is not based on selfishness and greed.[50]

For Cuba's renovative left, then, preserving the ethics of social justice and solidarity once associated with socialism and with the Cuban revolution is as important as figuring out the precise balance of state planning and market, social property and private enterprise, solidarity and individual liberty.

The ethical component of any renovated socialist project is gaining renewed attention within the Mexican left as well. In a society permeated by corruption, from the petty *mordida* paid to a traffic policeman to the infiltration of high government circles by powerful drug lords, many have welcomed as fresh air the strong ethical content of the Zapatistas' discourse, with its emphasis on traditional indigenous values. Chilean Manuel Antonio Garretón has captured the renovative left's growing appreciation of the importance of ethics, over and above any particular economic model, in orienting a socialist future:

> The fundamental of socialism is not a model of society—with predetermined economic, political, and cultural forms—but rather the ethical and institutional crystallization in each society of the principles of equality, liberty, fraternity or solidarity, which articulate the relationship between economy, politics, and culture and allow each society to transcend its most flagrant contradictions.[51]

With such formulations, the renovative left is attempting to reinforce the important ethical guideposts of a noncapitalist alternative without falling into the historical traps of defining socialism in rigid terms of particular economic institutions and models.

The current conjuncture, in which global capitalism is expanding and socialist and nationalist gains are being rolled back, is eroding another cornerstone of the left's old worldview: "the idea of needing to progress

---

50. Juan Antonio Blanco, oral presentation at the University of California, Berkeley, April 28, 1993.

51. Manuel Antonio Garretón M., "Socialismo real y socialismo posible," manuscript, May 1990, p. 7.

linearly from one stage through to the next," as Harnecker puts it.[52] Indeed, the idea of nearly inevitable progress to an imagined, superior socialist society informed much of the left's historic practice. Sociologist Walter Goldfrank elaborates the point:

> In Marxist theory, socialism is supposed to represent a higher stage of human development than capitalism, and of course as applied to individual societies, most Marxists thought that the USSR, or China, or Cuba had made some leap into the future, so that they were not merely morally superior but also "more advanced" ("more scientific and rational") than the decadent capitalist societies. History and its presumed teleology was a critical component of Marxists' self-confidence.[53]

In fact, the setbacks experienced by the world's lefts in the 1980s did seriously shake their self-confidence, as suggested in the quotes from Elvira Concheiro and Margarita Viera cited in the previous chapter. Moreover, "for the common citizen," as Haroldo Dilla noted, "there remain few doubts that the supposed superiority and irreversibility of [European] socialism were no more than a mythological construction."[54] Some of the people interviewed for this book occasionally expressed their sense that socialism or even social welfare states are unquestionably more advanced forms of society in calls to "preserve the advances of the revolution," or "stop the dismantling of the welfare state," or "halt the privatization of the national patrimony." Orthodox socialist intellectuals tended to express traditional assumptions about the indisputable superiority of socialism more frequently than did their liberal or renovative counterparts (e.g., "Socialism . . . can only be the highest expression and an enormous expansion of democracy in relation to limited bourgeois democracy.[55]).

However, there were fewer references to Marxism's teleology of progress than one might have expected, given the turn of world events. Goldfrank suggests that this may be because "Latin Americans have always been more 'moral' Marxists (defend the weak, fight injustice) than 'scientific' (advance historically into the future) ones."[56] Given the importance of moral and ethical questions in the political discourse of the

---

52. Marta Harnecker, "Democracy and Revolutionary Movement," in Jonas and McCaughan, *Latin America Faces the Twenty-First Century, op. cit..* p. 75.

53. Walter Goldfrank, correspondence with author, December 7, 1994.

54. Haroldo Dilla, "Cuba: La Crisis y la Rearticulación del Consenso Político," op. cit.

55. Marta Harnecker, "Democracy and Revolutionary Movement," op. cit., pp. 65-66.

56. Walter Goldfrank, correspondence with author, December 7, 1994.

left in Cuba and Mexico, I am inclined to agree with this observation as a partial explanation. Nonetheless, I suspect there is another, perhaps more important factor explaining why the recent reverses of socialist and nationalist achievements did not provoke more reflections by the intellectuals interviewed about Marxist, and, more broadly, Enlightenment, notions of progress.

As citizens of noncore societies, Cuban and Mexican leftists tend to be more acutely aware than the European and U.S. lefts of the extent to which access to the benefits of "progress" is determined by highly unequal relations of global power. Cuba's and Mexico's rise to the semiperiphery were more the result of arduous political and social struggles, indeed, national revolutions, than of any natural evolution of human progress through technological advances and ongoing rationalization. Any social gains won were always at risk of being lost again, to internal "class enemies," to U.S. "imperialism," or to "greedy" transnational corporations. Thus, just as the structural realities of life outside the core encouraged a skepticism among these left intellectuals about the possibilities or merits of "rational, liberal reforms," they also moderated the extent of the Latin American lefts' faith in the Marxist teleology of progress. Liberalism and Marxism were both ideological products of core societies and both were only partially embraced by the Latin American lefts. These lefts, consequently, are particularly well positioned to produce renovative, noncapitalist economic alternatives freed of old liberal and socialist orthodoxies.

Among Cuban and Mexican leftists, many key aspects of socialist discourse have been seriously discredited, particularly those that tended to equate socialism with the rigid, authoritarian statism of the Soviet Union. The orthodox voices that still cling to such discourse are few and marginal in Mexico and are seeing their position eroded in Cuba, as the deepening economic crisis encourages further economic liberalization. Economic liberalism has clearly gained influence among left intellectuals in both countries, as seen in their acceptance of the need to incorporate concepts of market competition and efficiency into their alternative economic programs, and in their recognition of the limitations of the state as economic protagonist. Liberal economic thinking tends to be on the rise among the left in still extremely statist Cuba and cautiously engaged by the left in now extensively liberalized Mexico.

Yet in both countries, liberalism's influence among the left is less than one might imagine based on Castañeda's account, or less than one might expect if a more simplistic class analysis were used to predict and explain the ideological perspectives of these intellectuals. The historic project of liberal reformism has collapsed along with communism and does not represent a viable alternative for semiperipheral Latin American societies in the brutal, globalized capitalism of the late twentieth century. If anything, the core ethical values of the old socialist project (solidarity, social justice, and equality) have gained (not lost) relevance as the neoliberal restructuring of Latin America over the past two decades has swollen the ranks of the poor and further polarized one of the most socially unequal regions of the world. Renovative left ideas have begun to transcend the limitations of liberal and socialist orthodoxies and to challenge neoliberalism's current ideological reign, a process that can only benefit from the most recent series of debacles in Mexico, the showcase of neoliberal reform. Moreover, despite predictions to the contrary, nationalism remains a powerful discourse in both nations, where the left still (and perhaps increasingly) insists on the important national character of its social and political project.

Part of the explanation for these observations is found in an editorial written in a Mexican journal in early 1990, as the state socialist dominoes continued to fall, as the full social impact of Latin America's "lost decade" was being assessed, and as the George Bush administration launched new military interventions abroad:

> The ideological crisis of socialism has not generated a new alternative ideology nor has it been able to strengthen the old American-democratic-liberalism. At the same time that the "socialist dictatorships," and supposedly socialist ideals, collapsed, the most traditional and archaic of imperialisms presented itself in Panama, El Salvador and—under the pretext of a war against drug traffickers—threatens to intervene in Venezuela and Colombia.[57]

In attempting to renovate a left project, the intertwining of social justice ethics and nationalist aspirations is particularly notable in Cuba and Mexico, homelands of the region's most thorough and enduring nationalist revolutions, perched on the edge of the century's most powerful nation. The end of the Cold War may have altered but did not end the historic tension between the regional hegemony of the United States and Latin America's aspirations for full economic and political sovereignty, the topic addressed in the following chapters.

---

57. "Entre la 'crisis de las ideologías' y la hipocresía," *El Cotidiano* (Mexico), No. 33, January-February 1990, p. 36.

CHAPTER 7. NATIONAL SOVEREIGNTY I

The Nation-State in the Post-Cold War, Globalized World-System

In twentieth-century Latin America, full national sovereignty came to be imagined as walking upon the two legs of political independence and autonomous economic development. For the left, these goals are inextricably linked to the construction of democracy and egalitarian economic alternatives, the themes of the previous four chapters. Full democracy, based on the representation and participation of the popular majority, is the only guarantee that the national interests of the broadest social sectors will not be hocked by powerful elites who perceive their interests to be closely tied to the fortunes of international capital. Autonomous, self-sustaining, national economic development is possible only if the great majority of the population is able to participate fully in the production and consumption of the nation's economic wealth. Although the left's current thinking on the question of national sovereignty cannot be completely separated from its reassessment of the political and economic alternatives available to each nation's citizenry, this and the following chapter focus more directly on the relationship of the nation-state to the modern world-system, understood as a capitalist world-economy organized politically as a group of interrelated states dominated by the core powers.

The Mexican and Cuban revolutions were certainly responses to internal inequities (vast social inequalities and undemocratic political systems), but they were also about national aspirations frustrated by the overwhelming presence of the United States. Genuine national sovereignty in the shadow of such a colossal power seemed possible only if Mexico and Cuba were able to achieve self-sustaining economic development. For Latin America's two most enduring revolutions, then, success and legitimacy became completely intertwined with the nation's ability to assert its political and economic autonomy within the world-system.

Mexico's boldest efforts in this regard came during the Lázaro Cárdenas government in the late 1930s. Cárdenas brilliantly used public hostility toward the crudely exploitative and monopolistic practices of

U.S. companies to help consolidate nationalist support for his domestic reforms. He simultaneously relied on mass mobilizations to strengthen his bid for increased independence from a United States temporarily preoccupied with recovery from the Great Depression and mounting conflict in Europe. A vision of national economic development through state-directed, import-substitution industrialization became the principal goal as well as the justification for nationalist unity and corporatist control of the masses. In carrying out this defining stage of the Mexican revolution, Cárdenas was able to count on the support of the Mexican left.[1]

Cárdenas's strategy was impressively successful relative to most other Latin American nations. In subsequent years, the Mexican left complained that the revolution had been either betrayed or unfinished, pointing to the persistence of social inequalities, the increasingly authoritarian political system, and Mexico's dependency on U.S. capital goods and advanced technology.[2] Nevertheless, for more than thirty years, Mexico diversified its economy, developed a powerful industrial sector, and sustained high rates of economic growth. It accomplished this while maintaining political stability and steering a cautious course between independence and collaboration with the U.S. in the international arena. By the 1960s Mexico had successfully fought its way into the semiperiphery, the cherished middle class of the world's hierarchy of nation-states, certainly one measurement of success for the assertion of Third World national sovereignty in the mid-twentieth century.[3] That, of course, was before the unprecedented crises and restructuring since the mid-1980s.[4]

---

1. On the role of Cárdenas and *cardenismo*, see Adolfo Gilly, *El Cardenismo: Una utopía mexicana* (Mexico: Cal y Arena, 1994); Arnoldo Córdova, *La Ideología de la Revolución Mexicana: La Formación del Nuevo Régimen* (Mexico: Ediciones ERA, 1973) and *La Política de Masas del Cardenismo* (Mexico: Ediciones ERA, 1974); Judith Adler Hellman, *Mexico in Crisis* (New York: Holmes & Meier, 1988); and Nora Hamilton, *The Limits of State Autonomy: Post-Revolutionary Mexico* (Princeton: Princeton University, 1982). On the left's relationship to Cárdenas, see Barry Carr, *Marxism and Communism in Twentieth-Century Mexico* (Lincoln: University of Nebraska, 1992).

2. There are many fine examples of such critiques, including two classics: Adolfo Gilly, *La Revolución Interrumpida* (Mexico: El Caballito, 1971) and José Luis Ceceña, *México en la Orbita Imperial* (Mexico: El Caballito, 1970).

3. See chapter 1 for a brief description of the semiperiphery.

4. On the crisis and restructuring see, Edward J. McCaughan, "Mexico's Long Crisis: Toward New Regimes of Accumulation and Domination," *Latin American Perspectives*, Vol. 20, No. 3, 1993.

The Cuban revolution's effort to break a long cycle of frustrated national liberation took a different form in a different world context; the substance of the goal, however, was arguably quite similar to that of Mexico.[5] Cárdenas's strategy for Mexico's rise to the semiperiphery is an example of what Wallerstein has called "seizing the chance."[6] Cárdenas undertook his radical reforms at a moment when the United States was not yet hegemonic, the world-economy was in crisis, and the mounting conflict in Europe dominated the international agenda. Fidel Castro, however, initiated the Cuban revolution's first reforms at the height of U.S. global power, world economic expansion, and the Cold War. United States' hostility to the Cuban revolution encouraged its early radicalization and a rocky first decade of experimental efforts to jump-start its own industrialization program in isolation from Cuba's historic, regional markets.[7] Fearing that continued economic and political instability would jeopardize the revolution, Cuba's leadership then turned toward an alliance with the Soviet Union, a "socialist" variation of what Wallerstein calls development "by invitation."[8] The Soviet Union would become the hostess setting a place for Cuba at the table of the semiperiphery.

Though the decision to join the Eastern bloc's CMEA (Council for Mutual Economic Assistance, formerly COMECON) in the early 1970s was controversial even among Cuban revolutionaries, it came to be accepted by many as Cuba's best hope for defending the revolution against U.S. aggression and for articulating with new international markets, given what Cuba perceived as its expulsion from the capitalist world market by the United States. Despite the fact that economic reliance on the Soviet bloc forced Cuba to completely reorganize its productive apparatus, many Cubans I interviewed regarded the generally favorable trade and aid relations with the Soviet bloc as an example of more equi-

---

5. For an excellent discussion of the history of Cuba's frustrated attempts at full national sovereignty, see Marfieli Pérez Stable, *The Cuban Revolution. Origins, Course, and Legacy* (New York and Oxford: Oxford University Press, 1993), especially chapters 1 and 2; on the radical nationalism of the Revolution, see chapter 4.

6. Immanuel Wallerstein, *The Capitalist World-Economy* (Cambridge: Cambridge University Press, 1980), pp. 76-82.

7. On the early period of the Cuban Revolution, see Marfeli Pérez Stable, *The Cuban Revolution*, op. cit., especially chapters 3, 4, and 5; Edward Boorstein, *The Economic Transformation of Cuba* (New York: Monthly Review, 1968); Leo Huberman and Paul Sweezy, *Socialism in Cuba* (New York: Monthly Review, 1969); and James O'Connor, *The Origins of Socialism in Cuba* (Ithaca: Cornell University, 1970).

8. Immanuel Wallerstein, *The Capitalist World-Economy*, op cit.

table North-South relations than those experienced by most noncore nations. As one Cuban, who was always critical of the Soviet model, put it: "With the Soviet Union we achieved what was supposed to be the new international economic order for the Third World. That is, we achieved the agreement to index the prices of their products with the prices of our products."[9] In that sense, many Cubans saw integration with CMEA as having improved Cuba's position in the world.

Indeed, through the 1970s and early 1980s, Cuba prospered in many regards, sustaining higher levels of economic growth than most of Latin America and achieving living standards far above those of comparable nations in the region.[10] Although sugar remained Cuba's main export, much of the harvesting was done mechanically and the processing plants were modernized. The nation's dairy production was transformed with genetic engineering techniques and modern, hybrid feed grains that increased output. Cuba developed a highly educated and skilled work force and an advanced scientific and technological capacity, including impressive, if small, biotechnology, medical equipment, and pharmaceutical industries. Cuba also established a strong presence in world affairs, pursuing an active and controversial role in Latin American and African politics, including a decisive military campaign supporting revolutionary forces in Southern Africa. Thus, by many standards, although it has not generally been thought of in these terms, Cuba, like Mexico, had found its way into the semiperiphery, if less securely. Moreover, Cuba had done so in a far more egalitarian if no less authoritarian manner. Finally, Cuba demonstrated its independence from the United States, even if the price was occasional subordination to a more generous, but equally arrogant, new Big Brother. That, of course, was before the crises of the 1980s and the collapse of the Soviet Union. Susan Eckstein has argued persuasively that many of the improvements associated with the first decades of the Cuban revolution, "proved by the 1990s to be contingent on a set of historical conditions that by then no longer existed."[11]

---

9. Juan Antonio Blanco, "Cuba: Crisis, Ethics, and Viability," in Susanne Jonas and Edward J. McCaughan (eds.), *Latin America Faces the Twenty-First Century. Reconstructing a Social Justice Agenda* (Boulder: Westview Press, 1994), p. 186.

10. On the performance of the Cuban economy, see Andrew Zimbalist and Claes Brundenius, *The Cuban Economy: Measurement and Analysis of Socialist Performance* (Baltimore: Johns Hopkins University, 1989).

11. Susan Eva Eckstein, *Back From the Future: Castro Under Cuba* (Princeton, N.J.: Princeton University Press, 1994), p. 205. Eckstein presents an indispensable, comprehensive overview of the changes in Cuba since the revolution and gives particular attention to the recent years of crisis. Also on the

Three significant developments in the international order climaxed as the millennium's final decade began, highlighting the extent to which the world had changed since the Mexican and Cuban revolutions first began their attempts to secure long-elusive national sovereignty. *Politically*, the international correlation of forces was altered by the demise of the Soviet bloc. The United States, as a world power, was freed from the constraints previously posed by the counterweight of a Soviet superpower. The developing world was freed from even the illusion of an alternative to the capitalist world-system (at least in the here and now). *Economically*, the ongoing internationalization of capital surged forward to new levels, as core-based capital continued the reorganization begun in response to the profit-crunch of the 1970s. The Third World debt crisis forced many developing nations to accept economic and even political restructuring under the neoliberal guidelines of international financial institutions. *Ideologically*, neoliberalism attacked the traditional concept of national sovereignty. Marco Rascón, an important leader of Mexico City's urban popular movements, explained that while the *neocardenista* sector of Mexico's democratic opposition continued to insist that political sovereignty was impossible without economic sovereignty, the Carlos Salinas administration saw sovereignty as a "backward concept that stood in the way of globalization." According to Rascón:

> The very essence of neoliberalism was to redefine the concept of sovereignty. . . . For the neoliberals, sovereignty had become an opponent of modernity and was therefore fiercely combatted: sovereignty was the equivalent of the Wall of China. . . . The sovereignty of [Latin American] nation-states lost strength in the face of [economic] integration, as the U.S. advanced across the southern hemisphere expanding its interests, given the weakening of the concept of *sovereignty*. Cuba, for example, was harshly punished for stubbornly clinging to this concept and for refusing to cede its sovereignty in exchange for economic dependence.[12]

How serious are the challenges posed by these changes to the Latin American lefts' traditional notions of national sovereignty? Does the

---

crisis of recent years, see Sandor Halebsky and John M. Kirk (eds.), *Transformation and Struggle: Cuba Faces the 1990s* (New York: Praeger, 1990) and Sandor Halebsky and John M. Kirk (eds.), *Cuba in Transition: Crisis and Transformation* (Boulder: Westview, 1992).

12. Marco Rascón, "La soberanía y Chiapas," *La Jornada*, February 21, 1995. In his article, Rascón goes on to point out the inconsistency of Mexican President Ernesto Zedillo's justifying the government's military assault on the Zapatista rebels in Chiapas in the name of defending the nation's sovereignty.

now quite advanced internationalization of capital alter the conditions for pursuing autonomous economic development? Has time run out, as Jorge Castañeda asks, "for many, if not all, of the developing countries . . . to construct nations like others: with their own national language, administration, market, and currency, and with a truly autochthonous local ruling elite"? In any event, according to Castañeda, "Nation-building in Latin American proceeded so slowly, is so unfinished and ill-defined, that it will probably not take place the way the left—and nearly everyone else—has supposed."[13]

In my interviews with left intellectuals in Cuba and Mexico, questions about the viability of nation-building and defending national sovereignty did not provoke responses that correspond so neatly to orthodox, liberal, and renovative tendencies, as found on the issues of democracy and socialism. While there were different interpretations among these intellectuals regarding the post-Cold War *political* order, there was also considerable consensus about the continued meaningfulness and viability of national sovereignty, even if on somewhat modified terms. In light of the dramatic changes of recent years, argues Sergio de la Peña, "the ideas of independence and national sovereignty inherited from the nineteenth century have lost their content. It is necessary to redefine them under the new circumstances."[14]

Assessing the Post-Cold War Political Order

As might be expected, the change in the international correlation of forces represented by the disappearance of the Soviet Union was felt much more strongly in Cuba than in Mexico, where the Soviets never had a strong presence. A Soviet-trained Cuban philosopher put it most strongly: "Cuba is absolutely more vulnerable today. There is a tendency in the world to reproduce a situation similar to that which preceded World War II. There is a dangerous new dividing up of the world into spheres of influence, which is why Third World unity is so critical."[15] A renowned Cuban historian with little sympathy for the former Soviet system expressed similar concerns that Cuba is far more vulnerable in a post-Soviet world: "Cuba needs a more flexible policy today toward the United States, because our very survival as a nation and as a state is at

---

13. Jorge Castañeda, *Utopia Unarmed. The Latin American Left After the Cold War* (New York: Alfred A. Knopf, 1993), p. 287.

14. Sergio de la Peña, "Tareas pendientes del socialismo," *Mundo* (Mexico), February 1991, p. 21.

15. Miguel Limia, interview with author, Havana, February 19, 1993.

issue."[16] Among those I interviewed, fewer Mexicans considered the new international order to be clearly unfavorable to progressive forces in Mexico and elsewhere. The most negative assessment in Mexico was made by a scholar of social movements, who argued that the new international situation leaves far less maneuverability for any "democratic popular government," which at most can only hope to act with sufficient agility so as to avoid "provoking the empire."[17]

While such echoes from an earlier era of the left's discourse on U.S. imperialism were rare in these interviews, the U.S. invasion of Panama, U.S. intervention in Nicaragua, the war against Iraq, and the United States' successful use of the United Nations to legitimize its actions were frequently raised as evidence of a dangerous new unipolarity in the world. Julio Carranza, a Cuban social scientist, told me:

> The correlation of forces has greatly worsened against the interests of progressive and revolutionary forces in Latin America. The socialist camp was a source of support, politically and sometimes materially, in the period of the struggle for power and as an economic alternative (even with all its problems). The United States now has great space and flexibility, which is reflected in changes at the United Nations. Poor and small countries like Cuba depend on an international rule of law to protect their interests. If the UN is not able to maintain a state of law, the situation for poor, small countries will be worse than ever.[18]

Rolando Cordera, a Mexican economist long associated with the revolutionary nationalist tendency of the Mexican left, is also concerned about the implications of an unrestrained United States. But he believes that the collapse of the Soviet Union just confirms something Mexicans had already concluded:

> A confrontation with the United States doesn't have any prospects. Now, without a bipolar game, it's clear there's no one to referee. But I think Mexico was already learning this, before the loss of bipolarity. From its own experience, in the very difficulty of the idea of a confrontation, which has never resulted in anything concrete but rather in a very aggressive rhetoric which is always counterproductive for Mexico. The loss of bipolarity forces Mexico to readjust its scheme of international relations.[19]

---

16. Jorge Ibarra, interview with author, Havana, February 21, 1993.

17. Jaime Tamayo, interview with author, Guadalajara, August 20, 1992.

18. Julio Carranza, interview with author, Havana, February 18, 1993.

19. Rolando Cordera, interview with author, Mexico City, September 2, 1992.

Particularly for Cubans, the prospect of a military confrontation with the United States remains a real concern and is seen by some as hampering internal reforms. One fiercely loyal but heretical Cuban Communist suggested that the threat of invasion by U.S. Marines prevents Fidel Castro from exhorting the masses to force more radical reforms on a reluctant bureaucracy.[20] Another Cuban social scientist explained that the cautious approach taken toward reforms at the Fourth Party Congress in October 1991, which contrasted with the more open tone of the Call to the Congress issued in March 1990, resulted from the unexpectedly rapid deterioration of the international situation following the Persian Gulf War and the collapse of the Soviet Union.[21]

Very few Cubans mentioned the political demise of Prime Minister Mikhail Gorbachev as a factor negatively influencing the international context, either because they were critical of his efforts or hesitant to broach what remains a sensitive issue in Cuba. Several Mexican respondents, on the other hand, identified Gorbachev's loss of power as a pivotal event influencing the character of the post-Cold War order. Mexican author Carlos Monsiváis, for example, lamented that the fall of Gorbachev and the rise of Boris Yeltsin had left President George Bush absolutely unchallenged.[22] Marco Rascón, the urban leader who has served as a federal deputy for the PRD, likewise regretted the international implications of Gorbachev's failure: "Had Gorbachev succeeded, he would have created a very different country, representing a clear alternative to neoliberalism in the world, but he didn't."[23]

Such gloomy assessments of the international situation, however, hardly reflect a consensus. Many respondents in both countries offered more balanced, occasionally even optimistic, assessments of the benefits and liabilities of a post-Cold War order. Jorge Castañeda, for example, notes the advantegeous disappearance of the communist "boogieman" of the East-West conflict. Moreover, he asserts that the South's leverage in North-South relations is actually growing, because global interdependence means that the effects of Third World poverty are global.[24]

---

20. Cuban intellectual who requested anonymity, interview with author, Havana, February 9, 1993.

21. Juan Valdés Paz, interview with author, Havana, February 25, 1993.

22. Carlos Monsiváis, interview with author, Mexico City, August 25, 1991.

23. Marco Rascón, interview with author, Mexico City, August 14, 1992. Also, recall the program notes by Mexican playwrite Héctor Ortega, quoted at the conclusion of chapter 2, which expressed a similar assessment regarding the consequences of Gorbachev's fall from power.

24. Jorge Castañeda, *Utopia Unarmed*, op cit., p. 443. Castañeda cites the 1992 Rio Earth Summit as an example of the new possibilities, though one that did not jell (ibid., p. 444). He warns that little can be accomplished along these

In another example, Alejandro Alvarez, a Mexican economist and political organizer from the non-Communist socialist left, maintained that the disappearance of the Soviet Union presented no real change for Mexico, other than socialism's loss of prestige; in fact, he maintained that there is greater multipolarity in the world today and that while some counterweights to U.S. power have been lost, new ones have emerged.

> The multipolarity of economic power has increased. Japan and Germany are very important economic powers, even if the U.S. economy continues to be a decisive power in the world-economy. Nor am I convinced that there is that much military unipolarity.
>
> The proof is that Saddam Hussein is still in power. What's the mysterious factor that explains why the U.S. forces didn't end up removing Saddam completely? The fact that there is a counterpower saying to the U.S., this is as far as you can go. This is part of the Russian military strategy; despite the disintegration of the Soviet Union, the military continues to be a point of cohesion for the independent states. And military unipolarity is not possible today without economic hegemony. The U.S. had to ask for money everywhere for the Gulf War, something impossible to imagine after Word War II.
>
> In terms of Latin America, any U.S. intervention here would be very costly for the U.S. And today the repercussions of such intervention would be very direct within U.S. domestic politics. The point is that new counterweights are emerging. The deepening integration of the region is so great that, now more than ever, the U.S. must be careful about its forms of intervention, or it could unleash uncontrolable processes. So, some counterweights are lost but others appear.[25]

Cristina Laurell, who comes from the same political tendency as Alvarez and is now a leading figure in the PRD, agrees that the disappearance of the Soviet Union does not greatly change the geopolitics in which the Mexican left must operate. But, she is less confident about new forces emerging to counter hostility from the United States and international capital in the event Cuauhtémoc Cárdenas should ever become president of Mexico:

> If the U.S. could not tolerate Nicaragua or El Salvador, it is unlikely to tolerate a Cárdenas government. The closest example we have in Latin America to what a Cárdenas government might look like is the

---

lines unless there is significant ideological change in the United States (ibid., p. 446).

25. Alejandro Alvarez, interview with author, Mexico City, August 28, 1992.

Salvador Allende government [in Chile]. And look how the U.S. responded to Allende![26]

Simiarly, Pablo González Casanova cites the whole combination of world changes, including the collapse of the socialist camp, the setbacks suffered by various national liberation and non-aligned movements, and the expansion of neoliberal policies, as having reduced the options for "alternative governments."[27]

Respondents from the former Mexican Communist Party, for whom the Soviet Union was a far more significant point of reference than it ever was for the non-Communist left, grant more importance to the collapse of the Soviet bloc, but also see certain advantages. A long-time Mexican militant who remains firmly committed to much of the old Communist agenda can see no new counterbalances to U.S. power in today's world; on the other hand, he argued, there is a great advantage for the left in what he sees as a disappearance of superpower, bloc politics and the so-called international communist threat. "Class struggle is no longer seen as an invention of Moscow."[28] Enrique Semo, a well-known theorist once associated with the "Eurocommunist" tendency of the defunct Mexican Communist Party, also sees pros and cons in the new international conjuncture. After ticking off a list of "great defeats for the world left in the 1980s" (the defeat of the civilizational project of the Soviet bloc, the defeat of the post-World War II belief in revolution in the West, the collapse of Third World unity, and the disappearance of most of the world's Communist parties), Semo mustered a cautiously optimistic observation: "If this was all that had happened, we'd have to say capitalism had won the battle. But look at what's happening to capitalism; it's also in bad shape." The global crisis has affected everything, stated Semo, and the left's defeats are simply part of "the death of the postwar world, which will mean eventually a defeat for the United States and for capitalism."[29]

While I did not interview a single Cuban who felt substantially less vulnerable in the post-Cold War order, many Cuban respondents also saw some ameliorating factors in the new conjuncture: "We have thirty years of building distinct social relations and a distinct way of life. These

---

26. Cristina Laurell, interview with author, Mexico City, August 6, 1992.

27. See P. González Casanova, "México: Hacia una democracia sin opciones?" in Jorge Alonso, et al. (eds.), *El Nuevo Estado Mexicano. IV. Estado y Sociedad* (Mexico: Nueva Imagen, 1992), pp. 273-74.

28. Eduardo Montes, interview with author, Mexico City, August 31, 1992.

29. Enrique Semo, comments at a public forum in Mexico City, September 4, 1992.

values will allow Cuba to counter the new vulnerability"[30]; "Cuba is still very strong militarily, even after the collapse of the USSR, and Cuba is unlikely to provide an excuse for intervention like Saddam Hussein did."[31] Cuba can no longer count on the USSR to provide some measure of balance, "but we also have to take into account the U.S. domestic situation. The threat of U.S. intervention can be greater or lesser depending on the internal contradictions in the U.S. An intervention in Cuba would not be another Iraq; it would cost the lives of many Americans, of 'our boys'."[32] While the collapse of the Soviet bloc means economic disaster, "this same situation actually reinforces our political independence."[33]

Cuban vice president and respected intellectual Carlos Rafael Rodríguez told a gathering of Latin American scholars that for all of the Third World, regardless of whether a country ever had ties with the Soviet Union, the politico-military bipolarity of the post-World War II era "was a guarantee of not being left alone, abandoned to the decisions of contemporary imperialism." On the other hand, citing Paul Kennedy's work on the decline of world empires, Rodríguez also noted that the United States was now a weakened power, forced to seek financial and political support for the Persian Gulf War.[34]

Several Cubans also mentioned increased solidarity from Latin America in the post-Cold War conjuncture as a factor that makes Cuba somewhat less vulnerable to U.S. aggression. A retired social scientist who immigrated to Cuba at the time of the revolution elaborated:

---

30. Sergio Baroni, interview with author, Havana, February 26, 1993.

31. Estervino Montesino Seguí, interview with author, Havana, March 6, 1993.

32. Beatriz Díaz, interview with author, Havana, March 5, 1993.

33. Ramiro Abreú, interview with author, Havana, March 8, 1993.

34. Carlos Rafael Rodríguez, presentation to the Latin American Sociology Congress, Havana, May 28-31, 1991. Three other thoughtful papers on these issues presented at the same conference by Cuban scholars were: Pedro Monreal, "Estados Unidos y América Latina y el Caribe: Geoeconomía, Conflicto y Coexistencia," m.s., n.d.; Juan Valdés Paz, "Notas Sobre el Nuevo Sistema Internacional, el Tercer Mundo y América Latina," m.s., May 1991; and Luis Suárez Salazar, "Cuba: Aislamiento Internacional o Reinserción en un Mundo Cambiado," m.s., January 1991. For two more official Cuban government perspectives on the new international order, see David Deutschmann, "Cuba, Socialism, and the 'New World Order': An Interview with Cuban Vice-President Carlos Rafael Rodríguez," *Focus on Cuba Series*, No. 2 (Melbourne: Ocean Press, 1992); and Mary Murray, "Cuba and the United States: An Interview with Cuban Foreign Minister Ricardo Alarcón," *Focus on Cuba Series*, No. 1 (Melbourne: Ocean Press, 1992).

Cuba's alliance with the USSR weakened Cuba in terms of our natural alliances with the world's peoples and with Latin America. The USSR provided us with arms, but in reality it also put us in the middle of a superpower conflict without any guarantee that we'd be supported or protected militarily in the event of an aggression. For many progressives, Cuba came to be seen as a Soviet satellite, which undermined moral support for us.

But international solidarity with Cuba has increased since the collapse of the USSR. Respect for Fidel among Latin American heads of state has increased. Cuba's early image as David against Goliath was a very important source of support; this was lost in our alliance with the USSR. We have to regain that, and we can if we don't make serious errors and if the Cuban revolution doesn't distance itself from the people. In that sense, we aren't much more vulnerable than before.[35]

Echoing the kind of optimism expressed by Mexico's Enrique Semo, an optimism that stems from decades of left militancy through the best and the worst of times, together with a strong dose of Marxist teleology, Cuban philosopher Fernando Martínez Heredia answered my questions about the new international order as follows:

Today there is a period of profound demoralization. Imperialism is working with all its strength, with a totalitarian production of public opinion. But in Latin America, there's no objective reason to believe that there will be even a medium-term, peaceful reign of bourgeois rule. New civilian governments are continuing the same economic policies of the dictatorships. There is no longer even a possibility of reformism, and without reformism it is not possible to reproduce hegemony. It's only possible to leave social demands outside of politics for a very short period of time. So there are two contradictory tendencies: more imperialist power and more potential for social movements.[36]

Thus, there is considerable diversity in the assessment of these leftist intellectuals about the nature of the post-Cold War political order. There may be broad general agreement that the United States remains the major (and problematic) regional power, but there is a wide range of opinions about the geopolitical significance of the Soviet bloc's collapse and about the balance of positive and negative elements in the new global political landscape.

---

35. Respondent who wished to remain anonymous, interview with author, Havana, February 18, 1993.

36. Fernando Martínez Heredia, interview with author, Havana, March 1, 1993.

Facing the Reality of a Single Capitalist World-Economy

While there is little consensus among the intellectuals interviewed about the nature of post Cold War *political* order, there seems to be general agreement, even among the Cubans, about one characteristic of the new *economic* order: There is, indeed, as Immanuel Wallerstein has long insisted, only one world-economy, and it is a capitalist one at that. As Cuban Minister of Culture Armando Hart put it, "We thought there was a socialist world, when in fact there was only a sphere of influence."[37]

For Cubans, this realization came through the experience of first being "expelled" from the world market by U.S. hostility, as several Cuban respondents characterized it, and then watching what they thought was their alternative, the Soviet economic bloc, suddenly collapse.[38] For Mexicans, the impact of globalization became increasingly evident throughout the 1980s as the debt crisis and political-economic restructuring ceded ever greater power over the economy to transnational capital. While the collapse of CMEA left Cuban socialism isolated and adrift in a sea of world capitalism, the formation of the North American Free Trade Agreement (NAFTA) hitched Mexico's future economic development ever more closely to the designs of U.S.-based capital.[39]

Julio Carranza, reflecting the increasingly influential liberal perspective among Cuban intellectuals described in previous chapters, stated the situation most plainly:

> Relations with the world market are necessary, especially for a country like Cuba with its scarcity of resources and especially now without the Soviet Union and Eastern Europe. There is now only one world economy, and there has been a generalization of the rules of supply and demand. Cuba has to deal with this reality.[40]

---

37. Armando Hart, interview with author, Havana, March 11, 1993.

38. For a candid Cuban assessment of how the Soviet collapse affected Cuba, see Juan Antonio Blanco, "Cuba: Crisis, Ethics, and Viability," in S. Jonas and E. McCaughan, *Latin America Faces the Twenty-First Century: Reconstructing a Social Justice Agenda,* op. cit.

39. There are several good sources on NAFTA; a fine place to start is Ricardo Grinspun and Maxwell A. Cameron (eds.), *The Political Economy of North American Free Trade* (New York: St. Martin's Press, 1993).

40. Julio Carranza, interview with author, Havana, February 18, 1993. For more of Julio Carranza's views, see his "Cuba: los retos de la economía," m.s. (Havana, 1992). Another liberal Cuban perspective on the need for Cuba to reinsert itself into the world market is found in Pedro Monreal, "Cuba y la nueva economía mundial: el reto de la inserción en América Latina y el Caribe," *Cuadernos de Nuestra América* (Cuba), No. 16, Jan.-June 1991.

Even more orthodox Cuban thinkers have been forced to similar conclusions, as suggested by this statement from Central Committee member Dario Machado:

> Cuba was practically expelled from the capitalist market by the U.S.—such an example of intolerance of pluralism! Cuba then copied an economic model that turned out to be inadequate for the specific needs of our country. We did this after a decade of attempts to elaborate and implement our own version of national development. Cuba was once able to choose to relate to the socialist system; now it has no choice but to relate to the capitalist world.[41]

Two theorists of the former Mexican Communist Party see globalization as having contributed to the failure of both state socialist and national developmentalist projects to create viable, autonomous national economies, making full integration with the capitalist world market inevitable. In the view of Américo Saldívar,

> Both crises are related to globalization and the third stage of the technological revolution. Only ten years later were we able to see that the new technological developments, such as biotechnology and transportation, would lead to the failure of the Stalinist model, because the authoritarian state hadn't allowed for such technological development. In Latin America, from the 1970s to the 1980s, we went from underdevelopment to stagnation; we moved backwards, in terms of increased poverty and almost all macroeconomic indicators. Globalization, internationalization of capital, and the technological revolution all imposed the crisis and imposed neoliberalism. Conditions are not ripe for another alternative.[42]

Sergio de la Peña offered a similar analysis:

> To a large extent I think the fundamental reasons for the collapse of Eastern socialism are found in the transformations of capitalism, which, since the 1960s, meant that socialism could not continue to compete, compensating ineptitude for competition in terms of living standards, with sacrifices at the level of consumption. But I don't think this is because socialism itself is so backwards, but because the qualitative leap made by capitalism is so great; it corresponds to an historical epoch.
>   I think it's important to include in any new formulations of alternative projects in Latin America that not only has the scheme of social-

---

41. Dario Machado, interviews with author, Havana, February 17 and 26, 1993.

42. Américo Saldívar Valdés, interview with author, Mexico City, August 4, 1993. Also see Saldívar's *El Ocaso del socialismo* (Mexico: Siglo XXI, 1990).

ism changed but also the scheme of capitalist nationalism, which have been the two great refuges and which had a similar historicity. [In this] new world context, there clearly can't be capitalism in one country, which is the counterpart of the historical possibility of constructing socialism in one country or one region. Countries like Mexico and Brazil can't develop in isolation from the world market. It's impossible. That's the great advantage of NAFTA for Mexico.[43]

Among Mexican leftists, one of the central debates about globalization and NAFTA has to do with whether such processes are inevitable and irreversible. Conclusions one way or the other have significant policy implications. It seems somewhat ironic that Rolando Cordera, an influential intellectual who was associated with Mexico's revolutionary nationalist tendency in the 1970s and 1980s, is now one of the most adamant proponents of globalization's inevitability:

> There is a reaction among the left to internationalization that has echoes of the crudest nationalisms. Really, the left's discourses about internationalization sometimes sound like the nationalists from the 1940s. Internationalization isn't an option, it's a world phenomenon, a given reality. You can't denounce a done deed. You have to take a position on it, on how to deal with it. But the left hasn't done that, and there is a price to be paid politically.[44]

Even among some young Cuban intellectuals, who were trained within a political culture that emphasized the invincibility of the revolutionary nation's political will, there is a growing tendency toward resignation to the notion that "processes of the world economic system can overcome 'national' interests."[45] A similar position is held by Américo Saldívar, who observed that "in the debates about NAFTA within the PRD, there are those, like Alejandro Alvarez, who think the NAFTA process is reversible. It's not. We simply have to strategize a means of survival and defense within it."[46] Saldívar was referring to economist

---

43. Sergio de la Peña, interview with author, Mexico City, August 16, 1992. Also see de la Peña's "Los cambios del socialismo en México," in *Zurda* (Mexico), Vol. II, Año 5, No. 9 (1991).

44. Rolando Cordera, interview with author, Mexico City, September 2, 1992.

45. Pedro Monreal, "United States and the New World Economic Order," manuscript, n.d., p. 5.

46. Américo Saldívar, interview with author, Mexico City, August 4, 1993. Regarding the PRD's debates on NAFTA, Cuauhtémoc Cárdenas attempted to steer a course between acceptance and absolute rejection, arguing "no to NAFTA" but yes to an alternative agreement. See Cuauhtémoc Cárdenas, "The

Alejandro Alvarez, a prominent figure in the now defunct Punto Crítico and an advisor to the PRD. Alvarez insists that globalization is neither absolute nor irreversible:

> Globalization is presented in neoliberal discourse as a world without borders, but in reality, while in some cases conventional borders have been overcome, in other senses there are still many obstacles to the free movement of goods, people, and capital. Together with globalization, there has been an intense process of regionalization, of forming trading blocs since the 1980s. This regionalization is not the same as globalization, because the regional blocs fragment the world economy, because competition has become more intense. Globalization is contradictory with regionalization, which is an example of why globalization shouldn't be understood as universal and irreversible.
>
> Nation-states have not completely lost their ability to control markets, to be able to influence national markets. The state's capacity for economic regulation remains more or less, relatively in tact.[47]

This difference of opinion illustrates the extent to which the crisis of statist paradigms has been felt most strongly by those political forces associated with the most extremely statist models in the past, the Communists, as represented by Saldívar, and the revolutionary nationalists, as represented by Cordera. As the collapse of state socialism and the advance of globalization seriously undermined their long-held faith in the state to direct economic processes, some left intellectuals have accepted much of the logic of neoliberal discourse. As we have seen, Cordera supported the Salinas administration, and Saldívar has lectured Eastern Europeans on the benefits of Mexico's neoliberal reforms.[48] Alvarez, on the other hand, whose political and ideological origins are in the 1968 student movement and the "new left," which was influenced by strands of critical Marxism and the new social movements of recent decades, was never as ideologically committed to the statist paradigm. This helps explain why he feels less challenged by neoliberal assertions and more confident in the nation-state's "relative" capacity to mediate the

---

Continental Development and Trade Initiative," in S. Jonas and E. McCaughan (eds.), *Latin America Faces the 21st Century*, op. cit. Also see PRD economic adviser Arturo Huerta's "¿Por qué el Tratado de Libre Comercio," in *Memoria* (Mexico), IV:33 (May-June 1991).

47. Alejandro Alvarez, "Integración económica y globalización," oral presentation given to the Seminario Permanente de Estudios Chicanos y de Fronteras, Instituto Nacional de Antropología e Historia, SEP, Mexico City, August 5, 1993.

48. Américo Saldívar, "Realidad y límites del neoliberalismo mexicano," *Memoria* (Mexico City), No. 57, August 1993.

process of globalization. Moreover, Alvarez is one of the notable left intellectuals who have avoided academic or bureaucratic isolation by remaining very closely tied to the popular movements of the past quarter-century, and who have emphasized the protagonistic role of popular social sectors rather than the importance of political divisions within the Mexican state.

As seen in previous chapters, close association with the popular struggles and social movements of recent decades, more than formal political or ideological affiliation, is a notable common factor among the left intellectuals in Mexico who today represent a renovationist tendency. Such immersion in grassroots politics contributes to a faith in being able to challenge the common wisdom of dominant ideology, in recent years, neoliberalism, through popular political struggle. An example of this faith is illustrated by the comments of Raúl Alvarez Garín, a cousin of Alejandro Alvarez, a prominent leader of the 1968 student movement, and a founder of Punto Crítico, who has served as a federal deputy for the PRD. Asked whether significant renegotiation of Mexico's foreign debt, a central plank of the PRD program, is a realistic option in the post-Cold War, globalized world, he replied:

> Renegotiation of the debt is possible as a political action, involving a political reorientation, clarification, and modification of the terms. If workers and others are strong protagonists in this effort, I think we could easily make significant social advances in Mexico.[49]

The dispute, then, between the activist Alvarez cousins, on the one hand, and intellectuals like Cordera and Saldívar, on the other, is not over the fact that globalization and further integration of the North American economies have advanced and altered the context for Mexico's future. Their differences are over the extent to which political struggle can still impose conditions on the powerful forces of transnational capital and the United States.[50]

---

49. Raúl Alvarez Garín, interview with author, Mexico City, August 27, 1992.

50. Cuauhtémoc Cárdenas expresses a perspective similar to that of Alejandro Alvarez and Raúl Alvarez on the need to confront an unfavorable international conjuncture with political will and mobilization of popular forces (as his father did in the 1930s under quite different circumstances), but without the corporatism that characterized the mass movements of the past. Cárdenas presents his views on these questions in an interesting interview by René Villanueva, "Los ochenta-los noventa: los cambios se harán por respaldo popular," in *Zurda* (Puebla, Mexico), No. 9 (1991), pp. 47-54.

For many Cuban intellectuals, national politics also mediate their views on the realities of globalization, though in this case it is the century-old politics of anti-imperialist nationalism. While there is widespread acceptance of the need to reinsert Cuba into the world-economy, there is relatively little openness to the idea of subordinated reintegration with a U.S.-dominated regional economy. This partly reflects the reality of ongoing U.S.-Cuba hostility, but it is also indicative of many Cubans' deep pride in having broken dependence on the United States. Rather than seeing a future integration of Cuba into a North American trading bloc, many Cuban revolutionaries are more concerned about what they perceive as U.S. designs to "recolonize" Cuba, particularly given the political and economic clout of the anti-Castro Cubans in Miami. Julio Díaz Vásquez, a reform-minded Cuban economist with liberal tendencies, thinks Cuba's economic reintegration into the world market is greatly complicated by politics, the historical differences between Cuba and the United States.

> There are long-time contradictions between Cuba's existence as a nation and its relationship with the United States. This is further aggravated today by the existence of the Cuban American community, which now has relationships with the U.S. establishment. This has led to a new project of recolonization.[51]

A rare exception to the Cuban position that age-old political conflicts stand firmly in the way of future economic ties with the United States was the comment of a one-time member of the prerevolutionary Communist Party (PSP), who is now a sympathizer of the "Democratic Socialist" opposition group:

> The logic of the current geopolitical/economic situation is that Cuba become the fourth piece of NAFTA. Cuba has to be prepared to soften its anti-imperialist stand somewhat in order to allow the Clinton administration to ease up. Cuba's eventual integration into a North American economic bloc is almost *inevitable*.[52]

---

51. Julio A. Díaz Vásquez, interview with author, Havana, March 12, 1993.

52. Respondent who requested anonymity, interview with author, Havana, February 11, 1993 (my emphasis). Such comments, suggesting any possible subordination to the U.S., are part of the fine and very sensitive lines that separate "dissidents" who are deemed hostile to the revolution, despite their commitment to socialism, from "revolutionaries," who often have even greater differences among themselves over other issues regarding Cuba's future direction. Nonetheless, given the rapid liberalization of views on other economic issues, as we saw in previous chapters, I imagine many Cuban officials

Positions on whether politics can or should be imposed upon what some consider to be inevitable economic processes are markers distinguishing renovators from liberals and orthodox leftists. As seein in the previous chapters, liberals on the left are somewhat more inclined to accept as unchallengeable the supposed "laws" of world capitalism, while orthodox thinkers remain more convinced of the need to struggle for socialism here and now, citing its superiority and "inevitable" eventual triumph over capitalism. Renovators insist on the importance of political and ethical goals, but attempt to adjust their strategy and vision to the new global realities, and tend to view nothing as inevitable. Such differences can also be found on the question of national sovereignty, but to a far less significant degree. With few exceptions, most left intellectuals interviewed still uphold the notion of national sovereignty, despite the advances of economic globalization. The following chapter examines their efforts to reformulate the concept in terms viable in today's world.[53]

---

would also quickly change their ideas about the possibility of joining NAFTA were relations with the United States normalized.

53. In assessing the situation of the world and the nation thirty years after the formation of Mexico's National Liberation Movement, long-time left scholar Alonso Aguilar Monteverde concluded that the struggle for national liberation was more imperative than ever, but under very different, and generally worse, conditions, requiring different forms of struggle. This is a perspective shared by most of the intellectuals interviewed. See A. Aguilar Monteverde, "La lucha por nuestra liberación, treinta años después," *Estrategia*, No. 100 (July-August, 1991), pp. 38-41.

CHAPTER 8. NATIONAL SOVEREIGNTY II

Toward a Relative Autonomy of the Nation-State

In an increasingly globalized, capitalist world-system, absent the once powerful state socialist bloc, do intellectuals of the Mexican left and the Cuban revolution offer any alternatives to the traditional pillars of national sovereignty: political independence and autonomous economic development? There is emerging among these intellectuals a more pragmatic but nonetheless firm defense of a *relative* national autonomy mediated by a variety of forces. Alone and isolated after more than twenty years of economic integration into the socialist bloc, Cuban intellectuals now strongly reject autarky, or even de-linking a la Samir Amin, as a viable option:

> Autonomy is not autarky. Autonomy means a nation's ability to choose the most useful and appropriate relations, to not accept economic relations that would reestablish capitalist relations of exploitation within Cuba.[1]

> We can't think in the extreme terms of the past about absolute autonomy. Reality confirms this. For example, Cuba has to rely on foreign companies to look for oil. But this doesn't mean that the country has to be subordinated to transnational corporations, because the revolution would no longer be possible in that case.[2]

> Independent national development is possible, but not an autarkic economy, which is not possible in the Caribbean. What is possible for Cuba is to achieve a certain level of broad reproduction on the basis of our own productive forces and resources.[3]

---

1. Sergio Baroni (Italian-born, Cuban urban planner), interview with author, Havana, February 26, 1993.

2. Julio Carranza, subdirector of the Centro de Estudios Sobre América (CEA), interview with author, Havana, February 18, 1993.

3. Miguel Limia, Soviet-educated Cuban philosopher, interview with author, Havana, February 19, 1993.

After several decades of ongoing, and recently accelerated, economic integration with the United States, Mexican respondents increasingly emphasize that national sovereignty and economic autonomy have to be reconceived within the realities of globalization:

> Autonomous national development is much more complicated now, and especially with NAFTA, the level of integration will be very advanced. National enterprises and markets are very trans-nationalized. Any national project will have to take internationalization into account.[4]

> The dangers today are global: the environment, poverty, unemployment, mobility of capital. These are problems throughout the world. But we can't deny that the concepts of nation, region, territoriality, group rights still exist. So we should be concerned with how to harmonize these two things, which the neoliberal model cannot do.[5]

> The levels of inequality, disparity that exist are too great to think that we're at the stage where we should consider dismantling nations and thinking about ourselves simply as one planet. The differences between nations have become greater; there is polarization rather than homogenization. There's enormous opulence, and yet there's a Third World even within the United States. In Mexico, the level of social stratification is brutal, barbaric. But that doesn't mean we should pursue autarky; that clearly hasn't worked.[6]

As the economic crises and threats to national sovereignty in both nations became increasingly apparent in the early 1990s, there was a renewed sense of urgency to find viable strategies and abandon hollow rhetoric. Novelist Carlos Fuentes captured the sentiments shared by many Mexicans and Cubans:

> A beautiful country, of magnificent people and uninterrupted culture, could slip between our fingers. We must recover the fatherland. The epoch of illusions, grandiloquence, and arrogant pride is over. Now is the time for work, modesty, and collective alka-seltzer.[7]

---

4. Enrique de la Garza Toledo, Maoist-influenced sociologist, interview with author, Mexico City, August 10, 1993.

5. Ifigenia Martínez, PRD leader and economist, interview with author, Mexico City, August 27, 1992.

6. Pablo Gómez, former Communist, PRD leader, interview with author, Mexico City, August 19, 1992.

7. Carlos Fuentes, "La hora del alka-seltzer," *La Jornada*, January 29, 1995.

The emerging consensus among Cuban and Mexican intellectuals of the left seems to be that, in the words of Cuban sociologist Niurka Pérez, *"relative* autonomy has always been the only option."[8] But what does that mean? For Nuria Fernández, a leading figure in the PRD, there is a theoretical as well as practical question, which is to understand "the relative autonomy of a nation, not just of a state," particularly in today's globalized economy. "We need a theory of the relative autonomy of a nation vis a vis the external sector, whereas traditionally the notion of relative autonomy has been defined only in terms of the state's relation to particular classes."[9] Cuban social scientist Juan Valdés Paz shares these concerns:

> Is relative autonomy possible? The world-economy globalizes and segments at the same time, and the Third World has to defend itself against both tendencies. Integration can happen in an autonomous manner or in a subordinated manner. But the left has no idea what autonomous integration might be; the left has never considered it a possibility.[10]

Indeed, there is no fully formulated conception of what relative autonomous national development might be under new world conditions, but respondents in both countries offered a variety of ideas about how such relative autonomy might be mediated.

1. The State. Despite evident erosion of the state's control over internationalized economic processes, most of those interviewed still place great importance on the state as a counterweight to transnational capital. The severity of the financial crises facing both countries has made reliance on foreign capital seem necessary. However, most Mexican and Cuban leftists still view foreign capital with great suspicion, more a necessary evil than the savior portrayed in neoliberal discourse. Cristina Laurell, editor of the PRD's journal *Coyuntura*, expressed concerns shared by many in the Mexican left when she told me:

> Much more relevant to Mexico than the collapse of socialism is the fact that big capital, transnational and national, has more power, more control in Mexico than ever. Since [President Miguel] de la Madrid, the state's partial control over certain strategic sectors of the economy has been completely eliminated through privatization, and big capital now completely controls the economy. How is that sector going to respond

---

8. Niurka Pérez, interview with author, Havana, March 1, 1993.
9. Nuria Fernández, interview with author, Mexico City, August 5, 1993.
10. Juan Valdés Paz, interview with author, Havana, February 25, 1993.

to a Cuauhtémoc Cárdenas government? We can't assume that it will continue to invest. Will it boycott? If so, we're screwed.[11]

Pablo Gómez, a former Communist now in the national leadership of the PRD, acknowledges that Mexico has to attract foreign capital, but insists that it must do so carefully and with state controls.[12] But is state regulation of the economy still possible? As noted earlier, Alejandro Alvarez insists that, contrary to neoliberal ideology, "The state's capacity for economic regulation remains more or less, relatively intact."[13] It is a question of having the political will and forces to take on the powers of transnational capital and the U.S. government.

Cuban revolutionaries seem even more resigned than their Mexican counterparts to the necessity of attracting foreign capital, given the near-total collapse of their economy following the breakup of the Soviet bloc.[14] Julio Carranza, a social scientist raised and educated under the revolutionary regime, is frank in this regard: "Cuba has had to seek foreign capital, because we don't have the necessary capital, markets, and technology. Foreign capital is principally interested in making a profit, so Cuba has to offer a profitable operation."[15] However, because the Cuban state retains firm control over most enterprises, Cubans expressed less concern than their Mexican counterparts about ceding strategic control to foreign capital. A reform-oriented urban planner, Sergio Baroni, for example, argues that foreign capital's threat to Cuban auton-omy is "moderated because Cuba retains control over the enterprises." As a result, "it is possible to preserve autonomy over the setting of pri-orities and strategic decision-making, while developing external rela-tions."[16]

Discussion of the possible role of the state as a mediator of national autonomy is given added complexity when the question of democracy is introduced. For many leftists in Mexico, where an authoritarian state is seen as failing to defend national autonomy, the future role of the state is dependent on the outcome of ongoing struggles for democratization. Indeed, for many Mexicans, national sovereignty is, as Pablo González

11. Author interview with Cristina Laurell, Mexico City, August 6, 1992.

12. Pablo Gómez, interview with author, Mexico City, August 19, 1992.

13. Alejandro Alvarez, presentation given to the Seminario Permanente de Estudios Chicanos y de Fronteras, Instituto Nacional de Antropología e Historia, SEP, Mexico City, August 5, 1993.

14. On the increasing reliance on foreign capital and other "marketlike reforms," see Susan Eva Eckstein, *Back From the Future: Cuba Under Castro* (Princeton, N.J.: Princeton University Press, 1994), especially chapter 4.

15. Julio Carranza, interview with author, Havana, February 18, 1993.

16. Sergio Baroni, interview with author, Havana, February 26, 1993.

Casanova insists, inconceivable without a full democratization based on the participation of the popular classes.[17] Typical of this view is the comment made by a Mexican leftist during a discussion about the left's traditional statism: "What force other than the state can confront the power of transnational corporations and monopolies? But it must be a democratic state, not a state like the one we have now."[18] For the Mexican left, which is a growing but still vulnerable opposition force, democratization also implies increasing its influence over state policies and therefore strengthening efforts to defend national sovereignty.

In Cuba, on the other hand, where the left has been in power for nearly forty years, the severity of the current crisis and recent experiences in the former socialist bloc make democratization and its potential destabilizing effects more problematic. As discussed in earlier chapters, broad national discussion about issues of democracy and decentralization in Cuba began following the March 1990 Call to the Cuban Communist Party's Fourth Congress,[19] but the discussion was quickly silenced as the Soviet Union began to self-destruct. As one Cuban political analyst told me, the "Call gave great impulse to such discussions," but with the disintegration of the USSR, "preservation of the state and of political power became the overriding question" in Cuba.[20] Nevertheless, as we also saw in earlier chapters, there are some influential Cubans who insist that democratization of the Cuban state is a precondition for saving the nation.

It has become almost commonplace, including among many left intellectuals in the United States and Europe, to argue that the significance of nation-states will disappear because they no longer play an important economic role. For Latin American leftists, acutely aware of the historical role played by the state in promoting economic development and of the current role played by activist governments in selling off strategic state enterprises at bargain-basement prices, such notions are far less credible. Mexican scholar and left activist Gilberto López y Rivas says that it is the nation-states controlled by sectors of the financial oligarchy, tied to transnational capital, that are at risk of deterioration, because they have condemned the majority of their citizens to misery and margi-

---

17. Comment made by Pablo González Casanova in response to my lecture on "National Sovereignty in Today's World," at the Centro de Investigaciones Interdisciplinarias en Humanidades, Mexico City, February 2, 1995.

18. Comment made from the audience at a conference on the Left and popular movements in Mexico City, September 4, 1992.

19. For key documents and analysis of the Fourth Party Congress, see Gail Reed, *Island in the Storm* (Melbourne: Ocean Press, 1992).

20. Juan Valdés Paz, interview with author, Havana, February 25, 1993.

nalization. These ruling sectors, he argues, have become antinational forces and therefore risk being displaced by popular, democratic, anticapitalist movements, which would further national development beyond the limits of what has been done in states under the hegemony of the bourgeoisie or the bureaucratic classes of "real socialism." López y Rivas warns that those who predict the rapid demise of the nation-state and of the state's economic role in the face of globalization are seriously underestimating the powerful resurgence in Latin America of a nationalism of resistance, survival and defense of the nation.[21]

2. *Latin American Integration.* In addition to a strong state, a commonly-cited source of sustenance for national autonomy is Latin American regional integration.[22] In Mexican activist Nuria Fernández's view:

> Any relationship with the U.S. has to be mediated first by Latin American integration in order to strengthen the position of Mexico vis a vis the United States. Any project to spur autonomous national development is about *how* to integrate regionally, not about whether to. If Mexico is still going to be a nation in the year 2000, it has to find a new form of association among relatively autonomous nations, along the lines of Gorbachev's proposal for a Confederation of Independent States.[23]

Several others in Mexico echoed her concerns, including Pablo Gómez:

> We have to have a policy of pursuing a union with countries similar to Mexico, which have a certain level of industrialization, which have to figure out how to join the postindustrial world, and which *can* do it. A country of a half-million people can't do it alone, but a country of 80-100 million, like Brazil, can. I ask myself, what would be the results of a full, open economic collaboration between Brazil and Mexico? There could be an immense complementary relationship between Brazil and Mexico.[24]

---

21. Gilberto López y Rivas, "Nación y neoliberalismo," *Memoria* (Mexico), December 1993, pp. 57-58.

22. For an excellent overview of the history of attempts at Latin American integration and its currency in the region today, see Ruy Mauro Marini, "The Paths of Latin American Integration," in S. Jonas and E. McCaughan, *Latin America Faces the Twenty-First Century,* op. cit.. For Cuauhtémoc Cárdenas's views on the need for Latin American integration in the face of U.S.-led neoliberal restructuring, see C. Cárdenas, "Por la unidad latinoamericana," *Coyuntura* (Mexico City), July 1991, pp. 3-7.

23. Nuria Fernández, interview with author, Mexico City, August 5, 1993.

24. Pablo Gómez, interview with author, Mexico City, August 19, 1992.

Raúl Alvarez Garín thinks the conditions for Latin American integration have improved since the 1960s and that the proposals themselves have matured. Alvarez commented, "the Latin American market offers interesting possibilities today, for example, to trade in the debt, to exchange devalued debt on the secondary market."[25] Jorge Castañeda summarized the arguments in favor of Latin American economic integration as follows:

> [It] represents an intermediate solution between a largely unsustainable status quo and a highly harmful progression toward the dissolution of sovereignties and economic and social options for developing nations. . . . Regional integration broadens markets, provides economies of scale, enhances regional autonomy, and concentrates trade and investment among equals, diverting it from other, far more economically powerful partners.[26]

Many Cubans also view Latin American economic integration as a potentially important alternative. Fidel Castro has even called it the only hope for an independent future.[27] However, several of the Cuban intellectuals interviewed for this book were skeptical about conditions for such integration any time soon. Ramiro Abreú, an official in the Cuban Communist Party Central Committee's international relations department, said, "Realistically, we can't expect in the near future any other exchange relationship like we had with the USSR. The best hope is Latin American integration, which is still a distant prospect."[28] Another Cuban social scientist acknowledged that "the tendency of the continent is to talk about Latin American integration," but warned that "the practical steps are not yet in sync."[29] A prominent Cuban historian agrees that regional *"concertación"* would be a positive development for the island, but feels steps in that direction depend more on the rest of Latin America than on Cuba.[30] Other Cubans were more explicit about the obstacles to

---

25. Raúl Alvarez Garín, interview with author, Mexico City, August 27, 1992.

26. Jorge Castañeda, *Utopia Unarmed. The Latin American Left After the Cold War* (New York: Alfred A. Knopf, 1993), pp. 313-314.

27. Fidel Castro in Tomás Borge, *Un Grano de Maíz. Conversación con Fidel Castro* (Mexico: Fondo de Cultura Económica, 1992), p. 156.

28. Ramiro Abreú, interview with author, Havana, March 8, 1993.

29. José Bell Lara, interview with author, Havana, March 1, 1993.

30. Jorge Ibarra, interview with author, Havana, February 21, 1993. There is no exact English equivalent of *concertación*, a term widely used in Latin American in recent years to refer to coordination or harmonization of interests or policies. At the March 1994 meeting of the Latin American Studies Association

Latin American integration. Social-pyschologist Beatriz Díaz, for example, cited U.S. economic influence as the main problem, pointing to Latin America's failure to create a debtors' cartel in the face of U.S. pressure.[31]

Julio Carranza identifies five factors limiting Cuba's ability to increase economic relations with the hemisphere: (1) Cuba's trade with Latin America declined significantly after the 1950s; (2) Cuba's economy, still mainly characterized by primary goods exports, is not generally complementary to the regional Latin American economy; (3) in those areas where the Cuban economy is complementary, e.g., biotechnology, pharmaceuticals, and medical equipment, it has to compete with transnational corporations that already dominate those markets; (4) Cuba has a debt with the most important Latin American nations; and (5) the U.S. trade embargo particularly affects Latin American businesses and governments, who are more vulnerable to U.S. pressures than are their European counterparts.[32] Carranza also places much of the blame for the difficulties facing regional integration squarely on the shoulders of Latin American elites:

> The Latin American ruling classes have demonstrated their inability to defend national interests. Look at their acceptance of neoliberalism, their acceptance of U.S. hegemony, their attempts to operate in a world market subordinated to the United States. Integration schemes like MERCOSUR aren't efforts at autonomous development, but simply attempts to get better treatment from the United States in a subordinated relationship. Argentina under Menem is the clearest case. If the forces that govern Latin America were to change, then prospects would be different. But Latin America is very weak and dispersed and not theoretically or practically prepared.[33]

---

in Atlanta, Cuban scholar Juan Valdés Paz spoke about the process of *concertación política* taking place in Latin America, which has excluded the United States, forcing it deal increasingly with multilateral actors around a variety of issues. He also noted that, thus far, Cuba has been absent from such efforts.

31. Beatriz Díaz, interview with author, Havana, March 5, 1993.

32. Julio Carranza, presentation at the Latin American Studies Association meeting in Atlanta, March 11, 1994.

33. Julio Carranza, interview with author, Havana, February 18, 1993. Regarding his assessment of MERCOSUR, there is considerable debate among leftists in the Southern Cone about whether it represents subordination or a challenge to the U.S. Other Cubans are equally skeptical about the prospects of progressive forces coming to power and/or substantially changing conditions in the region. Ramiro Abreú thinks the Latin American Left is in very serious crisis, with the possible exception of the Brazilian Workers Party (PT) and the

Alejandro Alvarez is dubious about the importance of Latin American economic integration for Mexico because, he argues, the preponderance of Mexico's relations are with North America.[34] This fact does not lead him to accept NAFTA, however, because he views that trade agreement as designed to further four geopolitical goals of U.S.-based transnational capital: (1) continue to weaken trade unionism and social opposition to economic restructuring in the United States; (2) weaken the trade unions in Canada and open up areas of the Canadian economy that remain protected; (3) lock-in the IMF-imposed restructuring in Mexico; and (4) use NAFTA for negotiating a better GATT agreement.[35]

How NAFTA may affect prospects for Latin American integration concerns some Cubans as well. Economist Hector Herrera notes that Mexico and Canada are two of Cuba's most important trading partners. He particularly wonders how NAFTA may affect Cuba's exports to Mexico: will it make Cuban products less competitive? Will Mexico be more vulnerable to U.S. pressures to enforce the trade embargo? On the other hand, reasons Herrera, should NAFTA contribute to a more dynamic Mexican economy, it could increase demand for Cuban products.[36] Still, despite such concerns, most leftists interviewed place great importance on Latin American economic integration, rather than further integration with the United States, as a key means of reinforcing relative national autonomy.

3. Transnational Social Alliances. In addition to Latin American integration, and instead of NAFTA, Alejandro Alvarez says the Mexican left has to "pursue alliances with social sectors in the United States and Canada that oppose the current model because they are excluded from it."[37]

Mexican PRD, "which have serious problems but good electoral prospects as fronts" (interview with author, Havana, March 8, 1993). Juan Antonio Blanco fears that even a political party like the PT runs the risk of simply managing the crisis for the bourgeoisie if they are elected to government (interview with author, Havana, February 9, 1993).

34. Comments made by Alejandro Alvarez during a seminar discussion at the Instituto Nacional de Antropología e Historia, SEP, Mexico City, August 5, 1993.

35. Comments made by Alejandro Alvarez to the Chicano/Latino Research Center, University of California, Santa Cruz, September 27, 1993.

36. Hector Herrera, presentation at the Latin American Studies Association meeting, Atlanta, March 11, 1994. It is interesting to note that Herrera is a researcher at CIEM (Center for Research on the World Economy), an institute that has provided the Cuban government with its current reform-minded minister of the economy and a prominent member of the National Assembly.

37. Alejandro Alvarez comments at Instituto Nacional de Antropología e Historia, op cit.

In other words, Alvarez believes that defense of Mexico's possibility for autonomous economic development rests to a large extent on political struggle by non-state actors, defined not so much in terms of a particular class protagonist but in terms of a broad alliance against a clear class antagonist, U.S.-based transnational capital. Is this simply a throw-back to 1940s-style nationalist populism, as critics like Rolando Cordera maintain? In its broad, cross-class appeal, perhaps. The new element, however, is the insistence by Alvarez and others that today's "united front" must be cross-border, bringing together all social sectors in the region that are being hurt by neoliberal restructuring.

The globalization of economic processes, they argue, makes such alliances more possible as well as more necessary. U.S. labor unions, for example, fought hard against the passage of NAFTA, which was also opposed by dissident (i.e., anti-PRI) labor organizations in Mexico. In recent years, with greater cross-border dissemination of books, music, and film, Mexican intellectuals have demonstrated increasing appreciation for Chicano cultural expressions, once derided by Mexican elites as mongrel. The 1994 battle against California's anti-immigrant Proposition 187 also forged broad cross-border alliances.

Arguably, pursuing such alliances is easier for the Mexican left, which has ready access to the United States, than it is for Cubans, given U.S.-Cuban hostilities. On the other hand, public sympathy for the Cuban revolution still runs deep throughout Latin America, where wildly enthusiastic crowds greet Fidel Castro on his state visits. Even in the United States, grassroots efforts to defy government policy and send humanitarian aid to Cuba have been impressive in recent years, and there are growing numbers of U.S. businesses eager to get a foothold in Cuba's opening economy.[38]

In both Cuba and Mexico, U.S. groups like Pastors for Peace (not the traditional, anti-imperialist, North American leftists) have played an increasingly visible role in challenging the U.S. embargo against Cuba and calling for peace in Chiapas. Important figures from U.S. cultural circles have begun to show more interest in Cuba and Mexico, as well. Robert Redford reportedly lobbied hard for a 1994 Academy Award nomination for the Cuban film *Fresa y Chocolate (Strawberry and Chocolate)*. Celebrities as diverse as linguist/writer Noam Chomsky, novelist Toni Morrison, and actor Edward James Olmos have visited Mexico, expressing concerns on a range of issues from Chiapas to the new U.S.

---

38. See the cover story on Cuba in the February 20, 1995 issue of *Time*, which notes, "It is a testament to the size of the prize that, despite the risks, an increasing number of Americans are sneaking into Havana with the hope of working out arrangement under the table."

credit package. The transnational social alliances imagined by Alvarez remain embryonic, but it is not unreasonable to imagine their growth in the future, as the unequal effects of globalization cut a vertical breach crossing national frontiers.

4. Scientific-Technical Capacity and Cutting-Edge Industries. In world-systems analysis, one of the important elements distinguishing core from periphery has been the former's domination of leading industrial technologies. Likewise, a defining feature of semiperipheral nations has been their ability to incorporate the industrial technologies that helped define the core in earlier historical periods. Thus, for example, production of steel and autos, once restricted to nations like the United States and Germany, became key components of industrialization in nations like Mexico, Brazil, and South Korea. Given the technological breakthroughs of the past decade, it comes as no surprise that respondents in Mexico and Cuba cite national scientific-technical capabilities and high-tech industries as essential to securing relative economic autonomy in today's world.

Cuba's José Bell Lara, for example, believes that one of his country's advantages relative to the rest of Latin America is its highly regarded scientific institutions and biotechnology industry:

> You have to define the notion of autonomous national develop-
> ment in relation to particular realities and conjunctures. It won't be the
> same for each country. Cuba today is not the Cuba of the 1960s. Today
> we have an industrial structure, with some technological problems be-
> cause of the Soviet model but also with some real possibilities. We have
> excellent education, scientific-technical development, a very highly
> skilled work force. Cuba is very much incorporated into the knowledge
> revolution. We have cutting-edge industrial sectors, such as biotech-
> nology and pharmaceuticals. The question is how to use these to
> achieve autonomous national development. We're walking on two
> legs, one developed and one underdeveloped.[39]

Several other Cubans likewise stressed the importance of Cuba continuing to develop its own technological capabilities, while others additionally emphasized the need to develop food and energy self-sufficiency, if the island is to maintain any degree of autonomy.

Some Mexican leftists gave similar attention to developing their country's technological capacity. Raúl Alvarez Garín, an engineer, suggested France as a possible role model for Mexico in this regard.

---

39. José Bell Lara, interview with author, Havana, March 1, 1993.

> I have the impression that the French model of strategic planning has very great virtues. You don't have the possibility of competing successfully in all sectors of production simultaneously; this is a world run by monopolies which control technology. But you may have the option to develop some leading industries and compete even with the monopolies. France had to reorganize education, develop nuclear energy, the air bus, and all the projects which have kept it partially competitive. I think this model makes certain sense in Mexico. We'd clearly have to prioritize areas where you could have an important presence. One area, of course, is oil, where you can develop a whole range of products that allow you a place in the world market in areas not yet developed. Obviously this requires investment, including investment to develop educational and technical capacities. But it can be done, it just requires making some decisions.[40]

Pablo Gómez made a similar point:

> What is it we don't have? The software, which is the property of a small number of companies in the world. The new revolution of world production depends on them. How do we join the new world without the software? Well, first there is some software that we *can* produce. We need to develop a group of the highest level scientists here in Mexico, which is a task of twenty years. Produce them and root them in Mexico, tied to production units able to compete worldwide. The state should promote this, not direct it, because it would direct it poorly. But there is no national capital to invest in this. National capitalists laugh at the idea of developing their own software, because they say all you have to do is buy it from the Americans, the Europeans, or the Japanese.[41]

Gómez says the main obstacle to developing Mexico's technological capacity is lack of democracy, because "in Mexico, society can't resolve problems; any problems that aren't resolved by the president aren't resolved by anyone." Like Alvarez, he points to France, "a society with a capacity for resolving its own problems."[42]

---

40. Raúl Alvarez Garín, interview with author, Mexico City, August 27, 1992. The validity of such an analogy between Mexico and France may seem questionable at first glance. However, they are countries of comparable population and natural resources. The French state has used strategic planning to defend its core status and avoid slippage into the semiperiphery. Alvarez is suggesting the Mexican state can employ similar strategies to further secure Mexico's place in the semiperiphery and perhaps edge it closer to core status.

41. Pablo Gómez, interview with author, Mexico City, August 19, 1992.

42. Ibid. Along similar lines, several Mexicans interviewed suggested that the Soviet Union's undemocratic system stifled scientific creativity and thus

5. National Culture. Finally, many intellectuals look to the strong national cultures of Mexico and Cuba to defend the nation's relative autonomy in a globalized world. Américo Saldívar, a former Central Committee member of Mexico's defunct Communist Party, remains a staunch defender of *lo nacional*, despite the fact that his perspectives on economic processes have been considerably "neoliberalized" in recent years. He explained:

> Economic nationalism is an anachronism, it's not viable. But in terms of politics, culture, and discourse, nationalism and autonomy are relevant. But the left is still very confused by, one, the internationalization of capital, and, two, the need for reasserting *lo nacional* in terms of culture and traditions.[43]

In a world-system in which nation-states progressively cede control over economic and even political processes to transnational actors, contestation of what constitutes and who genuinely represents *lo nacional* takes place increasingly within the cultural and ideological realm.[44] As Arturo Escobar has written:

> It is essential to recognize the importance of economic factors and their structural determinants. But just as crucial as the reconstruction of economies—and indelibly linked to it—is the reconstitution of meanings at all levels, from everyday life to national development.[45]

The Cuban Revolution's renewed emphasis on the legacy of national independence hero José Martí and the Mexican left's reclaiming of the

---

prevented that nation from keeping pace with the technological revolution that swept through the advanced capitalist nations. Such an explicit linkage between political democracy and technological creativity is made less frequently in Cuba, where the question of democracy remains sensitive and where Cuba's own technological advances may suggest such linkage is less clear cut.

43. Américo Saldívar, interview with author, Mexico City, August 4, 1993.

44. Two interesting examples of this were discussed in papers presented by Andréa Zhouri and Olga Celle de Bowman at the March 1994 Latin American Studies Associations meetings. Zhouri, writing on environmentalism in Brazil, and Celle, writing about the changing meaning of "cholo" in Peru, both described how meaning, signification, and national identity are being contested and reconstructed in two very different national contexts which have been radically affected by processes of globalization.

45. Arturo Escobar, "Culture, Economics, and Politics in Latin American Social Movements Theory and Research," in Arturo Escobar and Sonia E. Alvarez, eds., *The Making of Social Movements in Latin America. Identity, Strategy, and Democracy* (Boulder: Westview Press, 1992), p. 69.

banners of peasant revolutionary Emiliano Zapata and nationalist hero Lázaro Cárdenas are symbolic of the struggle to define and defend the meaning of *lo nacional*. One of the clearest examples of the cultural wars being waged over the meaning of the nation today was the conflict surrounding the Carlos Salinas administration's attempts to impose a new, official Mexican history text book for the public schools, in which the country's traditional nationalism was largely exorcised.[46]

Mexican historian Enrique Florescano noted recently that scholars are giving ever greater attention to the importance of cultural phenomena such as collective identities, national myths and heroes, and the construction of a nation's collective, historic memory. He sees no reason to believe that "globalization" will dilute the processes of constructing national identities and memories; it will simply occasion the creation of new self-affirming myths:

> Groups, nations, and states are going to continue cultivating, defending, feeding their myths of origin and their myths of identity. And more so when they feel pressured from the outside. Mexico demonstrates this. Since 1821, when it became an independent republic, it has had to face one of the world's most powerful nations. And instead of adapting to the myths of the dominant nation, Mexico always created more, new myths to differentiate itself from the neighboring country, from the great power. Today, many new, totally different myths are emerging along the border to differentiate itself from the U.S.[47]

Florescano cites the new Zapatista movement as one that draws upon historical myths but "with a proposal for the future, not to go back."[48] Along similar lines, activist poet Víctor de la Cruz argues that the insistence of the Worker-Peasant-Student Coalition of the Isthmus (COCEI) on speaking Zapotec and recovering communal lands is not about "a return to the past, but a more equitable route to the future."[49] In Cuba, writer Cintio Vitier looks to the legendary figure of José Martí, not

---

46. See Enrique Maza, "En los libros de texto se resalta lo que quiere para justificar el proyecto salinista," *Proceso* (Mexico), September 7, 1992.

47. Enrique Florescano, interview with Arturo García Hernández, in *La Jornada* (Mexico), March 9, 1995.

48. Ibid.

49. Víctor de la Cruz, "Brothers of Citizens: Two Languages, Two Poltical Prjects in the Isthmus," in Howard Campbell, et al. (eds.), *Zapotec Struggles: Histories, Politics, and Representations from Juchitán, Oaxaca* (Washington, D.C.: Smithsonian Institution Press, 1993), p. 246.

with expectations of turning back the national clock but for key markers of Cuba's national identity in facing the challenges of the 1990s.[50]

In light of the accelerated process of North American economic integration, Raúl Alvarez Garín ended one of our conversations by asking, "Is Mexico going to survive as a nation? And in what conditions? Are we going to end up like Puerto Rico: '*qué bonita bandera, qué bonita bandera*' [what a beautiful flag]?"[51] On the one hand, Mexico's deeply-rooted sense of national identity offers him some solace. It is true that Mexican cities receive cable television channels dedicated to broadcasting U.S. sports events and Hollywood movies, a fact which some cite as evidence of the so-called homogenization of global culture. But, Alvarez Garín shares Carlos Monsiváis's belief that national identity will endure. Nationalism, Monsiváis has argued, is the only language of internal communication for Mexican society; it is simply becoming a bilingual nationalism, reflecting the hybrid culture produced by the encounter between national culture and the U.S. cultural industry in the process of globalization.[52]

In spite of the penetration by U.S. consumer culture, there remains a strong, cohesive, distinctly Mexican culture, with many communitarian or collectivist values, even in an urban jungle like Mexico City, one of the world's fastest-growing megacities. Illustrative in this regard were the grassroots "self-help" initiatives and urban movements that flourished following the tragic 1985 Mexico City earthquake.[53] Those efforts, as well as the emergence of new urban leaders like the cartoon hero-inspired Super Barrio, are evidence of the sense of community, belonging, and

---

50. Cintio Vitier, "Martí y el desafío de los noventa," *La Gaceta* (Havana), September-October 1992.

51. Raúl Alvarez Garín, interview with author, Mexico City, August 27, 1992.

52. Carlos Monsiváis, interview with Marta Elena Montoya Vélez, in *La Jornada Semanal* (Mexico), September 13, 1992. On the issue of "hybrid" or "translated" national cultures in the era of globalization, see Nestor García Canclini, "Cultural Reconversion," in G. Yudice, et al., *On Edge* (University of Minnesota, 1992); and Stuart Hall, "The Question of National Identity," in S. Hall, et al., *Modernity and Its Futures* (Cambridge: Polity Press, 1992).

53. On the impressive array of contemporary urban movements in Mexico, including those that emerged around the 1985 earthquake, see Carlos Monsiváis, *Entrada Libre. Crónicas de la sociedad que se organiza* (Mexico: Ediciones ERA, 1987); and Vivienne Bennett, "The Evolution of Urban Popular Movements in Mexico Between 1968 and 1988," in Arturo Escobar and Sonia E. Alvarez (eds.), *The Making of Social Movements in Latin America*, op. cit.

citizenship among the urban popular classes in Mexico City, cultural factors often absent in urban metropolises of the late twentieth century.[54]

On the other hand, Alvarez Garín fears that the level of social disintegration caused by the past decade of crisis and restructuring could lead to a "worst case scenario in which Mexico devolves into another Yugoslavia, with regions fighting one another. Already workers are armed, campesinos carry machetes, demanding responses to their unbelievably miserable conditions."[55] Tellingly, the Zapatista guerrilla war begun on January 1, 1994, by Indians in Mexico's southern state of Chiapas both underscores his concerns about regional conflict and illustrates the cultural vitality of Mexico's revolutionary past as it accommodates to today's realities by using Zapata's image to press demands for democratic national elections. Monsiváis, a long-time chronicler of Mexico City's urban popular culture, agrees that the Mexican revolution profoundly transformed the national mind, and he has tremendous admiration for the vitality of Mexico's popular culture. However, he also believes that, after sixty years of corrupt and authoritarian rule by the PRI, it will take an entire generation to build a new *political* culture. For the moment, he fears that even the social movements, which he views as the great sources of resistance to neoliberalism, are concerned primarily with survival, not with transformation.[56]

Nevertheless, Alejandro Alvarez is confident that the strength and depth of Mexican culture, its nationalism, sense of identity and pride, sense of community, and social justice values, remain largely in tact. He considers them to be a very important integrating factor that gives historical cohesion to the left's project and makes Mexicans less susceptible to neoliberal discourse and to resignation before the supposedly inevitable forces of "globalization."[57] Surrealist poet Benjamín Peret has made a

---

54. See Robert Kaplan, "The Coming Anarchy," in *The Atlantic Monthly*, February 1994, for a provocative discussion of the role of culture in determining which peoples will survive the "scarcity, crime, overpopulation, tribalism, and disease [that] are rapidly destroying the social fabric of our planet." Kaplan sees the "formidable fabric" of Turkish Muslim culture playing a role somewhat analogous to what I am suggesting about national culture in Mexico, and perhaps to a lesser extent in Cuba.

55. Raúl Alvarez Garín, interview with author, Mexico City, August 6, 1993.

56. Comments by Carlos Monsiváis during a talk on "Intellectuals and the State in Mexico," University of California, Santa Cruz, April 10, 1991.

57. Author conversation with Alejandro Alvarez on a drive up the Northern California coast, September 28, 1993. For an insightful discussion of the endurance of nationalism and national culture in the era of neoliberalism, see Gilberto López y Rivas, "Nación y neoliberalismo," *Memoria* (Mexico City), December 1993. A thoughtful assessment of the Mexican left's attempts to

similar assessment in writing about Mexico's enduring myths and legends, such as that of Pancho Villa. Believing that the reconquest of our ability to imagine is as important as achieving equality and material well-being, Peret has described Mexico as a place where the creative, life-affirming myths of the revolutionary past remain "present in daily life, palpable in the street, the markets, there where the people gather and talk."[58]

Jorge Timosi, an Argentine-born journalist who has lived in Cuba for many years and now serves in a high-level post at the Cuban Ministry of Culture, also stressed national culture as the key to Cuba's national autonomy in the new world order:

> We need to rethink how to construct an authentic nationalism, cleansed of prejudices and old formulas. This needs to be done from a cultural point of view. The GDR [East Germany] was one of the socialist countries that had most resolved its economic problems. But it never thought through the national problem of culture. With the partitioning of the world after World War II, we all took for granted the logic of the Berlin Wall dividing communists and capitalists. But much of the culture remained the same, e.g., language and historical traditions.
>
> Today, economic reconstruction and reinsertion have to *pasar por la cultura nacional* [take place through the national culture]. Along with the economy, culture is the other most important and problematic area affected by world changes. There is no project today that cannot take into account the culture of the country. For Cuba, this is fundamental. Had Cuba fallen into the error of socialist realism, which it didn't because of its strong historical cultural traditions, things would have been infinitely worse. Because Cuba didn't, we now have an opportunity to refind our way on the basis of our culture. So today, autonomous national development depends greatly on reconstructing the national culture.[59]

Cultural Minister Armando Hart points to many intellectual traditions in Cuban culture that were not socialist but contributed to the essential values of equality, social justice, and solidarity that permeate the national culture. He notes that the great Cuban poet José Lezama Lima

---

construct a new nationalism is offered by Cristina Puga, "Un nuevo nacionalismo para México," *Mundo* (Mexico City), July 1991. For the perspective on nationalism of a prominent intellectual who supported Carlos Salinas's "modernization," see Héctor Aguilar Camín, "La invención de México. Notas sobre nacionalismo e identidad nacional," *Nexos* (Mexico City), July 1993.

58. Lourdes Andrade, "Benjamín Peret: Magia, revolución y poesía," in *La Jornada Semanal* (Mexico City), November 13, 1994, pp. 23-26.

59. Jorge Timosi, interview with author, Havana, February 25, 1993.

and other prominent writers associated with the respected literary journal, *Orígenes*, in the 1940s and 1950s, opposed socialism but understood
the "ideological and moral crisis" of prerevolutionary Cuba and were
subsequently incorporated into the revolutionary process.[60] Hart especially looks to the antislavery and anticolonial movements and ideologies
of the nineteenth century as the most important precursors of values in
Cuban culture today. In defending Cuban culture, Hart explains, "we
are defending that which exists as Cuban where the national and the
universal fuse into a single whole. That is what José Martí meant when
he said, 'My country is humanity.'"[61]

The severity of Cuba's current economic crisis will certainly put the
durability of the island's cultural fabric to the test, but Timosi and Hart
are not the only Cubans who believe that national culture is one of
Cuba's great strengths. Art critic Gerardo Mosquera says that, despite
artists' dissatisfaction with the restrictive political climate of the early
1990s, the situation in Cuba is very different from what existed in Eastern
Europe just before the fall of the Berlin Wall: "Cuban culture today is
very critical, but . . . the spirit is quite socialist."[62] The validity of his
claim is demonstrated by the remarkable Cuban film, *Fresa y Chocolate*, a
lovely testament to the resilience of Cuba's national culture in the midst
of crisis.

---

60. Armando Hart Dávalos, "The Traditions Behind a Socialist World
View," *World Marxist Review*, Vol. 33, No. 1, January 1990. In my interview with
Hart (Havana, March 11, 1993), he included himself among those who held
anticommunist views engendered by the Cold War before joining the
revolutionary struggle. Regarding Hart's assessment of Lezama Lima, there is
considerable controversy. In a recent book, *Mea Cuba* (New York: Farrar, Straus,
and Giroux, 1994), exiled Cuban novelist Guillermo Cabrera Infante maintains
that Lezama Lima was essentially suffocated by the Castro regime—never jailed,
given his reputation, but never allowed to leave the country. However, Ciro
Bianchi Ross, a friend of Lezama Lima who has edited a new collection of the
poet's previously unpublished letters, diaries, and other writings (*Como las cartas
no llegan*, Mexico: Editorial ERA, in press), insists that Lezama Lima never
repudiated the revolutionary regime and was never prevented from traveling
abroad by anything other than his own idiosyncrasies. See Alma
Guillermoprieto, "Cuba's Exquisite Martyrs," *The New York Times Book Review*,
November 27, 1994, p 9; and Homero Campa and Orlando Pérez, "Su amigo
Ciro Bianchi enfrenta la mitificación de Lezama Lima," *Proceso* (Mexico City),
October 3, 1994, pp. 60-65.

61. Armando Hart Dávalos, "The Traditions Behind a Socialist World
View," op. cit., p. 24.

62. Gerardo Mosquera, quoted in Jay Murphy, "Report from Havana.
Testing the Limits," *Art in America*, October 1992, p. 69.

Historian and philosopher Juan Antonio Blanco insists that "Cuban society, the nation, and the revolution will not be saved by economic changes but by culture. We have to find an ethical, moral resolution of the crisis."[63] He points to a consistent system of values, an ethical code, rooted in Cuban history and based on notions of social justice, solidarity, and a commitment to "the responsibility of all for all."

While Blanco counts these cultural values as strong assets, he offers no guarantees about the future of the Cuban nation. Historically, Blanco argues, this very set of values has led Cuba time and again into conflict with the United States as the former pursued independence and the latter manifest destiny. Moreover, as the current economic crisis deepens, Blanco foresees a growing conflict between two distinct ethical codes, one representing a project to save the Cuban nation and one a project of individualistic survival increasingly influenced by bourgeois values.[64]

The theme of "ethical crisis" arose repeatedly in my interviews in Cuba. An interesting recent discussion of values and morals in Cuban political culture is offered by Nelson Valdés, who suggests that the most polemical arguments in Cuban history have not been about democracy, power, or markets. Rather, he observes, "The themes of personal duty, political morality, patriotism, and the historic mission of the nation engaged Cubans from all political perspectives."[65] Thus while nationalism and patriotism give cohesion to Cuban society, Valdés warns that moralism and intolerance have often led to polarities and judgments rather than understanding.

Important disagreements emerged in discussing the options available in the globalized economy of the post-Cold war world-system for two nations whose old formulas for defending the nation's sovereignty and securing semiperipheral status no longer appear workable. There is significant debate, for example, in both Cuba and Mexico about the feasibility of Latin American integration. There are substantial differences, particularly among Mexican leftists, about the inevitability or advisability of economic integration with the United States. The Cuban intellec-

---

63. Statements made by Juan Antonio Blanco during a lecture on "The 1960s" at Casa de las Américas, Havana, February 9, 1993.

64. Ibid. For more on Juan Antonio Blanco's view of the ethical crisis, see Blanco "Cuba: Crisis, Ethics, and Viability," op. cit. For a classic analysis of the role of ethics and morality in Cuban history, see Cintio Vitier, *Ese sol del mundo moral. Para una historia de la eticidad cubana* (Mexico: Siglo XXI, 1975).

65. Nelson Valdés, "Cuban Political Culture: Between Betrayal and Death," in S. Halebsky and J. Kirk (eds.), *Cuba in Transition: Crisis and Transformation* (Boulder: Westview, 1992), p. 207.

tuals certainly do not view the relationship between democratization and crisis resolution through the same lens as Mexico's left opposition. Nevertheless, there seemed to be general agreement among all the Cubans and Mexicans interviewed that national sovereignty and autonomous national development remain meaningful concepts. Moreover, there is broad consensus that national sovereignty is not, and cannot be, the equivalent of autarky. Complete de-linking from the capitalist world-economy no longer seems a viable option.

Though it is not yet a fully defined notion, *relative national autonomy* seems to be emerging as successor to a once-imagined full national sovereignty. As summarized above, at least five elements were identified by respondents as key to mediating national autonomy in the new world order: a strong, democratic state acting in the interests of the majority; some form of Latin American regional integration; broad cross-border alliances with social sectors opposed to neoliberal restructuring; development of national scientific-technical capacity and industries in cutting-edge technologies; and finally, reconstitution of national culture in defense of *lo nacional*.

As Jorge Castañeda has observed, "the yawning domestic chasms in Latin American society, and the 'denationalization' of elites, . . . are powerful incentives for the left to retain a nationalism so unfashionable in these times, yet so necessary."[66] He regards crafting a new nationalism in the context of a post-Cold War, post-Marxist world as one of the left's most important challenges. I would suggest that the ideas offered herein by many Cuban and Mexican intellectuals make an important contribution toward that goal.

---

66. Jorge Castañeda, *Utopia Unarmed*, op. cit., p. 304.

CHAPTER 9. CONCLUSIONS

Past Imperfect, Present Tense, Future Conditional

As seen in the previous chapters, the lefts in Cuba and Mexico have experienced a great paradigm crisis, provoked by a chain of world events from the "revolution of 1968" and the new social movements of subsequent years, through the reorganization of the world-economy and the eclipse of liberal reformism by neoliberalism in 1980s, to the dramatic collapse of state socialism. This paradigm crisis undid old political and ideological alignments and produced a new, still unsettled, constellation of left discourse. Three ideal type perspectives among today's left on the questions of democracy and socialism have been identified: liberal, orthodox, and renovative. I have argued throughout this book that these three tendencies are defined largely around the degree to which they adhere to or depart from two world-systemic ideologies that dominated much of the past century: liberalism and socialism (in the statist form it took in practice).

Socialist discourse is clearly on the decline, having lost much of its legitimacy when caught in the cross-fire of an ascendent neoliberalism and a defeated communism. In Mexico, orthodox socialist discourse is found now mainly among a relatively small number of left intellectuals and aging militants. However, the ideals associated with socialism, or perhaps more precisely, with Marx's utopian vision of communism (full social equality among a self-governing "free association of producers") remain an important point of reference for the renovative current in Mexico, which still imagines a humane alternative to capitalism. In Cuba, orthodox socialist ideology remains more firmly entrenched, particularly within the ideological apparatus of the state-party regime, and especially in regards to the political system. Renovative Cuban leftists still view socialism as a necessary and integral aspect of their national society, but they imagine a radically democratized and decentralized socialism. Nonetheless, socialist orthodoxy is in retreat even in Cuba. Severe economic crisis forces the island in the direction of liberal economic reforms, which, ironically, are being undertaken in an effort to preserve the achievements of Cuba's socialist revolution.

Liberal ideology has clearly gained influence among leftists in both nations. Within the Mexican left, there are significant numbers of intellectuals who have adopted the restricted liberal notion of democracy as a representative, electoral, multiparty political system. They consider such democracy to be meaningful in and of itself, regardless of the social inequalities that may persist in their nation. Many intellectuals on the Mexican left also have come to believe in the value of free-market economies and fuller economic integration with the United States. These thinkers represent a liberal political tendency in the sense that Wallerstein has described historic liberalism, as a strategy of constant, rational reform to avoid social conflict and instability through incorporation of larger sectors of the population into the system. The liberal left in Mexico genuinely believes that capitalism can be made more humane, that electoral democracy can be made more meaningful, and, more importantly, that those goals are the best that can be hoped for. However, the liberal current within the Mexican left is far from dominant. There exists a very influential renovative tendency that accepts the liberal left's agenda as necessary *but insufficient* reforms. The renovators do not agree that liberal democracy can be truly meaningful in a socially polarized society and are not willing to settle for a version of capitalism that simply distributes some of the wealth more broadly.

Liberal economic tenets about the merits of market forces in promoting greater efficiency and productivity are also making gains within Cuba. In some regards, Cuba's emergency economic program resembles the adjustments implemented in Mexico and elsewhere: less state, more market, more foreign investment. But liberal economic reforms in Cuba are being attempted with great reluctance, more in the spirit that a cancer patient submits to chemotherapy, knowing it will kill some of the cancer cells and hoping it won't kill the patient. In contrast to the way neoliberal programs have been carried out in the rest of Latin America, the Cuban government has made serious efforts to preserve the great social accomplishments of the revolution: universal, free health care and education. There is considerable distress, even among the intellectuals advocating the liberal reforms, about the inevitable social inequality that accompanies them. In the political realm, liberalism has made only minimal inroads on the island. Fidel Castro, as well as many of the intellectuals I interviewed, continue to reject a liberalized, multiparty political system as a counterrevolutionary attempt to recolonize Cuba. Nonetheless, there are important renovative voices, including left dissidents as well as Communist Party loyalists, who insist that liberalization of the economy must be accompanied by radical democratization of

Cuba's political system. For them, democratization does not necessarily begin, or even end, with a multiparty system, but it certainly entails a thorough political reform of the party, state, and mass organizations, and a reconstitution of civil society.

To recap, in Cuba the renovative tendency is important but somewhat fragile, liberalism exerts its greatest influence over ideas about economic reform, and orthodox notions about democracy still prevail. In Mexico, the renovative current is quite strong, liberalism has been most influential in terms of the left's revaluation of democracy, and orthodox statism still informs the thinking of many regarding economic alternatives.

If orthodox socialist discourse is clearly on the decline and liberal discourse moderately more influential, nationalism remains strong among the left in both nations and cuts across liberal, orthodox, and renovative currents. Possibly the greatest source of legitimacy still remaining for the Cuban revolution and its leadership is their association with the defense and preservation of Cuba as a nation. In Mexico, the PRI's nationalist credentials have been further tarnished by the popular perception that the regime threatens to barter away the nation's sovereignty (symbolized in its nationalized oil industry and independent foreign policy) for another $40-50 billion of debt to the United States.

However, nationalist discourse also is changing, challenged by the realities of globalization. There are new notions about the relative autonomy of the nation-state replacing older concepts of full, uncompromisable sovereignty. Any nation's identity is constructed and asserted through discourse as well as political struggle and economic relations, and the cultural representation of the nation is increasingly important in Cuba and Mexico. In the post-Cold War, postrevolutionary, globalized world of the 1990s, much of nationalist discourse revolves around *what* constitutes *lo nacional* vis a vis the outside world and *who* represents *lo nacional* within. Thus the continued, perhaps accentuated, insistence on the uniquely Cuban and Mexican quality of music, film, art, literature, food, and language. Thus also the left's renewed efforts to claim the nation's great heroes as its own: José Martí, Che Guevara, Emiliano Zapata, and Lázaro Cárdenas, even in death, remain major players in contemporary national politics.

Having summarized the main findings of the research, let me now offer some explanations for the relative influence of the old and new ideological currents identified among left intellectuals in Cuba and Mexico. Five factors seem particularly useful for understanding what has been described above: (1) the structural position of Cuba and Mexico within the semiperiphery of the world-system; (2) the strength of the nationalist political and popular cultures that emerged from the Mexican and Cuban revolutions; (3) the impact of "the world revolution of 1968" on a generation of left intellectuals in both nations; (4) divisions within the ruling elites, which have resulted from the crisis confronting both state-party regimes and which affect the resources available for critical discourses; and (5) the reality of being a left-in-power vs. a left-in-opposition, combined with the related question of popular movements and their influence on left intellectuals. Let us now consider each of these factors.

1. *Semiperipheral status in the world-system.* I have argued that the different discursive tendencies among left intellectuals revolve largely around the degree to which they adhere to one or the other of two world-systemic ideologies: liberalism and socialism (in the statist form it took in practice). Liberalism has long been the dominant ideology of the capitalist world-system and hegemonic in the core. It effectively claimed "democracy" as its offspring. Socialism emerged as one of the most influential antisystemic ideologies of the nineteenth and twentieth centuries. Gradually formalized as the foundational ideology and justification of real power in the Communist regimes of Europe and Asia, socialism became increasingly identified with statism and authoritarianism. The Cold War reinforced and indeed exaggerated the false discursive opposition in no less subtle a form than the nuclear arms race. The forces of good and light defended liberal capitalism in the name of democracy against a socialism presented as inevitably totalitarian, an evil so great as to justify the risk of nuclear annihilation in the pursuit of its containment or destruction. With capitalism supposedly having won the Cold War, why is liberalism not the fastest-growing influence among left intellectuals in Cuba and Mexico?

We have to take into account how a nation's position within the world-system's hierarchy of nation-states *mediates and conditions* the appropriation of global discourses. The East-West conflict of the Cold War was not the only battle dividing the world-system of the twentieth century. As nations of Latin America, Africa, and Asia attempted to challenge the unequal exchange and unequal power relations between the world-system's core and periphery, nationalism emerged as another powerful, potentially antisystemic ideology. It did not always directly challenge the premises of capitalism, as Marxism and socialism did, but nationalism's assault on the structures of core domination mobilized the masses of the periphery in ways socialism never could.[1]

---

1. For a useful discussion of the role of nationalism in mobilizing mass movements, see Tom Nairn, *The Break-Up of Britain: Crisis and Neo-Nationalism* (London: Verso, 1981).

Liberalism never achieved hegemony in Cuba or Mexico, in part because their peripheral status in the global division of labor, imposed through violent European colonization, prevented them from accumulating the levels of surpluses that have made liberal reformism more viable in the core. Liberalism's critique of statism, understandably, has been met with skepticism in two nations which effectively used state-centered strategies to maneuver from the periphery into the more privileged status of semiperipheral states. Nationalism and partially successful nationalist development strategies played a very important role, I would argue, in steering left intellectuals toward privileging the state in their strategies for social change. That tendency was reinforced by the influence of Soviet-style socialism and Leninism, which made their ideological impact on the Cuban revolution, particularly after 1970, and influenced Communist and socialist sectors of the Mexican left dating back at least to the 1920s.

Recently, the left's more orthodox statist paradigms have been dealt a serious blow by the collapse of state socialism, the exhaustion of nationalist development strategies, and the increasingly obvious undemocratic nature of both. However, reformist liberalism also has collapsed, eclipsed by neoliberal doctrines of radical "free market" economics and narrowly defined electoral democracies. Consequently, the left's paradigm crisis in Cuba and Mexico has not given way to a generalized, hearty embrace of its old Cold War rival, the liberal reform paradigm. To a significant extent that is because liberalism's claims about the possibility of achieving prosperity, liberty, and democracy through gradual, rational reform are not credible within the realities of late twentieth-century, semiperipheral capitalism. The left's skepticism about liberalism and recent neoliberal prescriptions is reinforced by the mounting socio-economic crises that are undermining the old liberal consensus even in the wealthy core.

At the same time, because Cuba and Mexico managed to move into the semiperiphery through revolution and national development schemes, they have escaped the most extreme forms of social and political disintegration described by Robert Kaplan in his horrific account of "The Coming Anarchy" that is engulfing much of the Third World periphery.[2] Left intellectuals of the semiperiphery operate within societies of material and cultural conditions sufficient to nourish the pursuit of utopian dreams. The failure of the old left and liberal strategies does not mean the end of history or resigned defeat before a daily struggle simply to hold off starvation. In nations like Cuba and Mexico, the search for

---

2. Robert Kaplan, "The Coming Anarchy," *The Atlantic Monthly*, February (1994).

new, humane social alternatives is sustained by culturally cohesive and moderately abundant societies. As I believe the findings of this research suggest, the semiperiphery of today's world-system (including, for instance, much of Latin America, Eastern Europe, India, South Africa) is the most likely region to produce the new "antisystemic strategy for an era of disintegration" called for by Wallerstein. The seeds of such a strategy are present in the renovative discourse described in the previous chapters.

2. *The strength of national culture.* Among nations of the semiperiphery, Cuba and Mexico have the distinct advantage of strong national cultures. They are two of the world's most notable examples of societies mobilized to revolutionary action by assertions of nationhood in the face of vast social inequality and aggressive U.S. expansionism. The deeply embedded nationalist and social values of these postrevolutionary political cultures condition the left's discourse, weighing against the influence of liberalism and neoliberalism, and mediating the appropriation of European socialist traditions. Recall that even the most clearly "liberal" of left intellectuals in Cuba and Mexico still couch their arguments in terms of traditional left values and goals of social justice and equity. Similarly, even the most orthodox socialist voices on the left insist on the unique national quality of their project, legitimizing their stance with reference to the nation's historic struggles and heroes.

National revolutions in Cuba and Mexico, for all their many contradictions and authoritarian outcomes, fostered traditions of solidarity, community, social rights, and the state's responsibility for the well-being of its citizens. In both nations, these values permeate beyond the political culture into the broader popular culture, reflected, for example, in music and film. Two recent films in particular attest to the resilience of these national cultures. *Fresa y Chocolate*, with humor, compassion, and exquisite aesthetic qualities, treats various aspects of contemporary Cuban society. The film delineates the political and sexual intolerance, petty hypocrisy, censorship, and fear that erode the nation, but it also shows the qualities that hold it together: solidarity among neighbors, a creative daily appropriation of Catholic, African, and Communist traditions into a distinctly Cuban identity, and an irrepressible, sensual *joie de vivre*.

Mexico's *Danzón*, another celluloid gem of rare beauty, demonstrates the extent to which feminist sensibilities and changing attitudes about gender and sexuality are gradually transforming Mexico's traditional culture, even while society attempts to reappropriate and reassert life-affirming musical and social modes of the past. The strong social, as opposed to individual, identity associated with the postrevolutionary cultures of Cuba and Mexico give added cohesion to their societies, making them particularly fertile ground, within the larger semiperiphery, for renovated utopian projects.

The culture of solidarity, very palpable still in Cuba and Mexico despite the pressures of severe economic crisis and national disorder, contrasts, for example, with recent accounts of life in Chile. There, the Pinochet dictatorship of the 1970s and '80s successfully ruptured the nation's once strongly democratic and socially conscious political culture. Chilean leftists who have returned home after long years in exile express astonishment and despair at the prevalence of ruthless individualism and materialist consumerism in the Chile of the 1990s.[3] Some of the Chilean left itself, deeply traumatized by the brutal repression under Pinochet, has abandoned much of the social and democratic traditions it once so valiantly pursued. A few Chilean socialists have helped design and implement the neoliberal restructuring of the Chilean economy, occasionally even defending the continued repressive excesses of the post-Pinochet civilian regimes.[4]

My point is not that Chilean leftists are somehow less pure than leftists in Cuba or Mexico; that is hardly the case, as demonstrated by the efforts of a Chilean Marxist like Manuel Antonio Garretón to reconceptualize a socialism based on ethical principles.[5] Moreover, there is evidence that the Chilean left is beginning to revitalize itself, as environmentalism increases its influence, as feminism is on the rebound, and as left parties continue to attract their historic third of the Chilean electorate. My critical observations are meant to underscore that, in the absence of a strong national political culture, rooted in ideals of social equality, justice and solidarity, it is far more difficult for left intellectuals to formulate and pursue popular alternatives. The persistence of such cultures in Cuba and Mexico help explain the resistance to neoliberalism, the hesitancy to settle for liberal reforms, and the strong presence of renovative voices within the left.

---

3. This observation is drawn from conversations with Jaime Osorio and Patricia Olave, who only recently visited Chile after having lived in Mexico since shortly after the 1973 coup.

4. Galo Gómez Ogalde recently wrote about Chile: "A socialist minister of the past government . . . explained last year . . . that the police brutality against the left exercised while he was minister can be explained by the fact that 'violence in Chile is a sociological problem.'" He continued, "In Chile there is a law that allows for detention of any citizen simply for the fact that he appears suspicious in the eyes of the police." Galo Gómez Ogalde, "Silencio, Chilenos en Transición," *La Jornada Semanal*, No. 280 (October 23, 1994).

5. See Manuel Antonio Garretón, "Socialismo real and socialismo posible" (manuscript, May 1990).

3. The generation of 1968. I have noted that the liberal, orthodox, and renovative tendencies of the left in Cuba and Mexico today do not correlate neatly with past organizational affiliation or ideological orientation, because the paradigm crisis has shaken up old alignments. On the other hand, there is some logic to the current line-up of tendencies, and one of the explanatory factors seems to be the relative influence of the critical discourses and movements of 1968.

The most orthodox, socialist views and the most liberal perspectives within the Cuban and Mexican left today are expressed primarily by individuals from the historic Communist parties or by the most ardently nationalist thinkers, that is, by those once associated with the most statist traditions within the left. I suggest that this reflects the severity of the paradigm crisis as it has been experienced by forces that once accepted the false dichotomies of liberalism and socialism discussed earlier. With their ideological foundations undermined, they tend toward one or the other of two extreme reactions: retrench and deny anything has changed, or abandon their leftist past and embrace liberalism, occasionally even neoliberalism.

The renovators, on the other hand, tend to be people who were most closely associated with the critical Marxist tendencies and newer antisystemic discourses of what Immanuel Wallerstein has called the worldwide "revolution of 1968." He considers it "one of the great, formative events in the history of our modern world-system."[6] The antisystemic movements and discourses of the 1960s were of a different breed. They challenged the authoritarianism of state socialism as well as the inequality and cultural alienation of capitalism. Intellectual and political events throughout the world in the 1960s influenced the Cuban revolution and Mexico's student movement, both of which, in turn, became emblematic of the revolutionary changes afoot in those years. Activist intellectuals who embraced the new ethics of 1968 were critical of the old left's rigidity, antidemocratic nature, and increasing ineffectiveness.

The antisystemic discourses of the 1960s continued to influence many intellectuals and activists of the era, long after the "revolution of 1968" had been largely defeated. Note, for example, how many of the renovative Cuban voices cited throughout this book were associated with the unorthodox journal of the '60s, *Pensamiento Crítico*. One member of that circle, Juan Antonio Blanco, says that the subversive quality of the '60s (the questioning of capitalism's and real socialism's ethics and models) had a significant influence on the Cuban revolution's first decade. Blanco recalls that while the Beatles sang, "better free your mind

---

6. Immanuel Wallerstein, "1968, Revolution in the World-System: Theses and Queries," manuscript (1988).

instead" and "money can't buy me love," Cuba's popular Silvio Rodríguez sang that "the era is giving birth to a heart." But, says Blanco,
the baby was stillborn for many reasons, including the Soviet invasion of
Czechoslovakia, an event that "destroyed the hopes of 1968."[7] Cuban
historian Jorge Ibarra believes that if Cuba proves able to overcome the
current crisis, it will be as a result of "recontinuing along the lines of advances made in the first years of the revolution."[8] The critical perspectives of Cuban intellectuals who identified with the ideological currents
of 1968 have been somewhat reinforced over the years to the extent that
many of these intellectuals have been able to travel abroad and remain in
dialogue with progressive forces in Latin America and elsewhere, who
continued to renovate their discourse with the ideas of new social and
popular movements of the 1970s and 1980s.

Similarly, in Mexico, many of the renovators came of age politically
and intellectually during the 1968 student movement. Several of them
were associated with *Punto Crítico*, another unorthodox journal influenced by critical Marxists like Antonio Gramsci and post-Marxist ideas
that emphasized a greater plurality of social subjects and political arenas
other than the state. Writing about the effects of 1968 on the Mexican
left, former Mexican Communist Enrique Semo argues that it had two
original and lasting contributions: (1) It gave rise to a new political culture that insisted on liberty and democracy, which became diffused
throughout journalism, novels, poems, film, music, and even daily life;
and (2) it produced a cadre of thousands of activists who became popular leaders, engaged in social and political movements throughout the
country, and contributed decisively to broadening democratic spaces in
Mexico.[9] The 1968 student movement and its repression by the government is considered an *año fronterizo* (literally, border year) in Mexican
politics, and the twenty-fifth anniversary of the October 2 massacre was
commemorated in 1993 by tens of thousands of Mexican citizens.

The significant number of renovators in both countries who were
once radical young intellectuals associated with the revolution of 1968
suggests that a particular generational experience, shaped by the watershed events of the 1960s, also conditions how these intellectuals process
and appropriate world ideologies, taking them beyond the limits of old
socialist and liberal paradigms.

---

7. Juan Antonio Blanco, presentation on Cuba and the 1960s, Casa de las
Américas, Havana, February 9, 1993.

8. Jorge Ibarra, interview with author, Havana, February 21, 1993.

9. Enrique Semo, "1968, página abierta de una agenda vigente," *Memoria*,
No. 60 (November 1993), p. 9.

4. *Divisions within the ruling elites and the availability of resources.* In his study of the Reformation, the Enlightenment and European socialism, Robert Wuthnow concludes that such periods of cultural innovation occurred under particular conditions of economic expansion that produced divisions among ruling elites and increased the resources available to support critical discourses. New growth in the capitalist economy, he argues, led to a "transitional period in which the boundaries between ruling-class fractions became blurred, alliances became more fluid, temporary opportunities to promote new ideas opened up, and exploitable resources not tied to any single established fraction became available."[10]

In my case studies, new opportunities for export-led economic expansion in the globalized world-economy presented themselves as an alternative to Mexico's stagnated import-substitution industrialization and Cuba's shattered alliance with the now extinct socialist bloc. Neoliberal restructuring in Mexico was actively pursued starting in the mid-1980s by a fraction of the ruling class tied to transnational capital and represented by technocrats trained in elite U.S. universities. This led to serious divisions within the ruling party, including the eventual abandonment of the PRI by some of its most prominent center-left nationalists, such as Cuauhtémoc Cárdenas, Porfirio Muñoz Ledo, and Ifigenia Martínez, who are now leading figures in the left opposition.

Cuba's ruling circle only reluctantly began liberal economic reforms and the aggressive pursuit of new export markets through partnerships with transnational capital after the collapse of the Soviet bloc. The divisions created by such changes within the Cuban Communist Party may be less transparent than those of the highly-publicized splits within the PRI, but they exist nonetheless. Increasingly, more liberal-minded, technocratic intellectuals like Carlos Lage and José Luís Rodríguez are taking over leadership areas from more traditional party bureaucrats and ideologues. Moreover, important defections from the Communist Party have contributed to the formation of a new social democratic opposition within Cuba.

The resources and opportunities to promote new ideas have been increased as a result of such divisions. In Mexico, the democratic dissidents who left the PRI made enormous material and political resources available to the opposition, combining them with the resources of Mexico's traditional left parties, like the Communists, who turned their electoral registration and substantial infrastructure over to the newly formed

---

10. Robert Wuthnow, *Communities of Discourse. Ideology and Social Structure in the Reformation, the Enlightenment, and European Socialism* (Cambridge: Harvard University Press, 1989), pp. 572-573.

PRD. Divisions among the elites also contributed to the founding of the newspaper *La Jornada* in the 1980s, which is now one of the most respected dailies in the nation, gives constant and complete coverage to the left opposition, and regularly publishes opinion columns by many of Mexico's most prominent left intellectuals. A large, nonpartisan group of Mexico's intelligentsia, several of them former PRIistas or PRI dissidents, organized themselves as the "San Angel Group" in 1994 and provided an important critical voice in national politics. Similarly, divisions with the Catholic Church hierarchy have allowed Bishop Samuel Ruiz García to play a crucial role not only in mediating the conflict in Chiapas but in giving legitimacy to the new discourses emerging as a result of that conflict.

The inventory and distribution of resources available to promote new ideas in Cuba is considerably different and less favorable to the renovative tendency. Nevertheless, the recent changes are significant. Divisions within the party leadership, for example, allow for the official sponsorship of a wide variety of research institutes reflecting very different ideological currents. The Academy of Sciences remains largely the domain of orthodoxy. The Center for the Study of the World Economy is the base of influential liberal economic voices. The Center for the Study of the Americas is the home of several of Cuba's renovators. Another change resulting from divisions within the Cuban revolution is that prominent former cadre, like Vladimiro Roca, son of famed Communist Blas Roca, have added considerable legitimacy to the social democratic dissident left on the island.

The growing presence of foreign companies in Cuba has also made new resources available in sometimes interesting and unexpected ways. One of Cuba's prominent renovative intellectuals, for example, has been able to support a new nongovernmental research center partly as a result of the income and infrastructure available through his work for one of the new joint enterprises. Divisions within Cuba's Christian community also play an interesting role: a prominent Protestant minister was elected to Cuba's National Assembly in 1993, and the Communist Party has courted church support by liberalizing its stand on the compatibility of religious beliefs and revolutionary loyalty.[11] In a more mundane but critical example, extreme shortages of paper have made it very difficult for renovative Cuban intellectuals to publish; most of the written sources

---

11. It is interesting, given the typologies of left thought we have identified, that a recent study of the church in Latin America notes the presence of two tendencies, "Conservatives" and "Renovationists," the latter including the charismatic spiritualists, populists, and socialists. Carlos Alberto Torres, *The Church, Society and Hegemony: A Critical Sociology of Religion in Latin America* (Westport, Conn.: Praeger, 1992).

from Cuba used for this research were given to me in the form of manuscripts. In contrast, Mexico has several good journals available to the range of left currents.

The availability of discursive resources is also altered by recent economic changes and ruling class divisions. As the PRI has lost legitimacy as the Mexican revolution's rightful flag-bearer, the left opposition has been increasingly effective at claiming the heritage of the great national heroes. In addition to the obvious examples of the *neozapatista* and *neocardenista* movements, people costumed as legendary figures such as José María Morelos, Sor Juana Inez de la Cruz, and Father Hidalgo frequently appear at popular protests of the government's austerity measures.

Among Cubans, José Martí is claimed by all political factions from the extreme right in Miami to Fidel Castro to renovative Communists and social democratic dissidents. However, because the Sovietization of Cuba is associated with the more orthodox forces of the Cuban Communist Party, change-minded Cubans are better able to reclaim Martí's legacy than are orthodox leftists. Differences among Cuban Communists over how to assess the early years of the revolution and its subsequent Sovietization have also opened space for different political currents to assert allegiance to the still much beloved Che.

Divisions among ruling elites in the United States also have altered the relative fortunes of old and new discourses in these nations. Faced with the latest episode of Mexico's long escalating crisis in early 1995, the U.S. government, business sector, and academics were angrily divided over how to respond. The PRI could not automatically count on a U.S. bail-out, and the left opposition found itself some strange bedfellows in its unsuccessful efforts to block the contracting of additional debt. Some U.S. businesses appear increasingly eager to invest in Cuba, before their European and Japanese competitors completely shut them out of this new market, but many U.S. policy-makers remain fiercely opposed to normalizing relations with Castro's government. The position of liberal reformers in Cuba is somewhat strengthened by the growing interest of U.S. businesses, but orthodoxy also benefits from continued U.S. government hostility and threats to Cuban sovereignty.

Finally, the collapse of the liberal consensus in the core, combined with the deep social crises evolving in countries like the United States and England, birthplaces of neoliberalism, make it harder for ruling elites of these world powers to claim their model as the only reasonable option for peoples everywhere. Because transnational elites offer no real solutions to the planet's devastating problems, renovative leftists are in a better position to promote antisystemic alternatives as viable and necessary.

Thus in Cuba and Mexico, divisions within the ruling circles and a redistribution of resources has opened space for new ideas. The renovative left in Mexico has benefited far more from these changes than has the renovative current in Cuba. Cuban orthodoxy still controls considerable resources, whereas Mexico's orthodox left must settle for a fairly limited distribution of its ideas. In both nations, liberal-leftists enjoy support from certain sectors of their respective regimes, and neoliberalism enjoys only minimal support in either the Cuban or the Mexican lefts.

   5. *Left-in-power vs. left-in-opposition and the role of popular movements.* A significant difference between the left in these two countries has to do with the experience of being intellectuals of the opposition versus intellectuals of the ruling state-party. Orthodox socialist thinkers in Mexico tend to dismiss the possibility of reform and cling to notions of destroying the "bourgeois state," while the orthodox perspective in Cuba uncritically defends the popular and democratic nature of the "revolutionary state." Most Cuban renovators, still fundamentally loyal to the social pact of the revolution's original project, seek full democracy but are doubtful about the possibility of immediate, rapid democratization, given the severity of the crisis that threatens the nation's cohesion. Mexican renovators, fundamentally opposed to the neoliberal project that broke the old, postrevolutionary social pact, see immediate democratization as the first necessary step toward resolving the crisis. How one views power and the process of defending it, challenging it, or redistributing it, is clearly conditioned by one's current relationship to it. Overall, this difference has made the Mexican left far more determined than its Cuban counterparts to pursue a renovated vision of full democracy.

   Many of the renovators in Mexico appear to have something else in common: regardless of their past organizational or ideological affiliation, they tend to have remained very closely tied to the popular movements of the past quarter-century. Recall Samir Amin's observation about the Third World intelligentsia's "capacity to remain in living and close communion with the popular classes, to share their history and cultural expression."[12] Immersion in grass-roots politics has contributed to a faith among Mexico's renovative left intellectuals in being able to challenge the common wisdom of dominant ideology (in recent years, neoliberalism) through popular political struggle. Likewise, the close association with the new social movements of recent decades has provided

---

   12. Samir Amin, "The Social Movements in the Periphery: An End to National Liberation?" in S. Amin, et al., *Transforming the Revolution*, op. cit., p. 136.

fresh experiences that allow renovators to avoid the retreat to past formulations typical of the more orthodox tendencies within the left. As noted above, several former Communists and former revolutionary nationalists, i.e., those intellectuals most firmly rooted in the statist paradigm of the past, have been inclined to cling to orthodoxy or embrace liberalism in the face of paradigm crisis. However, notable exceptions to this trend are individuals who remained closely associated with mass struggles. Arnoldo Martínez Verdugo, former general secretary of the Mexican Communist Party, for example, expresses renovative ideas about politics and economics, and I suspect this has much to do with his consistent practice in popular struggles over many decades.

These experiences give Mexican leftists a decided advantage over their Cuban counterparts, who have operated in a political system in which mass organizations have been tightly controlled by the Communist Party and autonomous grass-roots organizing has been strongly discouraged. A disturbing illustration of this difference is that most of the women I interviewed in Mexico expressed renovative ideas, while most of the women I interviewed in Cuba were firmly entrenched in orthodoxy. I am convinced that this reflects the relatively greater strength of the feminist movement in Mexico and the Cuban Women Federation's subordination to the state-party regime. Thus an intellectual's relationship to popular and social movements also conditions his/her discourse and political stance.

This argument is also bolstered by developments in the lefts of the Southern Cone. As I have noted, military dictatorships unleased brutal repression against the lefts and their popular constituencies. Yet in Brazil, where many vibrant new social movements emerged during the long process of transition back to civilian rule, a strong, renovated left was born in close relationship to those popular struggles. Regarding Argentina, another nation whose left and popular movements were brutalized by the military's dirty war, it is interesting to note Donald Hodges' observation that while other sectors of Peronism moved to the right, the Peronists' populist labor organization, the CGT, "made a left-turn" and became "the nucleus of a united workers' front."[13] The Pinochet regime was particularly successful at disarticulating not only the Chilean left but also Chile's highly organized civil society. The Chilean left, after many years in jail, exile, or underground, and without the large, organized popular base that once existed, has had great difficulty renovating a new alternative, anticapitalist project. Yet even there, the gradual re-

---

13. Donald Hodges, "The Argentine Left Since Perón," in B. Carr and S. Ellner, *The Latin American Left From the Fall of Allende to Perestroika* (Boulder: Westview Press, 1993), pp. 166-167.

emergence of social movements like feminism and environmentalism is beginning to renew the left. The existence and strength of social movements is a critical condition for a renovated left project, and the prospects for resolving the crisis confronting the Cuban revolution could only be strengthened by the emergence of autonomous, popular organizations there.

Clearly, statist perspectives and problematic, antidemocratic traditions, like corporatism, *caudillismo,* and centralized power, remain deeply rooted in the left and the broader postrevolutionary political cultures of Cuba and Mexico. Yet, there is also strong evidence that the left has begun to listen to history, and perhaps it will not have to repeat itself so often in the future. I am inclined to predict that, in the long run, the nationalism, collective identity and pride, and commitment to social justice, which also characterize political culture in Cuba and Mexico, will give cohesion to the left's project in these countries.

The structural realities of life in the semiperiphery encourage the search for antisystemic alternatives but do not guarantee the outcome of such pursuit. Popular culture and political culture in Cuba and Mexico, products of the twentieth century's great nationalist revolutions, will help make the left in these countries less susceptible to neoliberal discourse and to surrendering before the allegedly inevitable forces of globalization and the limitations of free market, electoral democracy. At the same time, the manifest inability of ruling elites and old strategies to resolve the crises they have helped to create open an important space in which new discourses can gain influence. Conditions are such that the Cuban and Mexican lefts are in a better position than some to rescue what remains valid and worthwhile of old left social values, while simultaneously incorporating the best of liberal political traditions into a new left paradigm of democracy and social equality freed from false dichotomies of the past and appropriate to realities of the new century.

About the Book and Author

Based on in-depth interviews with seventy-four intellectuals of the lefts in Cuba and Mexico, *Reinventing Revolution* explores the rapidly changing thinking of progressives on the big—and enduring—questions of democracy, economic alternatives, and national sovereignty. Offering a unique world-systems perspective on the sociology of intellectuals and ideology, Edward McCaughan concludes that the collapse of state socialism, the rise of neoliberalism, and accelerated economic globalization have deeply challenged the old paradigms of Latin America's socialist and nationalist lefts and have given rise to renovative ideas that defy both Marxist and liberal orthodoxies. The book's findings are relevant not only throughout Latin America but in Eastern Europe, Russia, South Africa, India, and other regions of the world where political, social, and intellectual forces continue to defy predictions about the "end of history." *Reinventing Revolution* will be an invaluable resource for anyone interested in Latin American politics and political theory, the sociology of intellectuals and ideology, and nationalism and revolution in the Third World.

Edward J. McCaughan is assistant professor of sociology at Loyola University in New Orleans.

Index